REFUGEE TO REVOLUTIONARY

REFUGEE TO REVOLUTIONARY

A Transnational History of Greek Communist Women in Interwar Europe

MARGARITE POULOS

VANDERBILT UNIVERSITY PRESS
Nashville, Tennessee

Copyright 2024 Vanderbilt University Press
All rights reserved
First printing 2024

Library of Congress Cataloging-in-Publication Data

Names: Poulos, Margarite, 1967- author.
Title: Refugee to revolutionary : a transnational history of Greek communist women in interwar Europe / Margarite Poulos.
Description: Nashville : Vanderbilt University Press, [2024] | Includes bibliographical references and index.
Identifiers: LCCN 2024016858 (print) | LCCN 2024016859 (ebook) | ISBN 9780826507167 (paperback) | ISBN 9780826507174 (hardcover) | ISBN 9780826507181 (epub) | ISBN 9780826507198 (pdf)
Subjects: LCSH: Women and communism--Europe. | Women refugees--Europe.
Classification: LCC HX546 .P67 2024 (print) | LCC HX546 (ebook) | DDC 324.2495/07508209041--dc23/eng/20240517
LC record available at https://lccn.loc.gov/2024016858
LC ebook record available at https://lccn.loc.gov/2024016859

Front cover photos, from top left: Clio Dimitrievna Stai, Chrysa Hatzivasiliou, 3 Allegra Felous, (courtesy Jewish Museum of Greece Photo Archive), Chrysanthi Kantzidou, Stella Vamniatzidou, Inessa Fyodorovna Armand, Lidiia Ivanovna Petrova. All photos courtesy of RGASPI except as noted.

For Edmond and Xenia

Contents

Acknowledgments ix

Introduction ... 1

Chapter 1. Gendering Radicalization after Lausanne ... 16

Chapter 2. Upward Mobility and the Comintern Universities ... 54

Chapter 3. The Greek Sectors ... 81

Chapter 4. Professional Revolutionaries: Interwar Trajectories ... 113

Chapter 5. Chrysa Hatzivasiliou: An Icon without a History ... 146

Conclusion. The Transnational Social History of Greek Interwar Communism ... 160

Appendix 1. KUTV Curriculum for Academic Year 1925/26 168

Appendix 2. The Greek Communist Party and the Woman Question (1946) 173

Glossary of Terms 199

Notes 201

Bibliography 239

Index 257

Acknowledgments

This journey started in 2015 when I received the Women's Research Fellowship, an internal grant scheme designed to support and reinvigorate the research of female colleagues whose research so often falls between teaching, supervision, administration, and family responsibilities. I thank my colleague and then supervisor Brett Bowden, for insisting on submitting an application that had to be done at breakneck speed. Recalling my discovery of several Greek communist "files of interest" in the Comintern archives—made possible by the Library of Congress's role in the INCOMKA digitization project—I booked my first ticket to Moscow.[1] Thus began the odyssey that became this book.

    I'm immensely grateful to have been given the opportunity to look at files in the Comintern archive that have hitherto not seen the light of day. It would not have been possible without the immense goodwill and assistance of the librarians at the Russian State Archive of Social-Political History (RGASPI) in Moscow. Nor would it have been possible without the help of Arcadie Capcelea at the World Bank who put me in touch with my formidable Russian interpreter Olga Tikush, and her colleagues Irina Golovina and Inna Melnikova. I was blessed to be subsequently introduced to Russian native speakers of Sydney who assisted me most generously with translation. Thank you, Alla Khlebakova and a very special thanks to the wonderful Tatiana Davies. A final thanks for translation goes to my niece Elise Galati for her French language contribution.

    There are too many colleagues I'd like to thank. I must mention Sheila Fitzpatrick whose early advice on the balance of Soviet and Greek sources was invaluable. The insightful and encouraging words of all of the manuscript reviewers—I owe a debt of gratitude to the early reviewers who inspired me to push on, and of course, to the final readers whose incisive comments helped bring this project to completion. A sincere thanks also to my colleague at the University of Illinois, Chicago (previously at the University of New South Wales), Nicholas Doumanis, for his enduring support and friendship throughout my career, and Roger Markwick, at the University of Newcastle (Australia), for his clear-sighted comments on the final draft of the book—I honored every word. Most of all I thank my commissioning editor, Zachary Gresham, whose gumption made this research project real.

A final thanks goes to my family, past and present, the source of all inspiration.

Introduction

Isn't the life of an ordinary man just like that? He gives out a little flame at first, and then a bigger flame, and finally burns out. All that remains is a little useless ash. Man lives, works, establishes a family, brings children into the world, dies, and is mourned at best by members of his family and a few of his friends: a futile, superfluous life. When we look at our own life by contrast—a life of experience, danger, travel, imprisonment; with responsible tasks, with membership of the great family which we call "the Party," with a clear and firm objective as the cornerstone of a new world, with countless comrades to mourn us at our death—is that not something very different from the futility of a spent match?

WOLFGANG LEONHARD, *Child of the Revolution*

I spoke to a girl. "Where do you come from?"

"From the country," she said. "My family are peasants. I am studying to be a chemical engineer. At harvest time I go back to the village to help my family."

"Are you better off now than before?"

She looked at me, astonished. "Without the Revolution I should never have left my village! I should never have learned even to read and write. I'd have married at fifteen like my mother, borne children, cooked and washed and worked in the fields all my life."

ELLA WINTER, *Red Virtue*

My mother died in 1926, on her deathbed she said to us: "I am dying, and I see no shame in my children being communists. I believed in God, but God would not give me anything. For me Lenin is higher than God." And she asked me to avenge her sufferings. I am ashamed to say, that as I am writing these lines to you, I am crying at the memories of my childhood.

OLGA PAPADOPOULOU, "Letter to Khrushchev"

These statements, the first two collected by German-born Australian-British journalist Ella Winter and Soviet-educated German communist and writer Wolfgang Leonhard during their travels in the Soviet Union, and the last taken from a letter to Khrushchev by Olga Papadopoulou, a Soviet-Greek communist, are easily dismissed as propaganda, instrumentalized Bolshevik-speak, by the twenty-first-century reader, including this historian. As this project evolved, I came to acknowledge the entire human drama that is contained within them—the whole cacophony of material, social, and existential agonies and hopes that so many men and women invested in the communist movement in the previous century.

This book is concerned with a generation of young Greek women who aligned their aspirations and struggles with the goals of the Greek Communist Party (Kommounistiko Komma Elladas, KKE hereafter) in the era of Bolshevization, that is, from the date of the Party's passage into the Comintern fold in December 1924 to the installation of the Metaxas dictatorship (1936–1941). Its central subject is the cadre (*stelechos*), the aspiring "Bolsevika," and, in particular, the promising militants chosen by the Party to be trained as professional revolutionaries in the universities of the Comintern.[1]

It began with the discovery of prominent Greek Communist Party Politburo figure Chrysa Hatzivasiliou's Comintern archive file ID, while perusing the digitized archive index made available online by the INCOMKA project. It was a historic discovery for this researcher, who had long been curious and fascinated by the singular yet elusive figure of Hatzivasiliou, and it eventually became the catalyst for the first of several journeys to Moscow, to locate the file and to view its precious contents. As fate would have it, the file was successfully located, but it was very slim and revealed relatively little beyond what is quite well known about her background and political trajectory, including a verification of her years as a student in the Communist University for the National Minorities of the West (not the Communist University of the Toilers of East as widely thought), and confirmation of her learnedness and dedication to the Party despite chronic ill health. Her file was thus not the revelation I had hoped it would be, but it led me to the discovery of many more files of other Greek and Soviet-Greek communist women, many of them also graduates of the Comintern universities, a precious selection of which I was able to retrieve before COVID brought all international research requiring travel to a grinding halt. Reading Hatzivasiliou's file alongside the other files brought to my attention unanticipated aspects of the history of Greek communism, overturning some widely held assumptions, confirming others, and ultimately changing the course of my research. The files, in the first instance, revealed to me the scale of the Comintern's international cadre training program, that Hatzivasiliou was only one of an increasing number of young aspiring Greek and Soviet-Greek communist women (and men) who traveled to Moscow to receive their revolutionary training *together* at the universities of the Comintern between 1924 and 1938, before shifting Soviet foreign policy objectives, the Great Terror, and World War II brought the international cadre education system, and indeed the Comintern, to an end. The discovery that Soviet-Greek and "mainland" Greek students were systematically merged in the Greek sectors of the Comintern universities had, as one might expect, historic consequences for the development of Greek *and* Soviet communism, redefining my understanding of who the "Greek" actors in this history were, as well as affirming the fundamentally transnational character of Greek communism.

Important links quickly emerged between refugee displacement and radicalization; the overwhelming representation of Anatolian refugees, men and women, among the Greek and Soviet-Greek student cohorts of the Comintern universities places imperial collapse and emerging national states unequivocally at the center of the expansion of Greek and Soviet communism between the Wars. The conflict that brought an end to the Ottoman Empire was of particular consequence for Greek politics, economy, and society.

The Greco-Turkish War (1919–1922), a conflict known as the Asia Minor catastrophe in Greece, and as the Western Front of the Turkish War of Independence in Turkey, concluded with the Treaty of Lausanne (1923) that oversaw the first internationally ratified compulsory exchange of populations under the auspices of the League of Nations, essentially the first negotiated exercise in "ethnic cleansing" in the region.[2] It had profound ramifications for the new Turkish Republic, which absorbed hundreds of thousands of Muslim peoples from their Greek homelands, but especially for Greece, which by the end of 1922, the peak period of hostilities, had absorbed approximately 1.3 million Christians, predominantly Greeks, and thousands of Assyrians, Armenians, Jews, and Circassians from the shores of Asia Minor, Eastern Thrace, and the Black Sea.[3] For the Greeks, Lausanne constituted a major defeat for it ended the millennia-long Hellenic presence in Anatolia. At the time it constituted a major humanitarian emergency, with intervention by international agencies, both for short-term relief and for the long-term settlement of the displaced peoples.

The Greek defeat in Asia Minor and the subsequent influx of refugees wreaked political, social, economic, and ideological havoc. The period 1923 through 1936 was marked by military interventions, dictatorships, and constant political instability and government changes. The restoration of the monarchy in 1935 was soon followed by the Metaxas dictatorship, the Greek analogue to the contemporary German and Italian fascism. The impact of the refugee vote on the traditional balance of mass politics at the electoral level, and, in particular, on the electoral gains of the KKE in the 1930s, gave legitimacy to the communist threat and ultimately served as a pretext for the end of republican governance and the installation of the Metaxas dictatorship in 1936. As I've argued elsewhere, the nature and extent of refugee identification with Greek communism, while widely accepted, is not well understood, based entirely on assumptions about the voting patterns of male refugees who composed a minority of the refugee population.[4] The necessity of keeping a large number of men under arms in Thrace in order to protect the frontiers and to preserve the integrity of territories still left to Greece, in conjunction with the Turkish strategy of retaining all males of military age (eighteen to fifty) as hostages during the evacuation of Smyrna in 1922, the last phase of the Greco-Turkish War, many of whom perished before their release, accounted for the "abnormally high" numbers of refugee widows and girls, especially among the refugees of Asia Minor.[5] It was estimated that at least 200,000 children aged fourteen and under were fatherless; of these, 75,000 were also motherless. Eight thousand of the total number were placed in institutions by 1923 with the promise that many thousands more could be accommodated in orphanages by 1924; the remainder lived principally in camps with the adult refugees. The number of orphans increased daily owing to the deaths of mothers weakened by exposure and undernourishment.[6]

This book is an examination of radicalization outside the ballot box, in particular among the refugee women and youth who composed the majority of the refugee population, and whose political behavior fell outside the purview of the state and its institutions. As I learned, a considerable number of these young refugee women not only joined the Greek Communist Party but were among its highly trained, internationally mobile, "professional" soldiers.

A critical aspect of the context of radicalization is the convergence between the refugee crisis and the Bolshevization of the KKE, a process of internal transformation that preoccupied the Party starting in 1924. For historians, the term *Bolshevization* is used primarily to designate and date the processes by which the Comintern and its national sections were subordinated to Soviet policy, and to Stalin himself. From the point of view of parties affiliated with the Comintern, Bolshevization provided a blueprint for their transformation into the "true mass parties" they aspired to be, which amounted to eliminating political opposition, particularly factionalism, within individual parties and throughout the Comintern. The doctrine of "discipline and organization" committed parties to an overhaul of their organizational structure on the basis of cells (*pyrines*) and fractions (*fraxia*) to more closely resemble the Communist Party of the Soviet Union (CPSU).

The 5th Congress of the Comintern (June–July 1924), in the aftermath of defeat of the revolution in Germany, adopted the "Theses on Tactics" that made the "bolshevization of its sections" the most important task. While the definition of Bolshevization was contested, the actual task of Bolshevization, according to the Fifth Congress, was for national sections to "become real mass parties with the strongest and closest possible contact with the working masses." They needed to be "capable of manoeuvre" rather than "sectarian" or "dogmatic." They needed to be "revolutionary, Marxist in nature," and "centralised . . . permitting no factions, tendencies, or groups," but "based in one mould."[7] Bolshevization was thus, to borrow Zumoff's term, double-edged. It promised a strong party and undermined the party at the same time.[8]

Parties affiliated with the Comintern could be forgiven for accepting Bolshevization as good coin, given the ravages of factionalism that many sections suffered; subservience to the "center" did have a cohering effect on affiliated parties. This was especially pertinent in the case of the KKE; records of the Comintern, the 4th Congress of the KKE, and the Federation of Greek Communist Youth (OKNE) all attest to the seriousness of the factionalism that threatened to split the KKE and the necessity of Comintern intervention. The ascendancy of Nikos Zachariadis (1903–1973), the charismatic and autocratic leader of the KKE from 1931 to 1956, is widely acknowledged as the "point of no return" on the timeline of "Bolshevization as Stalinization," a period characterized by a distinctive subordination of the KKE to the "center." The reconstitution of the Party leadership by the Comintern in 1931, while heavy-handed and controversial, raised the ideological level of the Party and importantly, marked the decisive end to the internal factional battles that had dogged the Party for more than a decade, ushering in a period of relative internal stability that allowed for the development of the Party and the unprecedented growth of its support base in the most hostile of political environments.[9] To be sure, the shift toward centralism also set the scene for creeping authoritarianism and the personality cult that developed around Zachariadis, both harder to check in the context of intensifying state persecution and illegality that had dogged Greek communist movement from 1925. Full-blooded democracy was not compatible with underground activity.

Pertinent to this study, the Bolshevizing KKE expanded its transnational activities and networks on the one hand and focused on "doubling its forces" and invigorating grassroots activity on the other. Calls for the establishment of "[Party] cells in every factory, street, and village club and association" that were "controlled by local committees" were intensified, and interest and investment in the youth wing, the Omospondia Kommounistikon Neolaion Elladas (OKNE; Federation of Greek Communist Youth) were renewed, in recognition of youth's importance to Party renewal, both a stepping stone for membership in the KKE and vital to its succession plan. Indeed, many members of OKNE who joined in 1924 graduated to the KKE the following year.[10] The term *stelechos* itself shifted from its ubiquitous but vague usage, often as an honorific, an expression of respect toward persons sympathetic or affiliated with the movement, to a marker of specific duties, responsibilities, rank, or Party membership. Bolshevization demanded clarity and order on all organizational and operational matters including rank, duties, and mission; so too did the rank of *stelechos* begin to acquire clearer definition.[11] In early 1925, shortly after the Third Extraordinary Congress, an Executive Committee statement referred to the *stelechoi* as "organizers, editors, educators, propagandists, executive committee members, professional leaders," that is, the full range of elite to mid-ranking functionaries of the Party and its mass organizations, who served and were sustained by the Party on a full-time basis.[12]

From 1925, Party literature, directives, announcements, and declarations began to refer systematically to both female and male workers, to male and female youth, and pertinently, to the Anatolian refugees. The KKE's intensifying courtship of politically marginal demographic groups found an audience among girls and women, and in particular, among refugee women, a group "doubly displaced" by the upheavals of war and imperial dissolution. A select few were given the opportunity to access interwar communism's greatest engine of social mobility, the cadre universities of the Comintern. These graduates became low- to mid-ranking functionaries, veterans of grassroots organizations and propaganda work by the time Axis troops landed on Greek soil in 1940, and I argue, were pivotal to the mobilizational force among women that the KKE-led resistance movement, the Ethniko

Apeleftherotiko Metopo (EAM; National Liberation Front) would become during the War. Many decades after these tumultuous events, these *epanastatries* and *stelechoi* are but shadows in the history and the historiography of Greek communism.[13]

The history of Bolshevization itself remains relatively marginal in the historiography of communism overall.[14] Certainly, this phase is not credited with any special significance in the now extensive literature on communist subjectivities, or in feminist and non-feminist histories of communism, or in histories of Greek women's political activism. In histories of Greek communism, the mobilization of women is closely associated with the period of Axis occupation (1941–1945), which shifted the Party from the margins to the political center stage, able as it was to harness the misery and suffering of the occupation, and the appetite for resistance. This juncture gave rise to the EAM (National Liberation Front) whose defining feature was the mass mobilization of Greek women into all facets of the movement (1941–1945). The optimistic albeit brief interlude between Liberation in 1945 and the outbreak of full-scale Civil War in 1946 witnessed an increasingly organized women's movement seeking consolidation of the gains women made in the Resistance. This short period also saw the KKE establish priorities that favored women, including the election of modest numbers of women to the Central Committee and one woman to the Politburo.

The mass participation of politically marginalized groups in the EAM Resistance movement and the construction of political subjectivities through political action is a well-documented phenomenon in the now vast scholarship on Resistance "modernity," that is, the aspect of the Resistance project that aspired to modernize (Westernize) Greek politics and society. The goals of the EAM Resistance were two-fold: (1) national liberation—expelling the occupying forces and all traces of local fascism from the body of the Greek nation; and (2) social justice—constructing a modern (Western) inclusive national political culture that extended active citizenship rights to all traditionally marginalized groups. This environment paved the path for the unprecedented mobilization of women into political life, a defining feature of the EAM Resistance coalition, in contrast to other resistance groups, and also enabled some of the most accomplished female communist cadres (*stelexoi*) to come to prominence within the Party.[15]

This examination does not extend into the subsequent Civil War period (1946–1949), or beyond. The state of emergency did create opportunities for female leadership also, most notably as Political Commissars (Politikos Epitropos) a position deliberately created to manage and support the number of female soldiers fighting in the front lines of the communist Greek Democratic Army, which increased dramatically as the number of male reserve fighters diminished. The Civil War was not a growth phase for the Party; it ended in communist defeat, exile, and fragmentation. Its reconstitution in the compromised conditions of exile across the various countries of the Eastern Bloc marks a departure in the Party's organization and operation that lies beyond the scope of this study.

Electra Apostolou was among the female cadres who came to prominence in the Party during the War, and indeed acquired an iconic status for the Greek Left in part due to the circumstances of her violent and premature demise. She had been the editor of the Communist Youth newspaper *Neolaia* (Youth) in 1933, was elected to the Central Committee of the OKNE in 1935, and became the editor and head of the national liberation women's organization Lefteri Nea (Free Young Woman) established in 1942, a member of the Central Committee of the EAM's youth wing, the Eniaia Panellinia Organosi Neon (EPON; United Panhellenic Youth Organization) in 1943, and shortly after, head of propaganda of the Party's Central Athens organization (Kendriki Organosi Athinas, KOA), before she was arrested, tortured, and executed by Security police in 1944.[16] Chrysa Hatzivasiliou, elected to the Central Committee at the 6th Party Congress of 1935, had been instrumental in the reconstitution of the KKE leadership during the Axis occupation and in the formation of EAM, for which she was rewarded with election to the Politburo at the 8th Party Plenum in January 1942. In 1944 women gained five out of 180 seats (3 percent) in the Ethniko Symvoulio (National Council) of the Provisional Government established by the EAM during the War, specifically called the Politiki Epitropi Ethnikis Apeleftherosis (PEEA; Political Committee of National Liberation), a governing body equivalent to parliament. The five women were Hatzivasiliou (representing Piraeus); Kaiti Nisiriou-Zevgou (Athens), a member of the Central Committee since 1942; Machi Mavroeidi-Hiourea (Kalamata-Peloponnese); Foteini Fillipidi (Larissa); and Maria Desypri Svolou (Athens). Svolou had been a prominent member of the most influential feminist organization of the interwar period, the League for Women's Rights (Syndesmos gia ta Dikaiomata ton Gynaikon). She became sympathetic and collaborated with the communist movement in the 1930s in the context of the growing fascist threat and the conviction that the communists had greater potential to affect substantive social change. Svolou was married to Alexandros Svolos, a prominent socialist and legal expert and leader of PEEA, the Provisional Government established by the Resistance during the War.

FIGURE 1. Work session of the National Council 1944; Hatzivasiliou and Svolou at far left. Photo by Spiros Meletzis. Benaki Museum, Athens, Photographic Archives.

FIGURE 2. A presidium was elected to guide the work sessions of the National Council, which included Maria Svolou. Photo by Spiros Meletzis. Yiorgos Petropoulos, "The First People's Parliament in Greek History," *Efsyn*, May 27, 2016, http://www.efsyn.gr/arthro/i-proti-laiki-voyli-stin-elliniki-istoria.

The PEEA elections of 1944 were the first in which all Greek women could be voters and candidates. The equality of women and men was enshrined in law for the first time in Greek history under Article 5 of the PEEA Constitution, which declared that "all Greek men and women have the same political and civil rights."[17]

The 7th Congress of the KKE held at the conclusion of the War, the highest point in the Party's popularity and legitimacy, recognized and capitalized on its now much larger female audience/constituency. Tasks were set to boost the female Party membership to 50 percent and to establish a women's office/secretariat at every level of the Party structure, dedicated to supporting the "work among women." The Party's appetite to share political power at the highest levels was less forthcoming, although it outdid its Soviet counterpart.[18] Chrysa Hatzivasiliou was re-elected to the Politburo and the Central Committee, appointed to the directorship of the new Women's Secretariat of the Central, and appointed leader of the Panelladiki Dimokratiki Enosi Gynaikon (PDEG; Panhellenic Democratic Union of Women), the Greek branch of the Women's International Democratic Federation (WIDF), and a member of its council.[19]

A small group of women who had been very active in the Resistance, who had endured their share of imprisonments, beatings, and exile, and importantly, had not succumbed to disclosing information or signing repentance statements (*diloseis*) were elected to the Central Committee of the KKE, albeit as alternate, not permanent, members: Avra Partsalidou, Allegra Felous, and Rodi Katou. All were active in the organization of the first post-war Panhellenic Women's Conference, which took place in May 1946, in Volos, Thessalia, the last legal women's gathering before civil conflict engulfed the country.[20] Very little biographical information on Avra Partsalidou exists except what she provided in her own memoir of her time as an activist in OKNE and a handful of articles she published in the *Kommounistiki Epitheorisi* (Communist review).[21] She was a member of the Greek branch of the Women's International Democratic Federation (WIDF) and was married to communist leader Dimitris "Mitsos" Partsalidis. Allegra Felous was born in 1916 to a Jewish Greek communist family from Trikala, Thessalia. She joined the Party in 1936, and was very active throughout the Metaxas dictatorship, in the EAM Resistance, working in propaganda and serving as secretary of various *achtides* of KKE, and served as a Political Commissar for female soldiers in the communist Dimokratikos Stratos Elladas (Greek Democratic Army) during the Civil War.[22] Felous had been imprisoned and exiled with Electra Apostolou, Kaiti Zevgou, and

FIGURE 3. Allegra Felous, as an officer of the Democratic Army of Greece (DSE), during the Greek Civil War 1946–1949. (Greek Democratic Army, Vitsi, 1948). From the Jewish Museum of Greece Photo Archive, https://jewishmuseum.gr/en/psifiaki-ekthesi/synagonistis-greek-jews-in-the-national-resistance/https://jewishmuseum.gr/wp-content/uploads/2024/06/1-9.jpg

Rodi Katou. She fled to East Germany after the Civil War, became a permanent member at the subsequent 3rd Party Conference in October 1950, and returned to Greece after the collapse of the junta where she joined the Greek Communist Party of the Interior (KKE Esoterikou, later Synaspismos) that formed after the KKE suffered a major split following the 1968 Warsaw Pact invasion of Czechoslovakia and the suppression of the Prague Spring.[23] When she died in 2011, *Avgi* newspaper wrote that the Party was "deafeningly" absent from her funeral.

This book's focus on Bolshevization from "below" thus addresses an overlooked but important juncture in the growth of Greek communism's transnational female constituency and the overwhelming representation of refugees within this constituency. It argues for a reconsideration of the interwar era as an important turning point in communist women's relationship to the Party, a factor that was critical in the KKE's development toward the mass organization it would become during the War. Like the existing English-language scholarship on Bolshevization, which is primarily occupied with the extent of Bolshevizing national parties' subservience to Moscow, the scholarly preoccupation in the historiography of Greek communism has been with the ambitions, strategies, delusions, and failures of the KKE leadership.[24] In a similar fashion, the general scholarship on the Comintern universities and the foreign cadre training system has been captive to the objectives of the national parties for sending their militants to study in Moscow, and in turn, the motives of the Comintern—and the Kremlin—for training them.

At the heart of this study thus lies the vexed question of communist agency, and communist women's agency in particular; the quest to historicize the aspirations and activism of women who threw themselves into the KKE and its struggles between the Wars is also the quest to intervene in a historiography still too eager to reduce them to indoctrinated adherents of a movement that did little more than use and exploit them as anonymous ancillaries in furthering Comintern and KKE policies and, ipso facto, the interests of Stalin's Soviet Union.[25] It is a view also shared by some Western feminist scholars who are skeptical of the "desire of feminist revisionists" to find women's agency in an anti-capitalist Marxist past.[26]

This book draws on both Greek and Russian language sources, the most important of which are the individual personnel files (*lichnye dela*) of individual Greek students, kept by the Soviets for all Soviet citizens, foreign students, and Comintern officials, which accompanied individuals throughout the course of their professional and educational life. The bureaucratic possession of what Fitzpatrick calls the file-self has prompted many to regard the personal files as mechanisms of oppression as "they are impervious to reconstruction," although Fitzpatrick herself has noted that the content of file-selves was not static and indeed could change in accordance with shifting state policy.[27] However fragmentary and contrived, I would argue that the files are invaluable primary sources for case studies of people and organizations like the Comintern that elude detailed and comprehensive analysis by nature, illuminating the agency of people who for the most part remain in the shadows.

Each file contained an *anketa* (questionnaire) completed by the student—sometimes with the assistance of a more literate peer or superior—which included key classifications like "social position," and "nationality." The *anketa* was accompanied by an autobiography (*autobiografia*) which included a brief account of an individual communist's life and educational and professional achievements. Autobiographical reflection, for all the particularities of the Bolshevik genre, was, as Hellbeck has written, "an important subjectivizing practice; the core of the personal narratives of struggle and triumph that characterizes many autobiographies depicts the author's personality as an unfolding subject of revolutionary consciousness."[28] Many followed established guidelines, written in the Bolshevik idiom or "Bolshevik-speak," while others are surprisingly personal, reflecting that Comintern and Soviet authorities' effort to instill a single subjectivity were not always or perhaps ever successful. This study does not set out to draw a distinction between narrative and experience, however, or see the autobiography only as a "narrative artifice," which would be to deny agency in the manner that it precisely sets out to challenge. All autobiographies, even those that appear unreflective and constructed, tell us something about the author and her experience, and as Laamanen states in relation to Swedish communists, serve as an allegory that illuminates the culture and the history as a whole, a wider culture that can only be understood when ideology, gender, opportunism, conviction, and adventurism are all evaluated in their context, or to borrow the historian Carlo Ginzburg's words in reference to the importance of microhistory as historical method, "in history (as in cinema), every close-up implies an off-screen scene. In any close-up the global perspective is implicit. Every singular case assumes the possibility of a generalization."[29]

The primary materials consulted in this study are drawn predominantly from the Comintern archives held at the Rossiiskii Gosudarstvennyi Arkhiv Sotsialno-Politicheskoi Istorii (RGASPI; Russian State Archive of

Socio-Political History), Moscow; Archeio Syghronis Koinonikis Istoria (ASKI; Contemporary Social History Archive), Athens; US Foreign Office and CIA documents (digitized material); Kendro Mikrasiatikon Spoudon (Center for Asia Minor Studies), Athens; Elliniko Logotechniko kai Istoriko Archeio (ELIA; Greek Literary and Historical Archive), Athens; Charilaos Florakis Library, Athens; Library of the Greek Parliament, Athens; National Library of Athens; Greek Communist Party archives, Athens; and Benaki Museum, Athens.

The book begins with an examination of the geopolitical and institutional contexts that brought women into the KKE/Comintern fold, with particular emphasis on the refugee experience. The first chapter draws out the gendered aspects of poverty, displacement, and workplace exploitation in post-Lausanne Greece, in conjunction with the mobilizational practices adopted by the Greek Communist Party to draw women and youth into its ranks in its Bolshevization phase. The nature and extent of refugee identification with communism is broadly assumed in the historiography but has not been interrogated, hitherto based entirely on the voting patterns of male refugees. This chapter delves into patterns of radicalization outside the ballot box among refugee women and youth, whose political activism intensified but had no institutional measure. Chapter 2 draws out the theme of upward mobility that is central to my interpretation of Bolshevization and its historical significance. The focus for this examination is the Comintern cadre university, a key vehicle of mobility for communists between the Wars. It illuminates the context in which select groups of young communist women and men, those regarded as "promising" militants, were sent to the Soviet Union to train at the cadre universities of the Comintern to become the KKE's professional revolutionaries. It illuminates a central paradox of Bolshevization whereby diminishing Party autonomy and the pressure and expectation to bring internal Party culture and operations into alignment with Comintern principles accelerated the formalization of women's greater access and participation in the emerging Party "apparatus." Chapter 3 shifts the focus to the history and development of the Greek sectors of the Comintern universities and reflects on the appeal of these institutions "from below." The tables in this chapter convey the expanding representation of women in the Greek sectors over time as well as the class and ethnic composition/nationality (Greek nationals or Soviet Greek) of the female cohorts across all three Greek sectors throughout the Comintern university period. It establishes a foundation for the subsequent chapters, 4 and 5, which focus on the background and trajectory of individual cadres, revealing a common experience of displacement, disadvantage, and aspiration. Chapter 4 sheds light on the relationship between these Cominternians with the Greek Communist Party, their transnational activities, achievements, and struggles, before, during, and after the era of the Comintern. In Chapter 5, dedicated to the communist who inspired this book, Chrysa Hatzivasiliou, I fuse some of the precious few data from her Comintern file to add some volume to her sparsely documented life. It includes a brief contextualization of her essay "To KKE kai to Gynaikeio Zitima" (The KKE and the woman question), written in 1946, more than twenty years after she joined the Greek Communist Party, in the radically different political environment of the post-war period. The inclusion of the English language translation as Appendix 2 serves to introduce this important essay to a non-Greek-speaking readership for the first time, and in its entirety. The book concludes with reflections on the confluence of (Ottoman) imperial collapse, Soviet ambitions, and the Bolshevization moment and its profound social impacts, which remain conspicuously absent from the relevant historiographies, and which this book only begins to address.

1

Gendering Radicalization after Lausanne

In a somewhat overlooked examination of Greek communist autobiographies of the interwar period, Christian Gonsa argues that recruits came to communism through one or more of the following identity attributes or characteristics that also determined the trajectory of individuals within the movement: social background (intellectuals, workers); geographical background (refugees); minority background (Jews); and gender.[1] Gonsa's acknowledgment of gender is not followed by further comment, however, as are the other "identifiers." This is not inconsistent with an ambivalence about gender and women's place in the historiography of interwar Greek communism. Historians, including feminist historians of the interwar period, have focused much of their attention on the vibrant first wave of the feminist movement in Greece, vaguely aware of the female presences in the early history of Greek communism but discouraged by their "negligible" numbers, and the perception of their status in the pre-antifascist communist movement as too ad hoc, disorganized, and informal to be worthy of scholarly investigation. The dearth of Greek archival material is compounded by the very small number of published autobiographies and memoirs of communist women that reference the interwar period, among which the writings of Avra Partsalidou (née Vlassi), Kaiti Zevgou (née Nisiriou), and Elli Alexiou are among the most important and well-known.[2] The (mis)perception of communist women like Partsalidou and Zevgou as auxiliaries of their more prominent spouses has perhaps also provided grist to the mill of this enduring historiographical marginalization.

This chapter recasts the interwar period (1924–1936) as a critical juncture for women's growing identification with and further integration into the Greek communist movement, a phase in the development of the Party that laid important groundwork for the mobilizations of the subsequent period of war and Axis occupation. Very little is understood about the arc of women's involvement with the communist movement during this period; the shift toward broad-based antifascist resistance is conventionally credited as a turning point for women's greater political participation. The so-called popular front period in Greece was inaugurated with the Panhellenic Anti-fascist Congress held in June 1934, an event organized by the KKE and other prominent intellectuals, including the writers (and sisters) Galateia Kazantzaki and Elli Alexiou. The Congress of the World Committee of Women Against War and Fascism, a subcommittee of the World Committee sponsored by the Comintern, took place in Paris in August 1934. Greece was represented by the Panhellenic Committee of Women Against War and Fascism, a coalition of prominent feminist and communist activists.

The turning point for women's shifting relationship with the KKE and the communist movement, however, had occurred much earlier, following two key overlapping events. The first was the transplantation of approximately 1.3 million refugees into Greece, primarily women and youth, whose labor drove the expansion of Greek industry between the Wars. The second was the KKE's entry into the Comintern fold at the Third Extraordinary Congress of December 1924, which marked the beginning of its transformation into a "revolutionary party of the proletariat," in accordance with the Comintern's Bolshevization drive.[3] The vigor with which the process of Bolshevization was undertaken shifted the Party from obscurity to the center stage of Greek politics as the single greatest threat to the stability of the political order. This chapter argues that the synergies between the particular predicament of refugee women and youth, on the one hand, and the momentum of Bolshevization of the KKE, on the other, laid the groundwork for women's greater participation and formal integration into the Party, a phenomenon that has been overlooked in historical evaluations of the Party's growth between the Wars.[4]

A Revolution in Cheap Labor

The particularities of early twentieth-century Greece—late industrialization, a small bourgeoisie, a significant petty bourgeoisie, and a tertiary sector that defied political profiling—situate the Greek case outside the norms associated with the development of communism in Western Europe.[5] For Potamianos, Bolshevik ideology has its greatest challenge in the strength of Greek nationalism, associated both with Antiquity (and, via Ancient Greece, Europe) and also with the Eastern Orthodox Church and the high culture of the Ottoman Orthodox populations.[6] Despite these setbacks, communist internationalist politics entered Greek political life, inspired, no doubt, by the success of the October Revolution.

The Greek Communist Party began life in 1918 as the Sosialistiko Ergatiko Komma Elladas (SEKE; Socialist Labor Party). It was a party of limited influence and very few members in its first years and functioned for the most part in a state of quasi-illegality (*nomimoparanomia*). It was but one of various small groups and organizations operating in the left-wing political space that were constantly at odds with each other and among themselves, frequently splitting and reforming, their potential hampered by delayed industrialization in Greece.[7] In the early 1920s the number of Greeks who could be classified as industrial proletarians was negligible, especially as compared to the number of shopkeepers and merchants. This changed dramatically with the arrival of the Anatolian Greek refugees due to the Greek defeat in the Greco-Turkish War (1919–1922). By late 1922, most of Anatolia's ethnic Greeks and members of other Christian minorities such as the Armenians, Assyrians, and Circassians had either fled, been deported to labor camps, or been killed. Those remaining were transferred to Greece under the terms of the Treaty of Lausanne.

In the years between 1922 and 1928, more than 130,000 refugees had settled in the nation's capital, Athens, effectively transforming it into a new city. According to the 1928 census Athens grew from a city of 297,000 in 1920 to a city of 131,810 natives, 129,380 refugees, and 198,021 internal migrants in 1928.[8] In 1928, when the population of Greece was approximately 6.2 million, the urban working population numbered approximately half a million.[9] The figures for women's participation in paid employment, traditionally concentrated in textiles and dressmaking, tobacco, and paper production, were at 16 percent in 1907, 20 percent in 1920, 23.2 percent in 1928, and 26.8 percent in 1951.[10] According to Jecchinis, one third of industrial and commercial workers, about 150,000, were women after 1923, and about one third of these were refugees from Asia Minor, many of them orphans as most married women held skilled jobs in weaving and received wages on a piecework basis.[11] Industrial production, in particular, absorbed large numbers of female refugees. In 1928, 36.2 percent of women industrial workers were refugees compared with 23.8 percent of male workers, with significant numbers working in the northern tobacco centers of northern Greece—Kavala and Thessaloniki—and in the central mainland city of Volos, Thessaly.[12] The focus here is therefore on refugee communities settled in the urban centers of Greece, most of whom entered the industrial labor force. Rural refugees, whatever their losses after the exchange of populations, were less disgruntled and less inclined to rise against a state that had given them land (abandoned by the Muslim owners expelled from Greece) and effectively transformed them into landowners.

There is a widespread consensus among historians that the reduced circumstances of the once prosperous and established Anatolian communities combined with a persistent and assertive Anatolian "otherness" opened them to outsider politics. This was also a view shared by contemporary observers including political elites who expressed concern that the new composition of the population—religiously diverse, multicultural, multilingual, Bolshevists from Russia, communist tobacco workers, leftist agricultural workers, and so on—in conjunction with a yet unconsolidated national consciousness, economic underdevelopment, and despair constituted fertile terrain for the cultivation of ideas, "pregnant" with danger for the state and the nation.[13]

But as mentioned, the connection between the refugees and the growth of communism, while broadly accepted, has never been the subject of a focused study. Doubly obscured is the extent to which the swelling ranks and unregulated conditions of female industrial labor (both refugee and native), were represented in this momentum of radicalization. Following the traumas of the war, including mass rape, and the forcible removal from their homeland, the postwar settlement saw the women of Asia Minor and their children transplanted into a land that was largely unknown to them, where their gender would once again render them doubly vulnerable.

In parallel, the Greek Communist Party's membership increased almost ninefold in the span of thirteen years from fewer than 2,000 in 1923, to 6,000 in 1934, to more than 17,500 in 1936, accompanied by an increased electoral share from 4.38 percent in 1926 to 9.59 percent in 1935 and gaining fifteen seats in the Greek parliament in 1936. This trajectory is widely attributed to shifting voting patterns of the refugee community to the Left in the 1930s, an important pretext for the installation of the Metaxas dictatorship in the same year.[14] But there is little to be learned about the dynamics of women's political behavior from shifting electoral data in the era of universal male suffrage.

Greece was a predominantly agricultural society well into the twentieth century; most Greek women worked in primary industry, that is, agriculture and animal husbandry. With the exception of women who worked as hired labor for more prosperous farmers, the range of tasks performed on the land and in the home were considered to be part of women's domestic duties. As unpaid work, it was not (usually) counted in the census. According to the historian Efi Avdela, the increase in female employment figures between far exceeded the increase in overall employment figures and was a defining characteristic of the period.[15] Between 1907 and 1920 the increase in women's employment was at 68 percent while the increase in total employment was 50.5 percent. Between 1920 and 1928 the increase in women's employment was at 35.4 percent and total employment was 28.7 percent; 80 percent of this difference can be attributed to female refugee labor.[16]

While lower in absolute numbers than elsewhere in Europe, the largest growth sector for female paid labor in the first half of the last century was the manufacturing industry, surpassing domestic service by 1928. Greek women and girls had been working in the manufacturing industry since the first factories appeared in Athens and the Piraeus in the 1870s, their numbers growing rapidly in the context of territorial expansion, especially after the Balkan Wars, migration, population growth, and urbanization. Girls and women of "productive age" (*paragogikon ilikion*) worked across a range of industries with the largest concentrations working in cotton mills and silk factories, but also in paper mills, tanneries, and the tobacco and chemical industries.[17] The percentage of female industrial workers rose from 16 percent in 1907 to 20 percent in 1920 to 23.2 percent in 1928, 36.2 percent of whom were refugees.[18] Female industrial workers were predominantly very young (ten to nineteen years old), barely literate, and usually worked to support at least one other family member besides themselves. After 1922, approximately one third were refugees who had lost one or both parents. On average female workers were paid 43.6 percent less than male workers in the period between 1913 and 1935.[19]

The reports of resettlement bureaucrats made it abundantly clear that the arrival of the Anatolian refugees redefined the Greek economy, by their sheer numbers but also by the considerable range of their skills and business acumen. Sir John Hope Simpson, the vice president of the Greek Refugee Resettlement Commission (RSC; Epitropi Apokatastasis Prosfygon), tasked with monitoring and administering the resettlement of the refugees, wrote that silk factories, cloth factories, and factories for pottery were all inaugurated with the arrival of the refugees.[20] League of Nations official

TABLE I. EMPLOYMENT DATA FOR 1907 BY JOB CATEGORY AND GENDER

	Total	Men	Women
Agriculture (paid labor only)	331,660	324,682	6,978
Fisheries	5,870	5,856	14
Mining	4,365	4,325	40
Manufacturing industry	123,561	102,853	19,708
Transport sector	87,624	83,497	4,127
Commerce/trade	72,793	71,904	889
Private services (domestic service)	33,862	14,404	19,458
Freelance	31,580	26,435	5,145
Public service	32,376	32,231	145
Clergy/faith	3,394	3,374	20
Unspecified	40,610	31,283	9,327
Unemployed	1,146,416	251,931	894,485
Total	**1,914,111**	**953,775**	**960,336**

Data counts workers over the age of ten years. Source: Census statistics from 1907 (Ministry of the National Economy of Greece) reproduced in Saliba, *Women Workers in the Manufacturing Industry*, 21.

C. A. Macartney wrote in 1930 that the refugees did not just swell the labor ranks and remain "dependent solely on the efforts of the Greek Refugee Commission or on Government assistance," but also expanded Greek trade and industry, initiating many of the businesses and industries set up at this time.

> Merchants, industrialist bankers and shipowners who had migrated to Greece brought with them a large amount of capital besides a great business capacity.... The production of woollen stuffs and fabrics rose from 1.4 million metres in 1922 to 2.2 million in 1925. Industrial progress was also marked by the increased importation of machinery. The fishing industry has made astonishing advances. New silk factories have sprung up, which absorb the produce of the cultivators of Macedonia.[21]

The most numerous and important of the factories that sprang up were the carpet factories; Macartney reported that "the famous Smyrna carpets [were] now manufactured exclusively in Piraeus." In this industry the refugees [women] are expert, and it has been introduced since their arrival. The industry is increasing very rapidly, and in the year 1927 the exports of Greece to America was valued at over half a million pounds sterling. "About 10,000 women now earn their living by this trade that brings in more than 50,000 pounds a year."[22] According to Pentzopoulos, the carpet industry in Greece only truly developed with the transfer of the Ionian Greeks.[23]

RSC reports, however, were often self-indulgent. Most refugees came from the less-well-to-do elements of the Asia Minor community and found work in the traditionally female-dominated sectors of industry, sometimes laboring in the businesses and industries owned by their better-off kinsmen, as the KKE was soon to point out and capitalize upon in its quest to mobilize them. While the RSC did bring some solutions to a seemingly unsolvable humanitarian crisis, the commission's policies governing the agricultural and urban settlement of refugees in Greece created new crises and incited intense animosity among native Greeks toward both the refugees and the incumbent Greek government. The focus of the RSC was agricultural, with Macedonia as the main area of settlement, the rationale being that the homes of forcibly deported Muslims would be turned over to the refugees. Large estates were carved up among refugees, as were large swaths of uncultivated land that had been formerly owned by Turkish landowners. However, the redistribution of Turkish lands posed an unexpected problem. In the delay between the evacuation of the Turkish landowners and the settlement of the refugees, local Greeks and non-Greeks had settled or purchased the unclaimed land, leading to the division of villages into distinct quarters based on ethnic identity, where the natives remained in the old part of the village while the refugees occupied enclaves away from the village center.[24]

Only in 1924 did the RSC begin to undertake the settlement of the 500,000 refugees living in urban areas. For years after arriving in Greece, refugees lived in camps on the outskirts of Athens, Piraeus, and Thessaloniki where disease was rife, and food and medicine were extremely scarce. One report stated that forty to fifty Greeks died every day in the camps from 1922 to 1924, hundreds more dying in rudimentary hospitals. These circumstances were glossed over in the RSC reports. In cities like Thessaloniki, urban space was drastically transformed in order to accommodate the refugees. The settlement of the refugees in specific districts was based on a logic of class stratification. The removal of the city's 25,000 Muslims after 1923 cleared space for the settlement of the more affluent refugees from

Anatolia in undamaged areas of the city. On the other hand, poor refugees were settled in eighteen refugee housing districts on the city's outskirts, consisting of little more than shanty towns with squatter houses.[25]

Many of the factories built during this period, especially carpet factories, were located near the urban settlements in Athens and Piraeus where labor was abundant.[26] The League of Nations loans protocol documents of 1923 refer to the numerous lots of land at the Athens settlements that had already been sold to carpet manufacturers for the purpose of building factories containing forty looms each. The document makes optimistic projections about the success of the industry in Greece given the many skilled carpet makers and weavers to be found among the refugees. Simpson reported that the commission provided sites for the erection of factories "on very advantageous terms, in the vicinity of the various settlements, and that this arrangement has been valuable both to the refugees and the industrialists who have taken advantage of it."[27] This of course made the refugee settlements into perfect sources of cheap labor for industry, and the surplus of refugee girls and women made women's labor even cheaper.

Macartney and Simpson's admiration for refugee ingenuity obscures the dark underbelly of the industrial phenomenon that unfolded in the 1920s, when masses of refugee women and youth from Anatolia and Eastern Thrace were thrust into an unregulated and opportunistic labor market, seemingly impervious to protective legislation. Moreover, they were firewalled from trade union representation by prejudice and law that demanded membership of individuals aged sixteen and under and women required the written permission of father and husbands respectively.[28] As Papastefanaki notes, both the communist and the feminist movements would have to battle against these constraints to improve representation and achieve equal rights for women workers, refugee and nonrefugee, in the unions.[29]

From 1913 to 1935 women workers' wages generally amounted to 22.3 to 58.6 percent of the average male's wages, even in the tobacco industry where the number of women employees was almost equal to men. Among the most poorly paid were women who worked in workshops that produced undergarments, gloves, and paper bags. In 1935 the average daily wage in tobacco work for men was 79.05 drachma, and for women, 33.33 drachma.[30] The working day of women far exceeded the eight-hour limit stipulated by the law, and sanitary conditions in the factories were reportedly appalling. The conditions in tobacco and textile industries, for example, were especially unhygienic, which in combination with very long work hours, resulted in serious illness, particularly tuberculosis, for many female workers.[31] In many cases women's wages were so low that children also had to work so that the family could make ends meet.

Greek feminist and socialist leader Maria Svolou outlined the predicament of working women thus:

> The position of the female worker who tries to reconcile her professional duties with her duties at home, and, in particular, the care of her children, is genuinely tragic. She returns from work late at night, exhausted after twelve to twenty-five hours of work, and then must prepare what little food she has for the following day, fetch water to clean the house, and tend to tend to her children as best she can. There is no rest, no joy. Saturday evening and Sunday is reserved for the loads of washing, mopping, and darning. Recreation is something unknown—a day out, a visit to the countryside, a breath of fresh air, are dreams rarely realized by the female industrial worker with a large family, or who is the sole breadwinner. In any case, there are no organizations catering for workers' recreation and leisure. The absence of welfare provisions for mothers obliges women to either interrupt their work duties to care for their children or deprive themselves of a wage that is essential to the survival of their families, or take up unskilled work that enables them to stay at home. Pregnant women are obliged to remain working right up until the last days before the birth, or again be deprived of a wage when it's most needed. These women often have to send their older children out to work or have them stay at home to care for the younger ones so that they may work. In all these cases, the outcomes are equally sad: Premature employment for the children, chronic illiteracy, and an entrenched cycle of economic disadvantage for the working family.[32]

As for the celebrated carpet industry, dominated by female refugee labor, Svolou's account of labor inspector Anna Makropoulou's presentation to the Greek Ministry of the National Economy is instructive:

> The one ray of light which fell upon the hell in which the Greek woman worker works, illuminated the horror: Women who work twelve- and fourteen-hour days with a half hour break at lunch time, spent on the work stool. Ten- and twelve-year-old children huddled next to their mothers and grandmothers the whole time, their chins resting on their knees, their fingers destroyed by the knots they have to tie, their bodies bent forever. Dry bread for food eaten on the work stool at lunch. Workshops raised in

places formerly used as stables and storage cellars. Daily pay rates that stave off nothing more than starvation, where all strength is drained by intensive endless work. Which obliges mothers to drag their children alongside them, depriving them of the light of learning, the joy of their youth, the joy of play. Daily pay rates lay the ground for every moral exploitation.[33]

Svolou's reference to moral exploitation is very likely a reference to the spread of prostitution among working refugee women for the purpose of supplementing meagre incomes. Indeed, 40 percent of undocumented sex workers admitted involuntarily to the Andreas Syggros Venereal Diseases Hospital in Athens, between the Wars, were refugees from Asia Minor.[34]

As labor inspector Anna Makropoulou had noted, the enforcement of the law that prohibits the recruiting of minors under fourteen in the factories always ran into the absence of state oversight and social welfare measures; 72 percent of the children working in the factories had lost one parent, usually the father, and their small wages were indispensable for the family budget.[35] Most of the children working in industry and the manufacturing sector were girls; in fact, a large part of the child industrial workforce consisted of female labor. Girls were predominantly employed by the large textile factories for unskilled and low-paid tasks while boys opted for small workshops where they could get an unofficial apprenticeship in skilled, preferably artisanal, work, a figure that increased exponentially after the arrival of the refugees. The induction of young girls into industrial labor closed off educational opportunities and had a downward pull on wages for unskilled labor.[36]

The work of historian Efi Avdela on protective labor legislation for women and children examines the inadequacy of trade union representation and the overall lack of legal and institutional support for working youth and women in the interwar period. The particularly fragmented structure of the labor market in Greece as well as the chronic inadequacy of the newly founded Labor Inspectorate, whose purpose was to oversee the legislation, rendered the enforcement of Venizelos' protective laws (1912) for women and children ineffective.[37] These laws aimed to restrict night work, work on Sunday, and heavy unhygienic labor, and capped the working day at ten hours.[38] But employers blatantly ignored labor legislation with the silent complicity of the police, while the women themselves were often reluctant to make use of protective measures for fear of retribution and firing.

Although the number of women in Greek industry increased in the 1920s, the country did not experience significant gender competition in the job market or open hostility from trade unions toward women's industrial work as happened elsewhere in Europe. In general, with the exception of the tobacco industry, women's work did not appear to represent a threat to men's work, and so trade unions did not show a great deal of concern for women's membership and representation. Overall, reports of the Labor Inspectorate constantly confirm that providing redress to the problem of ongoing and severe exploitation of the female labor force was caught between the defective enforcement of protective legislation, the characteristics of women's labor that rendered the enforcement of protective legislation impossible, and trade union indifference.[39] Increasing state hostilities toward trade unions and escalating police violence against strike action, which became conflated with communist subversion, further entrenched the challenges to women's trade union organization.

The Limits of Feminist Intervention

The growing feminist movement of the interwar period, a protagonist in the fight for the political economic and institutional equality of women, was not much more successful at capturing the attentions of female industrial labor. The most influential of the feminist organizations, the League for Women's Rights (Syndesmos Gia ta Dikaiomata ton Gynaikon) fought doggedly for the universal human rights of women on the basis of equality, joining trade unions in defense of the principle of equal pay for equal work, and the establishment of a minimum wage that was the same, for both women and men workers. Yet, as Avdela observes in both cases, this never extended beyond principled declarations. Feminists expressed only occasional concern for the plight of female industrial labor and refrained from criticizing the trade unions' contradictory demands for both women's protection and equality.[40]

An article that was published in the largest refugee newspaper, *Prosfygikos Kosmos* (Refugee world), by a writer known as Elvira, was a rebuttal to the articles (*kosmografimata*) of a Mr. Kosmografos, in which he criticized female refugees as insensitive and indifferent to the plight of refugees for their rights and for their daily bread, and for not being feminists. Elvira wrote:

> I don't know what Mr. K means by feminism. I don't know for example if his perception of feminism is the same as that of "Women's Struggle" and the old rich and ugly women that have no other way to pass their time,

and out of atavism and snobbery, pursue useless electoral and other rights without first securing the most basic rights of women and children. Perhaps it's because that's what women in England are also doing. If on the other hand the point of well-meaning feminism is the dawning of women's economic independence and emancipation, on that score, refugee women have achieved great progress out of necessity, incomparably greater progress than that achieved by native women (*dopies*).[41]

The crisis of female industrial labor, especially refugee labor, generated sporadic and relatively few articles in the League's journal, *O Agonas tis Gynaikas* (Woman's struggle). Fewer than twenty articles were dedicated to the subject of industrial labor between 1923 and 1930, the peak crisis years. In chronological order, these articles focused on unemployment among refugee women, child labor and illiteracy, professional and vocational training, squalid working conditions and exploitation, wages, equal pay for equal work, and the indifference or inertia of working women preventing them from pursuing their own interests and helping themselves.[42] The League was keenly aware of the filthy conditions and worsening exploitation, but ultimately deemed that it "could do little more than to report it to the general public."[43] As Avdela notes, League feminists were much more engaged with the equality/difference debate, as it related to the demands of women office clerks, than with workers in general who voiced no demands at all.[44] The singular exception here was Maria Desypri (Svolou), a co-founder and secretary of the League, who in fact resigned from it in 1932, disillusioned with the inability of bourgeois feminist politics to address issues of systemic class-based privilege and power, in which, she argued, both women and men were equally implicated.[45] She turned to socialism and sympathized with the communists although she was never a member of the Greek Communist Party.

KKE and the Refugee Moment

The fact of endemic and extreme workplace exploitation does not necessarily evolve into self-conscious, organized political action or radicalization; the coinciding circumstances of the Greek Communist Party in the throes of "revolutionary transformation" were also a vital feature of the context. At first, like the rest of Greek society, the SEKE/KKE treated the destitute refugees who arrived on Greek shores as a foreign body.[46] The Party saw the refugees as a mere electoral tool of Venizelism, a negative force in the labor market, a threat to wages and conditions, the cause of rising unemployment. Throughout the interwar period, the refugee labor force, largely women and children, was often used as a reserve labor force, to counteract trade union campaigns. The period witnessed many cases of un-unionized refugee workers being used as strike-breakers. As the director of the International Labor Office, A. Thomas, stated in March 1927, "the working class is unable to defend against employers who respond to every organised worker campaign with mass sackings, replacing the unionised workers with unprotected refugee labour."[47]

By 1925 the Bolshevizing KKE decided that it was "precisely the right moment for our Party to appear among the refugee masses and to lead their struggle."[48] It had begun to recognize that, like the native population, refugee communities were characterized by class division and exploitation, that the "native Greek plutocracy was in cahoots with the upper refugee classes against the great majority of the refugee populations."[49] By the end of the decade the Party made no distinction between native and refugee labor, appealing to *one* working class and a united class-consciousness: "Greece is not divided between natives and refugees but by rich and poor, by people who cannot work to live, and people who work but cannot live. . . . Each of us has to choose between the rich refugee who aligns himself [sic] with the rich native, and the poor refugee whose comrade is the poor native worker."[50]

Class-based politics enabled the KKE to call out the exploitative nature and vested interests of the various refugee "mediators" in the community, highlighting internal class divisions and realigning the political loyalties of refugees accordingly.

The communist daily *Rizospastis* ran with the treachery of the Venizelos government and that of its rich refugee clients, inciting the betrayed refugees to fight "with the native oppressed masses under the banner of the KKE, not their overlords (*tsorbadzides*), and to demand full compensation for the estates they left in Turkey (as stated in the Lausanne Convention), and the cancellation of all debts owed to the Greek Refugee Resettlement Commission, the state, and the banks."[51]

The communist campaign was vindicated when the Ankara Agreement of 1930 withdrew these obligations, ending any hope for repatriation and compensation and paving the way for the shift leftward of the refugee vote.[52] The Refugee Settlement Commission was also disbanded in 1930. Up to this point, the vast majority of refugees, a portion of whom belonged to the middle classes of Asia Minor and Bulgaria, remained Venizelists, staunch supporters of the liberal statesman Eleftherios Venizelos, despite their reduced circumstances.

The refugee's overwhelming support for Venizelos accounted for much of the conflict and volatility that defines the period of the Second Hellenic Republic (1924–1935).[53] Venizelos and Venizelism, the characteristics of which included irredentism, liberalism, civic nationalism, secularism, republicanism, cosmopolitanism, centrism, and pro-Westernism, shook the conservative royalist political culture associated with "Old Greece," which consisted of pre-Balkan War territories. The old elite was often lukewarm about national expansion because its powerbase in the old core of the state would be diluted by the addition of new lands whose inhabitants often worked in new industries. Venizelos's "bourgeois revolution" gave rise to a new class based on manufacturing, shipping, the professions, and other fresh forms of enterprise; it attempted to end the patronage/clientelism system, the manipulation of votes and other tools of the old oligarchical parties, none of which was welcomed by the political heirs of the old notables and landowners.

A major fault line known as the Ethnikos Dichasmos (National Schism) emerged between this bloc and "New Greece" (territories gained after the Balkan Wars of 1912–13) represented by the liberals (Venizelists) that remained a feature of Greek politics till the Second World War. As Macrakis notes, Venizelos was a politician who combined a bold modernist vision tempered by a pragmatic approach with an understanding of Greece's need to maintain strong ties with the West, especially Britain and France.[54] This vision had long appealed to major Greek communities living outside Greek borders (Ottoman Greeks and diaspora Greeks), especially those settled in urban commercial centers, who, as Kitroeff states, were almost by definition predisposed to endorse a pro-Western stance because it strengthened their own status.[55] Even though the refugees had become toiling proletarians, it was only after Venizelos extinguished all hopes for compensation and repatriation with the signing of the Greco-Turkish Friendship Treaty in 1930, that they began to act and behave as members of the working class.[56]

Refugee representation in the Party leadership had started to increase from as early as 1925. Eleftherios Stavridis, born near Istanbul, moved to Greece in 1911 and assumed leadership of the Party from 1925 to 1926; Pastias Giatsopoulos, born in Bulgaria, migrated to Greece in 1919 and became general secretary in 1926; Andronikos Haitas, a Pontian communist from Sokhum, Georgia, came to Greece in 1922 and took the helm in 1927. KKE chief Nikos Zachariadis was born in the Ottoman province of Edirne

(Adrianoupoli in Greek) in 1903 to an ethnic Greek family. Zachariadis was among the thousands of men who flocked to the expanding ports of the Ottoman Empire to work as stevedores, boatmen, and coal heavers, eventually becoming involved in the labor movement in Istanbul.[57] After the Greek defeat in the Greco-Turkish War and the population exchange between the two countries, the Zachariadis family, like so many others, was forcibly relocated to Greece in 1922 and fell into poverty. Inspired by the Russian Revolution, Zachariadis traveled to the Soviet Union soon after, where he joined the Communist Youth of the Russian Communist Party, the Komsomol, and at later stages studied at the Kommunistichesky Universitet Trudiashchikhsia Vostoka (KUTV; Communist University of the Toilers of East) and the Mezhdunarodnaia leninskaia shkola (MLS; International Lenin School). He returned to Greece from the Soviet Union in 1923 to organize the OKNE and eight years later was appointed general secretary by the order of Stalin to restore order in the highly factionalized KKE. Zachariadis was a member of the Central Committee of the KKE (1924–1927), a member of the Politburo (1931–1935), a deputy in the Greek Parliament (1936), and a member of the ECCI (1935–1943). Like many other Greek communists, he emigrated to the Eastern bloc after the communist defeat in the Greek Civil War (1946–1949). He was removed from his position in the Party after Khrushchev's secret speech of 1956 and expelled from the Party in 1957. According to KGB claims, Zachariadis ended his own life in Surgut, Siberia, in 1973.[58] Chrysa Hatzivasiliou, a refugee from Aydin (Aidinio in Greek), an ethnic Greek–majority province of Western Anatolia who had joined the Party in 1925, would not be elected to the Central Committee until 1935, and to the Politburo in 1942.

The majority of the Central Committee of the KKE and almost all members of the Politburo after 1931, the year in which KKE and Comintern interests became inextricably intertwined, were not "domestic cadres" but refugees from Asia Minor and the greater diaspora, including the Pontos, the Balkans, and the Greeks of Russia.[59] A significant percentage of this group had also been trained at one of the Comintern schools.[60] On one hand, the growing refugee representation in the leadership, Moscow-trained or otherwise, gave substance to the argument that after 1924 the Party became disconnected from and could not respond to Greek political realities.[61] On the other hand, it cannot be discounted as a factor in the eventual leftward shift of the refugee vote, in addition to the disappointments of the Ankara Agreement of 1930 and the effects of the global economic crisis. Rapid industrialization and the proletarianization of the refugee population both occurred under the pincer of the debt burden which created an explosive radical mix. To give one example, between 1928 and 1938 labor productivity increased by 43 percent and wages increased by 24 percent; consumer prices between 1922 and 1935 increased by 207 percent, whereas wages rose by only 83 percent. This brought social struggle and left-wing politics to the forefront of a decaying political system whose main cleavage remained the same: Venizelists versus royalist populist factions.[62]

The "Woman Question" Revisited

By May 1925, an important month on the communist calendar, factory cells across the country pursued the directive to engage energetically with the daily life of men and women workers, to organize them, and to engage in direct political action.[63] Every member of the Party was obliged to enlist one new recruit, who would then be initiated by that member into his/her cell. The status of the new members was provisional; permanent membership could be bestowed after a process of review by local committees.[64] Party publications underscored the importance of ongoing recruitment as an essential prerequisite for the existence and life of the Party: "If recruitment stops, the replenishment of the blood of the Party organism stops; the development of the connection between the Party and the masses stops, the Party cannot advance its aims, it begins to shrivel and decompose."[65]

Accordingly, the Party's commitment to the "woman question" was invigorated at this time, and perhaps even earlier with the Party's introduction of International Women's Day (IWD) in Greece in March 1924, some months before the Third Extraordinary Congress of December 1924. For Angelika Psarra, IWD was the first act of Bolshevization regarding women, an event that became "central in communist women's course along the path of politics."[66] Gender representation and equality was not a new principle for the SEKE/KKE; it was the first Greek political party to have written the "full civil, political, economic, and social equality of women and men" into its charter, but Bolshevization called for a renewed focus and clarification, in Greece, as elsewhere, of the so-called "work among women."[67] As noted in the previous chapter, 1925 saw the inauguration of the Women's Office, and Greek representation at the Comintern's Organization Conference of the Enlarged Executive on the "Work Amongst Women," followed by frequent attendance of Greek delegations at international Comintern congresses, where they presented reports on various aspects and problems of the Greek movement, including progress reports on the "work among women."[68]

A small and very active cohort of aspiring *Bolshevichki* had been writing on the woman question in the Party's theoretical journal *Kommounistiki Epitheorisi* (*KOMEP*; Communist review) and in the communist daily *Rizospastis* since 1919, reflecting the influence of the Comintern on the political and intellectual climate in the KKE that had been established the same year. Inspired by the new Soviet state, *Rizospastis* and *KOMEP* began to publish translations of key revolutionary texts and theoretical articles that heralded the new gender relations that would emerge out of the classless society or deliberated on the form and content of communist propaganda and the work among women.[69] The writings of Ioanna Komioti, the best known and most prolific of these early contributors to *Rizospastis*, emphasized the familiar mantra of gender equality (*isopoliteia*) as essential for the establishment of the classless society and vice versa.[70]

The increasing subordination of the KKE to Comintern authority allowed Comintern delegates to appoint the Party's leaders directly or indirectly, and to determine and monitor the implementation of policies, including those regarding women. The Women's Office was inaugurated in January 1925. In the same month it issued a call to girls and women in the pages of *Rizospastis*: "All working girls and women of the city and the meadows . . . walk beside us under the banner of the Greek Communist Party, alongside our counterparts in the other countries, and fight for the establishment of a new society of working and free peoples."[71]

In the following months Greece sent a delegation to the Comintern's Organization Conference of the Enlarged Executive on the "Work Amongst Women," by A. Sgrudeos.[72] In 1925 the newly inaugurated Women's Office of the KKE was visited by a representative of the Communist Women's International, sent to Greece by Ruth Fischer, to help organize the communist women's movement in Greece.[73] In 1925, the first Greek translation of Zetkin's *Converzations with Lenin* was published in Greece. In 1925 the KKE sent its first "promising" female militants, Smaro Kritikou and Olga Paterouli, two refugees from Istanbul, to the Soviet Union, to study at the Communist University for the Toilers of the East (KUTV).[74]

The Party's renewed interest in its youth wing, OKNE, founded in 1922, led them to make it a "section" (*tmima*) in 1925, subject to the "political direction of the Party, whose program it must accept and according to whose political line it must act."[75] When members turned twenty-five, following recommendation by the cell, they automatically entered the Party.

Thus starting in 1925 the OKNE's status as a "feeder" organization for the Party became systematized. Members could also graduate into the Party at nineteen years, subject to the agreement of regional committees of the Party and the OKNE. All aspiring and new members had to be introduced or sponsored into the Party by two existing members, after which their membership would be brought to a vote at the next Party meeting.[76] Party documents claimed that membership numbers began to see a "serious increase" in 1925 and 1926.[77] This was despite intensifying persecution under the Pangalos dictatorship, including its establishment of a new police unit, the Special Security Services (Ypiresia Eidikis Asfaleias), for the purpose of monitoring "foreign propaganda" and communist activity, and its outlawing of the KKE in January 1926.[78]

According to Party historian Christos Tzitzilionis, the first communist youth cells were formed within institutions of learning at this juncture. "Male and female students were recruited from high schools and universities for the first time, paving the way for multiple ongoing student strikes."[79] Reports compiled by the Greek military and the police regarding communist activity corroborate the particular success of the communist movement's efforts within institutions of learning, a phenomenon attributed to their "progressive spirit," the impressionable nature of youth, and a proliferation of "fanatical" communist teachers enabled by the liberal democratic state.[80] It was also understood as a strategic response of the communist movement in the face of intensifying state efforts to stifle access to workers.

> Illegal protests and demonstrations could not take place under the new measures. Communist leaflets aimed at school and university students, soldiers, sailors and working youth did not circulate widely due to ongoing close surveillance of various communist cells. Thus, OKNE activists focused their propaganda efforts on students. There are countless cells across the city's high schools. Female students in thrall to propaganda were also discovered. As far as higher education is concerned, the university holds the record for students inspired by the anarchic ideas of communism. . . . The greatest danger to the status quo, at present, does not come from the toiling masses, organized or otherwise. The most serious threat emanates from the emboldened ranks of communist youth who are well placed to lead a revolutionary charge once the order is given.[81]

Achilleas Kalevras (1878–1972), a Greek merchant, politician, senator, minister, and prefect (*nomarchis*), wrote profusely on the short-sightedness and shortcomings of the Greek state, and in particular of the Minister of Public Education and Religious Affairs, Ricardos Livathinopoulos, for not taking adequate measures against communist high school students and returning them to the right path.

> We are tragic witnesses to a miserable social scene: To observe the communist family constantly and actively inspired by a fanaticism of unimaginable cruelty, sending mini apostles of the "idea" to schools, to then blow up (dynamite) society and by extension the bourgeois family, more or less passive, oblivious, fatalistic, bourgeois family that expects all will be sorted by the intervention of the state.... No sermon by a teacher can shake the spirit of the communist high school student influenced as he [sic] is by his fanatical father and even more by his fanatical mother.... Today in many high schools the dominant students are communists. Because they abide by some kind of faith.... The youth of the bourgeoisie have no faith. Tired, anemic, weakened that they feel nothing for the image of the Greek flag. This youth has a need for an intense and exceptional psychic motive to rise to the bullet of an ideal.[82]

It was during this period that the students who would play a historic role in the history of OKNE and the women's movement were recruited: Electra Apostolou (1926/1927), "Raika" (1926), and Avra Vlassi-Partsalidou (1926), who recalls the network of comrades (*syndrofisses*) who oversaw the process of her own induction into the OKNE, which involved studying "the ABC of communism, once a week for three months, with five other women, under the instruction of another student, Eleni Roussaki."[83] Following the arrest of Apostolou, Vlassi-Partsalidou, and her sister Persa Vlassi in 1931, authorities described them as well-known communists responsible for propaganda among female workers and students.[84]

An extract from the autobiographical entry of the Comintern file of Electra Apostolou (pseud., Koula Drakou and Tasia Georgiadou) offers insights into the culture and process of Bolshevization from a young woman's point of view.

> I have never been a member of any other parties or organizations. In May 1927 I joined the Komsomol of Greece. I was recommended by my older brother who had been a member since 1921. Until the spring of 1929 I had been working as a rank-and-file member of the cell. And then I was elected as a member of the regional leadership.... In 1930 I was co-opted

by the county leadership of Athens. In 1931 I started working as the editor of our Central mass newspaper which I did till 1933.... Currently (1935) I am working as an organizer of a factory cell. During my Party life I have recruited 14 members to the Komsomol and two to the Party. There were six women among them.[85]

Raika's writing on the woman question dominated the critical period between 1925 and 1927. Appointed by KKE general secretary Pandelis Pouliopoulos to lead the Women's Office in 1925, Raika defined the nature of women's liberation for communist women in the same terms as Komioti: "The only natural ally of women's emancipation, the only healthy positive element we can depend upon, is the working class."[86] This was faithfully buttressed by the critique of bourgeois feminism and its inherent contradictions, and of suffrage as the panacea of women's liberation.[87] Raika argued that the vote would be granted by Parliament only when it was deemed necessary "for its own legitimation"; it would never change the lot of women.[88] Her term ended when she was purged in 1927 by association with Pouliopoulos and the Trotskyists.[89] Like Komioti, Raika's works, including her real name, have faded from view.[90] As Katsiamboura notes of this earlier period, "both the personalities and their writings have been virtually written out of the historiography."[91]

The increase in the communist output on the "woman question" has been interpreted by scholars Katsiamboura and Psarra as a response to the intensification of feminist campaigns for the women's vote in Greece at this time.[92] This is only partly correct. Between the worsening plight of an expanding and unprotected female industrial labor force and the KKE's drive to "double the forces of the Party," the "meagre" numbers of Party women and the sporadic, "fluid" nature of their activism and membership gave way to a larger and more embedded female constituency, many of whom were urban refugees.[93]

To be sure, the mass injection of refugee labor worsened the exploitation that had long defined female industrial labor since its beginnings in the nineteenth century. Many refugee women workers brought attributes to the workplace that opened new opportunities for organization. They were frequently single or widowed. Their former social world destroyed, they entered a new working environment in which they found opportunities to create new personal and political identities and to forge new kinds of relationships. Many of them were very well educated and able to enter the labor market, creating new forms of employment and acting as a driving force for

Greek women in general. Indeed, contemporary sources convey the resolve of refugees to "not give up to misery," but rather to "unite and to react," as characteristic of refugee communities as a whole.[94] For example, working widows and children in Thessaloniki formed the Enosis Hiron kai Orfanon Dikaiouchon Andallaximon (Union of Entitled Widows and Orphans), which was "very successful" among refugees, and whose membership grew dramatically in a very short space of time. *Prosfygikos Kosmos* wrote:

> What happens in their offices even on a Sunday is beyond description. During working days hundreds of toiling women storm the offices of their association to join. But that which most beggars belief is the asphyxiating crowds that gather there on Sunday, women of all ages and backgrounds lining up to sign up from all over Thessaloniki. The masses of haggard human ruins provoke pity and reflect the misery. The vision of thousands of miserable beings cannot but move all but the most hardened hearts. All those widows drag themselves to the association believing that only their united efforts will secure their rights if an inhumane government decides to challenge them. Without question the uprising of the female world against the callousness and irresponsibility of the present government will have a direct impact on the rest of Greece.[95]

Refugee women joined trade unions and became agitators for higher wages and better working conditions. Within the variously supportive structures of union activism women found themselves in positions in which they could be taken seriously. Chrysa Hatzivasiliou, for example, found her way from the trade union into the highest echelons of the Party. Born in 1903 in Aidinio (Aydin), Turkey, to a family of well-to-do peasants, Hatzivasiliou moved to Greece with her father in 1922 after the exchange of populations. She had completed secondary school and worked as a typist and accountant in private firms in Salonika and Athens between 1922 and 1924, becoming a member of the Greek Union of Office Workers and OKNE in 1924. She joined the Greek Communist Party the following year, and soon after became a member of the Athens and Salonika OKNE regional committees and the district committee of the KKE in Athens. She was also employed as a typist for the Central Committee of the KKE and at the Soviet Embassy in Athens; all of this culminated in a Party recommendation to study at the Communist University for the National Minorities of the West in 1928.[96] But many women resisted or remained out of reach of the agencies of political organizations of the era like the trade unions (*somateia*), presenting a particular struggle for the communists—and feminist organizations—that tried to mobilize them.

Red Tobacco

Tobacco had always been among the biggest employers of working women, along with textiles, dressmaking, and paper production.[97] The arrival of the refugees, especially the women, transformed these industries, and also created new ones such as the carpet industry. The tobacco plant owned, for example, by the Matsagou Brothers in Nea Ionia, Volos, founded in 1890, was a small enterprise with modest production and few workers till 1919. After 1922 and the absorption of female refugee labor, its production and exports doubled, as did the size of the factory building site. By 1930 it employed five hundred workers.[98] Betas notes that the most important component of the firm's workforce during the interwar period was women, mainly refugees from Asia Minor. In the 1928 census, 57 percent of the tobacco workforce in Volos was refugees, of which 77 percent were women.[99] The predominance of a female refugee workforce in tobacco was seen not only in the cigarette factories of Volos but in tobacco warehouses and factories across the country. The tobacco industry in interwar Greece is thus central to any examination of refugee radicalization between the Wars given the preponderance of female refugee labor in tobacco, and the historic ties between the tobacco union and the communist movement. The Greek Tobacco Workers' Federation (Kapnergatiki Omospondia Elladas) was also referred to as the Red Trade Union of Tobacco Workers. It was the oldest and most militant and stoutly organized union in Greece, and the only "autonomous" union, which according to Koumandaraki, accounted for its militancy, in contrast to the traditional subservience of the Greek trade union movement to the state. The autonomy and militancy of the tobacco union, in turn, is attributed to the deep influence of the Communist Party in the tobacco regions of Macedonia and particularly Thessaloniki, tobacco being the most underpaid sector.[100] Indeed, working in the tobacco industry was considered by many as the first step before joining the Party.[101]

According to official data there were 21,426 women employed in Greek tobacco in 1927, compared with 29,175 men; by 1932 the number of women and men had reached parity (19,500: 20,000) although the number of employees dropped due to increasing mechanization of the industry.[102] Most of the girls and women were of working-class origin, and most had received little formal education. Some came from "tobacco families" who had worked in tobacco for generations in Anatolia and gravitated naturally to it upon arrival in Greece. It is perhaps the case that some among them had already been exposed to labor activism in their land of origin given the militancy of the tobacco industry throughout the Ottoman Empire, from Egypt to the Mediterranean. Khuri-Makdisi states that the tobacco industry had been producing a culture of contestation and an inclination toward radical politics dating back to the late nineteenth century.[103] The centers of tobacco production within the Ottoman Empire—Istanbul, Izmir, Thessaloniki, and Egypt—were all characterized by the prominence of Greek families in cigarette production.[104] Indeed, Greek subjects constituted the majority of Orthodox Christian factory workers across the Empire in the industrializing late Ottoman period.[105]

Balsoy describes a persistent "mutual distancing" between labor history and women's and gender history that accounts for the lacuna in the historiography of the Ottoman Empire regarding women's work in tobacco and cigarette production. Using photographic archives, her work on the Cibali Régie Factory, one of the largest tobacco processing and cigarette manufacturing factories in the Ottoman Empire, reveals that a substantial segment of the factory's labor force consisted of female workers, who, given their uncovered hair, were presumably non-Muslims, probably Greek or Jewish due to the specific location of the factory near the Greek and Jewish quarters.[106] Photographic evidence also reveals a history of worker protest involving female workers. In 1904, Cibali factory workers organized a major strike to reclaim weekly payments withheld from them. Of the 250 protesters, 50 were female workers.[107]

On arrival in Greece, large numbers of refugees were absorbed as cheap factory labor by an expanding tobacco industry, most destined for the tobacco towns of Kavala, Volos, and Thessaloniki, although tobacco warehouses and cigarette factories proliferated across the country in response to mechanization and technological advances. Mechanization itself, as Betas has argued, was driven by the availability of large volumes of cheap(er) and very talented female refugee workers, mostly from Asia Minor, who were known to work "faster than the machines themselves."[108]

Extracts of the autobiographies of future Comintern students Stella Vamniatzidou (pseud. Elena Arnova) and Elena Anemelou, both refugee tobacco workers, offer rare insights into the strong links between organized female tobacco workers and the communist movement in the interwar period. Vamniatzidou refers to her induction thus:

I was born in 1910, in Fragia, in Raedestos. My nationality is Greek. My father was a peasant of modest means, later a refugee; we lived very poorly. I started working at the tobacco factory at the age of twelve. For ten years I worked at various factories in the city of Kavala. I am married to a tobacco worker, a party member since 1929. I have been a member of the Red Trade Union of Tobacco Workers since 1924, a member of Ergatiki Boitheia (Greek branch of International Red Aid) since 1929 where I held various elected positions, the most senior of them as a member of the regional committee of the MOPR. I did not go to school at all, I eliminated my illiteracy later after I joined the party. I have practically no party-political education with the exception of attending the propaganda classes in the cell. Before I joined the Party, I had not been a member of any other parties. I joined the Communist Party in 1931 in the city of Kavala. I was a member of the cell bureau almost since the very start after I joined the Party. In 1932 at the party conference of the city of Kavala I was elected a member of the regional party committee. As a party member I carried out work in the masses of the tobacco workers, organized strikes, meetings, rallies, I was appointed by the regional committee as the leader of one of the cells.... I was arrested in May 1932 during one of the meetings of the underground trade union. I was sentenced to one month in prison.[109]

Elena Anemelou (pseud. Dimitrieva) was born in December 1911 in Panormou, Asia Minor, to a "workers" family. She had completed two years of high school before she had to find employment to support the family. "My father was a sailor, my mother was a tobacco worker. My father died in 1912. In 1922 we became refugees and went to Kavala in Greece. In 1923 I started to work in a tobacco factory and worked there until 1928. In 1924 I joined the Red Union of Tobacconists and in 1925 I joined the Greek Komsomol."[110]

However, the status of women in the Greek tobacco union was precarious. As Efi Avdela has shown, starting in the late 1920s, the steady trend within the international tobacco market toward cheaper leaves promoted gender conflict; new technologies and the mechanization of production combined with fluctuations in the crop's market prices and overproduction led gradually to an extensive restructuring or "feminization" of the entire tobacco labor market, which had a destabilizing effect on the situation of male workers. One of the most important developments related to this restructuring was the introduction of cheap processing methods employing mainly women, so that "skilled" male unemployment increased significantly. In the 1930s, despite the fact that women were by then accepted as union members, the unions tried repeatedly to restrict their employment and to secure male predominance in numbers and wages, culminating in what Avdela refers to as the masculinization of the dominant trade union representation alongside the feminization of the actual labor force.[111]

While Party literature lauded the successful organization of female tobacco workers, it expressed continuing concern for their persistent underrepresentation in the tobacco union and in trade unions overall. In 1928 *Rizospastis* stepped up the call for women's full trade union rights and their right to vote and to be elected. Special attention was directed toward the tobacco union given women's very high numbers in that industry and the especially unhygienic conditions in both the tobacco (and textile) industries. In combination with very long work hours, the conditions let to serious illness, particularly tuberculosis, for many female workers.[112]

In her study of the textile industry in the port-city of Piraeus, Athens, between the wars, Papastefanaki states that by 1927 the organization of women workers in Piraeus had become a focus of the local KKE cells, which had been reconstituted and revitalized according to the tenets of Bolshevization. Indeed, seamstresses of military garments, tobacco workers, and carpet workers in the cities turned out in droves to labor union meetings and to strikes, even without party efforts, further illuminating the potential of women's mobilization in the battle against capitalism if only there was an effort made to rally them. The aims regarding the women's movement were established thus: to form a strong women's committee capable of directing a program for action and work among women workers; to fight to organize women into their trade unions, especially the textile and carpet workers, so they would have equal rights with their male counterparts; to publish a fortnightly newspaper for women; and to infiltrate the large textiles and carpet factories where they worked. KKE documents refer in particular to the exclusion of women textile workers (3,500 to 4,000 in Piraeus) from the communist labor organizations in which 60 percent of men in the trade participated, a problem attributed by the Party to an inadequate appetite for resistance, the apathy of the members. Unlike the tobacco sector, the textiles sector was not known for its "revolutionary traditions," but interest in it steadily increased as reflected in reports published in *Rizospastis*; the publishing arm of the youth wing, *Neolaia*; and the KKE trade union paper *Syndicalistis*.

The "Work among Women"

At the Fourth Party Congress in 1929 it was noted that "work among women" was undermined by ongoing indifference toward organizational work within the women's movement; their organization required the establishment of support committees from the center to the local organizations in order to succeed; the participation of women in the fractions needed to be boosted, especially within the trade unions that have lots of women members; and the women's movement needed a centralized publishing organ.[113] The newspaper *Ergatria* (Woman Worker) was established immediately after the Congress, published and distributed by the staff of the Athens Women's Office of the communist-dominated Enotiki Geniki Synomospondia Ellinon Ergaton (EGSEE or Enotiki; Unitary Greek General Workers' Confederation) formed in February 1929. *Ergatria* was distributed in factories and door to door throughout working-class neighborhoods. It was a four-page affair that focused on the lives of working women, which sold—or rather didn't sell—at the Socialist Bookshop.[114] Nevertheless, it was a big success among women workers on the factory floor because it was written in plain language and dealt with their issues.[115]

Avra Partsalidou recalls the exceptional militancy of the refugee female carpet workers (*tapitourgines*), whose many strikes and demonstrations were covered regularly in the pages of *Ergatria* but who had not made any connection with the Party. Staff from the Women's Office of the Party and OKNE would visit their homes in Podaradon, Kaisariani, Kallithea, and other red working neighborhoods to distribute copies of the newspaper and to get to know them, in this way helping the local cells to approach them.[116] The sight of communist women distributing issues of *Ergatria*, seeking the attention of women workers outside the textiles factories in parts of Athens, such as Podaradon, became commonplace. Partsalidou recalls, "The workers passed by us in groups. None of them stopped for fear of being seen by their employers. Some stared at our women as oddities, others looked with fondness because they understood very well, especially those who had relatives on the left in the district, that the women standing on the bench spreading propaganda, however strange and awkward, belonged to them."[117]

The deterrents to organizing girls and women began in the workplace itself. In 1931, sparked by the strike action taken by carpet workers in the industrial precincts of Piraeus, Kokkinia, Drapetsona, and Tambouria, the newspaper dedicated an issue to the plight of women workers for whom the right of association had little meaning. They were regularly followed and monitored by supervisors, or by favored employees. . . . The bosses deployed various methods to maintain control or at least to undermine cohesion or any attempt of the women to organize themselves. One worker claimed that in order to thwart any organization by the women, bosses would become "godfathers" to their children in return for loyalty, or otherwise exercise outright terror and threaten them with sacking.[118]

There were gender-specific obstructions to membership and activism across all the mass organizations including OKNE and the Party, as it demanded absolute commitment, long days, and many hours spent away from home, work, studies, and families. Strict honor-based codes of conduct, restricting the movement of girls and women in particular, frustrated the work of activists and obstructed the recruitment of others. Electra Apostolou spoke often of her own struggle, constantly marveling at how some other girls (*sindrofisses*) managed to "escape from their homes" to get to the OKNE offices.[119] Anti-communist discourse was very keen to portray the KKE as a "construct of immoral types," whose main purpose was the common ownership of women, the destruction of the family, and the abolition of religion. Newspapers would regularly run full-page stories depicting the promiscuous lives of KKE and OKNE women, often with photographs of the women themselves, which would result in family chaos and at times the loss of employment.[120] This was compounded by biomedical discourse that characterized the communists as "sexual paranoids," driven only by libido, the Party, and the Soviet Union. In this discourse, even the KKE's controversial policy on Macedonian autonomy was intrinsically linked with communist ideology on "self-sovereignty in sexuality," regarded as the major cause of sexually transmitted disease in the population.[121] When the Comintern endorsed and sanctioned the revised Bulgarian Communist Party policy that called for a united and independent Macedonia (and Thrace) within a Balkan Communist Federation, KKE's association with the Comintern—and the policy—caused a major general outcry branding the KKE as national traitors and equating communism with sedition. As pressure from outside and from within its ranks mounted, the leadership of the Party abandoned the policy in 1935 and adopted a new resolution emphasizing "equality for minorities."[122]

During the economic-crisis-ridden 1930s, deteriorating working conditions and increasing job insecurity preoccupied multiple labor sectors from tobacco to bakers. This led to waves of worker protests and strikes across the big industrial centers that provided a pretext for the end of parliamentary politics. The task of winning over working women gained greater traction following the election gains of KKE in 1933, but as Partsalidou wrote, it was both "easy and difficult." It was easy because the growing despair of women workers and their willingness to fight was evident, as demonstrated in the tenacity of the female tobacco workers of Volos, Kavala, Nigrita in the summer of 1932, the strikes of workers for higher wages at Sakka and Vlachaki plants of Thessaloniki, and the demonstrations of unemployed tobacco and textile workers across the country, "all of which demonstrated how capable women were of understanding and fighting for their dues."[123] It was difficult because of the constraints placed on women as both breadwinners and (often single) mothers. This was compounded by entrenched cultural prejudice against women's involvement in politics—especially communism—and the ever-intensifying state persecution of trade-unionists and communists, both men and women.

Radicalizing Tradition: Red Aid

The Greek Communist Party argued that the obstacles to women's organization could only be dealt with by creating Support Committees (Epitropes Ypostirixis) for women workers, a strategy tabled at the 1929 Congress but that had not been adequately or uniformly implemented. Support Committees would need to be formed for women workers, unemployed women, and farmers within the frameworks of their respective associations/unions, as decided at the 5th Congress of the Profintern and by the Women Workers' Conference at the first Congress of the General Confederation of Greek Workers (Enotiki Geniki Synomospondia). The Red International of Labor Unions, commonly known as the Profintern, was an international body established by the Communist International in 1921 with the aim of coordinating communist activities within trade unions.[124] At the 5th Profintern Congress (Moscow, 1930) and the 8th Conference of the Central Committee of the Profintern, Lusovsky reiterated the importance of electing women workers to every factory committee, strike committee, and administrative section of all factory-based Revolutionary Union Units (Ergostasiakes Epanastatikes Syndikalistikes Omades). He laid out instructions for the development of the appropriate support structure to achieve these goals in the form of separate women's committees on the factory floor, especially when the numbers of women were high. He was also careful to emphasize that the organization of women workers was an issue that had to be dealt with not only by these women's sections, but the whole organization, from the bottom to the top.[125] Partsalidou recalls that trade-union work was closely monitored by the Party thereafter. "Every communist had to be a member of (his) union and to be very active within it."[126]

The KKE became aware that the mass organizations, and especially those with strong neighborhood and community ties, had to be harnessed in the effort to approach women. Women had to be approached very carefully using particular methods, as they had particular problems, and they lived and worked under particular circumstances. In a 1933 article published in the *KOMEP* (Communist Review), Avra Partsalidou stressed the importance of

> holding early meetings and avoiding late night meetings and demonstrations for newly recruited women workers, who often encountered arguments or worse, when they got home. The great majority of women workers are not emancipated, nor can they break ties with the home, as it suits. . . . Nor can we expect women workers to abandon all their petit bourgeois perceptions and habits (grooming, makeup, dances, religious beliefs) when they enter our organization. Instead of cursing them as we have so often done, we should understand the social context, and educate them.[127]

The most important of these mass organizations were the Omospondia Ergatikou Athlitismou (Greek Workers' Sports Federation) and Ergatiki Boitheia Elladas (EBE; Labor Assistance Greece). The former, founded in 1927, was the Greek chapter of the Red Sports International formed by the Bolshevik Party of the Soviet Union in 1925, whose purpose was to "use sports consciously as a medium for the mobilization of workers and peasants around the Party and the trade unions, to draw them organically into political and social activism." Accordingly, the chief targets of the Greek organization were to facilitate contact with the large numbers of women workers, especially Jews and refugees, who were drawn to sport, many of whom were members of "reactionary athletic associations," especially in the big cities of Athens and Thessaloniki.[128] The second organization, EBE, was a mutual aid organization founded at the Third Extraordinary Congress in 1924; EBE was the Greek chapter of the Comintern's Mezhdunarodnoye Obshchestvo Pomoshtchi Revolutzioneram (MOPR; International Red Aid, or, more precisely, the Organization for Aid to Revolutionaries). The objective of MOPR, as declared at the Comintern's Fourth Congress in November/December 1922, was for member parties to "take the initiative . . . to organize material and moral assistance to vanguard fighters for the cause of communism who are locked in prison, forced into exile, or for any reason excluded against their will from our fighting ranks." MOPR branches were to be founded in every country, especially those dealing with white terror. In Greece, the EBE became a very powerful network of daily support and solidarity for militants and their families against the backdrop of intensifying persecution of communists.[129]

The care-based focus of EBE, the provision of moral and material support to the victims of white terror, appealed to and was able to draw large numbers of women into its ranks, offering them a form activism within the traditional gender bounds that was both familiar and less likely to meet with resistance or suspicion. It enabled the participation of women who had children and could not easily gather at cafes or trade union headquarters where the meetings often took place but could possibly gather on weekends at meetings of the women's sections in their own suburbs.

EBE's use of gendered metaphors was designed to appeal to their maternal instincts, as the locus of their revolutionary potential. The following excerpt from an EBE Bulletin issue exemplifies Papastefanaki's observation of communist mobilizational rhetoric in which the "pioneering" woman and the mother nurturer archetype co-exist uncritically:[130]

> The voice of the Mother of the poor and downtrodden. . . . EBE is not just a dry organization. [She is] a living, moving, throbbing organism. (She) is as upright, strong, and haughty as she is snuggly, comforting, and lifeguarding, the mother of the poor man, whichever poor man, who is fighting for his life. Tireless, willing, and moved, the poor mother wanders from village to village, town to town, from the shack to the palace, from the church to the police precinct, and from the school to the factory, asking of her children to give what they can for their brothers and sisters who still live on dried-up islands and in prisons.[131]

The task of making contact with women fell largely on the shoulders of organized female communists like Partsalidou; special women's sections within the Greek chapters of EBE and the Workers Sports Federation were established in 1931. According to the organization, "With the minimum of effort of one or two *syndrofisses* (female comrades), the women's sections of EBE sprouted like mushrooms." The Party claimed that "wherever the support committees came to fruition the results were miraculous."[132]

Echoing the organizational approach of the KKE and the OKNE, the basic organizational unit at the founding of EBE was the local committee (*topiki epitropi*); the club or association (*omilos*) came to dominate operations. This club was set up inside all businesses, factories, shops, offices, universities, schools, suburbs, villages—anywhere and everywhere possible where there were at least five organized EBE members. The club in each village, factory, et cetera, was directed by the nearest local EBE committee, to which it was subordinated.[133] The basic source of income for the activities of the EBE came initially from subscriptions of members and the organization of fundraising cultural events like dances, debutante balls, plays, and day trips. A statement published by the Central Committee of EBE in November 1934 on the organization's economic status lays out the distribution of monies (*drachmae*) as shown in Table 2.[134]

Cultural and fundraising events were often combined with information sessions about the work and aims of EBE. For example, a report on the trip to Podaradon, Athens, mentions that "eighty people participated, forty men and twenty-nine women, most of whom were workers from local factories (Kirkini, Papadopoulou, Nathanail, and others). While they did not visit nearby factories and villages to make more connections, the trip showed how effective clubs could be in mobilizing women of nearby factories."[135]

There are no firm data, however, on EBE membership numbers or gender composition, but ubiquitous references across the sources point to EBE membership as a springboard for women's further involvement in the communist movement, and also indicate that OKNE or KKE membership invariably led to EBE involvement. Incidental references to membership numbers by region or town indicate that the organization in Kavala had more than one thousand members in 1927, one thousand in Athens in 1928; five hundred in Piraeus in the same year; Mytilene had three hundred and Corfu one hundred. According to one statement, the Athens organization reached a membership of seven thousand in 1929. In a protest telegram to the Greek government sent by the Central Committee of the EBE in 1933, the organization claimed to have eleven thousand members in total, including 1,200 in the Peloponnese. In 1935, according to the Greek representative at the 7th Conference of the Comintern, the membership totaled thirteen thousand. In 1936, this number had climbed to eighteen thousand.[136]

The recollections of Greek communist, writer, refugee, and sister of Dido Sotiriou, Elli Pappa, shed light on the culture that characterized the Party during this period, in particular, the activities of the "women's section" (*tomeas ton gynaikon*) of EBE that centered on the refugee neighborhoods.

TABLE 2. EBE BUDGET 1934

Incoming (drachmae)	Outgoing (drachmae)
Remainder – 11,188.90	Recurring costs – 4,834.60
Divisions – 1,543.00	Exile/prison – 1,794.20
Fundraising, reinforcements – 1,200.00	Agit – 4,544.00
Financial reinforcing/support – 300.00	Organizational costs – 4,631.00
Patronage – 3,163.90	Loans – 3395.70
Campaign for Spanish proletariat – 1,250.00	
Loans – 5,998.70	
Total = 19,249.50	**Total = 19,249.50**

> From 1933 I worked at the grassroots (*vasi*) with Electra Apostolou—that modest and true communist—who made my initiation much easier and faster.... We loved walking those endless streets trying to gain the attention of the women from the textile factories (*yfandourgines*) of Nea Ionia, the tobacco workers of Piraeus, and the lively populations of Kaisariani and other neighborhoods. At first, we lent a hand to EB, helping with workers strikes and soup kitchens, liaising with working families, helping them get medical care, etc. We did the rounds of Iraklion, Patisia, Tourkovounia, Ambelokipoi, Vyronas, Dourgouti, Kallithea. We left no stone unturned. The doors of common people and refugee tents opened to greet us with a kind word, some coffee, and above all, understanding. In the beginning of course, it was difficult. They were suspicious of us. They resisted understanding our message, our warnings about the threat of fascism and war that were brewing in our country. They saw us as charity women who handed out books to illiterates when what they needed was work and bread. But we didn't lose heart, we explained to them that we were not charity ladies, did not speak empty words, and wanted to show them the road to having a chance in life. We struggled to establish co-operation with the first enlightened women workers and housewives, but they went on to become the yeast (*prozimi*) of our struggle.[137]

The heavily charged political climate of the interwar period was evident in the frenetic pace of politicization and activism. When Olga Bakola (pseud. Aliki Kanda) found work as a weaver at a cotton mill in Athens in 1933, at age sixteen, she became a member of the Trade Union of Textile

Manufacture Workers, and a correspondent for the communist newspaper *Rizospastis* "within 20–25 days." By 17 April she had joined the OKNE and begun working with EBE. In September, she became the secretary of the reconstituted cell at her factory, and in October, a member of the Union administration and the Panhellenic Antifascist Committee, whose Conference she helped organize.[138]

The organization of women eventually became the focus of the EBE even if it was not so at the time of its founding in 1924. In 1935 the organization's stated task was to increase the numbers from fifteen to thirty with five women; to create EBE bases in shops that didn't have any; to organize women's committees for the women's movement; to hold regular monthly meetings; and to secure houses in which to carry out the work of the association.[139] By 1935, as stated clearly in the EBE bulletin (*Deltio*) itself, women's activism constituted the engine of EBE operations; the women's associations in EBE (*omiloi gynaikon*) and the work of its female members dominated across the regions of Greece, especially in the area of fundraising that was critical for the acquittal of debts of the *collectives* (prison populations). Women's associations proliferated in the refugee neighborhoods of Peristeri, Gouva, Melissia, and Kaisariani, and even extended to the affluent suburb of Kolonaki. Donations were given both by individual women (and men) and by women's associations in Petra, Pilio (Lachanada), Messinia (Loga), Thessalia (Volos Association of Tobacco Workers), Serres, Kamenik, Arahova, Edessa, and Thrace.[140]

The increasing subordination of the EBE to the communist-dominated union movement cannot be underestimated in assessing the relationship between women and the communist movement between the Wars. By 1926 the KKE leadership was directing half of the proceeds of Labor Day to the coffers of EBE, and in the same year KKE support of EBE intensified with the directive that "all members of the KKE and OKNE are required to become members of EBE, and to not do so will be punished. The Central Committee obliges the executive council of the EBE to refrain from assisting any Party or OKNE member who is not an EBE member in the event of their imprisonment or exile."[141] The KKE's request that the EGSEE and its organizations be organically integrated with the EBE clearly signaled the EBE's subjugation by the Confederation and by KKE. By the 1930s, whether deliberately or not, the membership and cadres of EBE were mostly members and cadres of KKE.[142] At the MOPR's first international congress in Moscow in November 1932, attended by sixty-nine national sections, the Greek branch was represented by the KKE's Miltiades Porfyrogenis.[143]

The subsummation of the EBE by the EGSEE—and the KKE—was not an unfavorable development for women. According to Papastefanaki's study of the textile industry in Piraeus, women workers were far more drawn to the methods of the communist union over the reformist Ergatiko Kendro Pirea (EKP; Labor Center Piraeus). The latter preferred to use pleadings, consultation, mediation, and so on, while the communists insisted on the convening of general assemblies, the constitution of strike committees, strike guards for guarding factory entrances, and collective marches to the ministry over broadening the strike. The strategies of the EKP were condemned by the communists as treacherous, that is, cooperating with the government and with employers, which prevented the workers from guarding the strike and assembling.[144] The large numbers of women involved in or affiliated with the EBE, and the intimate links between the EBE, the EGSEE, and the KKE, mark out the EBE as an important bridge to communist involvement until its dissolution under Metaxas.

Liberal Responses to the Communist Offensive

The aims and methods of Bolshevization to bring the mass party into existence, in conjunction with the worsening plight of a young, expanding, unprotected, and activist female industrial labor force, especially tobacco, must be part of any history of the development of class consciousness, worker protest, and the growth of communism in Greece between the Wars. Papastefanaki has also argued, based on her study of the textile industry in Piraeus, that the electoral base and social composition of the KKE was not limited to the agricultural sector and nonindustrial workers (tobacco plantations), but it also encompassed the (female) industrial proletariat.[145]

The KKE invaded the political space with a completely new political culture, bypassing the methods and limitations of bourgeois political culture, with the introduction of a new "language field," which endorsed new social categories and employed new political methods that expanded the field of political actors.[146] As a response to the particular predicament of working women, the KKE's explicit call to girls and women in their own habitats and language, attention to the gender-specific constraints on political involvement, and a community-oriented approach to mobilization and activism were strategies that facilitated girls' and women's identification with the communist movement and offered them opportunities for social, economic, intellectual, and political participation unmatched by Venizelist liberalism, nationalism, or feminism.[147]

The Greek state's determination to secure a strong grip on labor organizations predated the rise of the Greek Communist Party as a player in Greek politics; a series of legal amendments were introduced to this effect dating back to as early as 1918.[148] The Party's growing influence in the 1920s reverberated across the political spectrum, but it was the Venizelist government that reacted most vehemently to the challenge posed by the left. Confirming the growing influence of the KKE in Greek political life, an escalation of anti-communist measures led by the second Venizelist administration (1928–1932) introduced the Idionymon (Special Crimes Act) in 1929. The Idionymon aimed to "secure the social order and protect citizens' liberties" by imprisoning anyone who was perceived as threatening them. It marked a turning point in the Greek state's legislative arsenal against communism, and indeed was retained, expanded, and institutionalized under the Metaxas dictatorship.

Between 1929 and 1932 there were 11,400 arrests and 2,130 convictions, while the security service arrested two hundred people, including, for the first time, communist women. Partsalidou recalls one of the first women to be arrested at this time was Chrysa Ladopoulou, a refugee tobacco worker who also took part in the first hunger strike staged by women political prisoners (for the right to have books in prison).[149]

The Idionymon enabled the government to restrict entry of Pontic Greek refugees into Greece, thus exposing the perceived connection made by the Greek state between the refugees and the growth of communism in Greece. The government imposed conditions of entry to ethnic Greeks of the Pontos, who were stranded in the Soviet Union, despite their legal right to migrate to Greece as stipulated by the Treaty of Lausanne.[150] The Minister of Foreign Affairs justified the measure as a "public security issue since it has been observed many times that those who lived under the Bolshevik yoke drift toward communism when they arrive in Greece."[151]

Venizelos' second term also saw a continuation of his efforts to restructure and reorient the Greek education system, which was seen as anachronistic but also as a hotbed of radicalization. The constitution provided for six-year free and compulsory elementary education. But in many parts of the country only four-year elementary schools existed, if any at all, and generally the law was not enforced. The rate of illiteracy increased with the arrival of the refugees, reaching over 70 percent in rural areas and exceeding 90 percent among women. The majority of (male) students who continued beyond elementary schooling pursued secondary level education, rather than commercial, technical, or other more practical training. Secondary school enrollments among girls were far behind those of boys, and there were glaring regional disparities.

Access to secondary schools and the institutions of higher learning was not well-controlled, nor based on achievement criteria. Most concerning were the numbers of secondary school graduates who could not be absorbed by the economy nor by certain faculties at the university of Athens that were overcrowded (e.g., law). In his pre-election speech in 1928, Venizelos duly announced his support for vocational education and the restriction of "classical" studies to the "select few" who would be the future leaders of society.

The reforms were introduced in 1929: new elementary schools reaffirmed the previous provision of compulsory attendance over six years. Elementary education would include schools of general or vocational education, whose combined purpose was to prepare pupils for life and provide them with basic elements required for the formation of good (virtuous) citizens. The new laws abolished the previous secondary education system; henceforth the full secondary school course was to extend over six years (following the six-year elementary school) and was to be provided in secondary schools (*gymnasia*) and scientific (practical) lycea. Admission into the secondary schools would require successful completion of elementary school *and the passing of an entrance examination*. After the third year (grade 9) the secondary school would offer two streams: classical and "practical."[152]

This elitist conception of education was another blow for the impoverished refugees, for whom classical secondary education was synonymous with social advancement and the eradication of social inequality. As Kazamias states, the 1929 reforms were designed to meet existing deficiencies, to modernize the educational system on the lines of contemporary pedagogical and social thought.[153] But the desire of Greek politicians to limit access to secondary education *in order* to reduce the urban mass of jobseekers and unemployed graduates of secondary schools was also intended as a bulwark against political instability. Regarding the proposal that children sit for rigid exams in order to have access to high schools, they argued that "these exams will make the primary school pupils understand that high school is not a game, and is not for all those who merely decide to go on to secondary education."[154] On the eve of the education reforms, the minister of Public Education and Religious Affairs, Constantinos B. Gondicas (1928–1930) made a direct reference to the threat posed by the refugees, denouncing the existing education policies of the previous governments (including the Pangalos dictatorship) that led the refugee world into the streets (as unemployed), doomed to ignorance and countless moral dangers.[155] State intervention in the problem of education was twofold. In addition to the reforms, the Idionymon enabled the state to address the moral dangers and communist inclinations (*kommounistikes ropes*) within the education system by putting an end to "scandalous teaching methods" and distortions of Greek history being taught in high schools, and by hounding the perpetrators relentlessly, teachers and students alike, for suspected subversive activities.[156]

But in the words of the police commissioner of Piraeus, neither the police nor the courts were able to suppress the momentum of the communist movement.[157] The collective and militant manner in which the KKE, the new outsider par excellence of bourgeois politics, mobilized factory floors, schoolyards, neighborhoods, men, women, and youth culminated in the massive electoral gains of the KKE in 1936 that would bring the Greek political arena to boiling point. In the elections of 1932 and 1936, thirteen and fifteen communist MPs were elected respectively, one of whom was from Piraeus.[158] In the parliamentary elections of 1933, the KKE gained 4.6 percent of the vote (but no seats)—12.4 percent in Nea Ionia, 12 percent in Kaisariani, 11.2 percent in Kokkinia, 10.5 percent in Vironas, all refugee neighborhoods (*prosfygoupoleis*). Kokkinia included two very large carpet factories, Eastern Carpet and Oriental Carpet, both employing at least five hundred women workers each, predominantly refugees. During the municipal elections of February 1934, the first elections in which Greek women were able to vote (conditionally) took place. The Venizelos government extended this right only to women who had completed elementary school and were over thirty years of age, although it is estimated that only 10 percent of those eligible actually voted—the Athens newspaper *Akropolis* reported a link between female labor and the communist vote.[159] Specifically, *Akropolis* noted that "the communist ballot (*kendro*) in Athens was surrounded mostly by 'fanatical' women, factory workers and office workers, including women of a very young age," while in Xanthi, it was a matter of fact that the communist candidate could expect at least one thousand votes from female tobacco workers.[160] The tobacco center of Kavala did indeed elect a communist mayor in 1934, Dimitris Partsalidis, and registered the highest percentage of communist votes in the legislative elections of January 1936.[161]

Three months later, on Wednesday April 29, 1936, in line with the decision of the Tobacco Workers' Union, twelve thousand tobacco workers in

Thessaloniki, 70 percent of whom were women, went on strike, demanding an increase in wages according to the 1924 agreement.[162] The tension between the state and organized labor reached a climax the following month during the "Bloody May of 1936," when police confronted a massive general strike of tobacco workers and other unions in Thessaloniki, opening fire on the protesters, killing twelve and wounding hundreds. Among the dead were three refugee women tobacco workers: Anastasia Karanikola, sixteen-year-old Anna Haralambidou, and Anna Laoumatzidou. General Metaxas came to power three months later, as the events of May made it clear "that the democratically elected government [Venizelos' Liberal Party] was incapable of restoring internal order and harmony, but rather handed the country over to communists who surely believed they were on the cusp of social revolution."[163] Metaxas reflected on the prominence of women, refugee and non-refugee, in the upheavals of the period, the outcome of "despair, and fashion, that led sections of Greek society into the embrace of communism—especially young women—as, by their nature, woman becomes impassioned by new things. She likes to put herself on display. This is why one can often observe among the world of women, the sight of communists, who are most fanatical."[164]

Illegality and increasing state repression of the communist and labor movement during the interwar period favored and indeed created an urgency for the creation of a professional cadre class specially trained in underground work. The next chapter highlights the era of Bolshevization as a juncture for social mobility through activism and higher education. The groundbreaking work of scholars such as Sheila Fitzpatrick has illuminated the significance of the educational policies that coincided with the first of Stalin's Five-Year Plans (1928–1932), and linked Stalin's regime with the massive upward mobility of the industrializing 1930s in the Soviet Union.[165] Less understood is the significance of the Comintern's educational programs for its affiliated parties, which equipped them with the means by which to produce knowledgeable, loyal, and highly trained functionaries and potential leaders as intended, but that also functioned as a much yearned for and elusive path to personal development and upward mobility for the vast majority of the students.

2

Upward Mobility and the Comintern Universities

Disentangling Bolshevization

The KKE's entry into the Comintern fold, many have argued then and since, estranged the Party from its grassroots as the once pluralistic Comintern and its constituent communist parties were increasingly subject to pressure by the Kremlin. But this was very much a reciprocal relationship. Comintern membership was instrumental in the KKE's consolidation as a coherent entity, effectively ending the sectarianism that had been a feature of the Greek Party from its inception and an impediment to its development. Increasing centralization also gave national parties access to the goods of the Comintern. One entered and progressed through the system based on affiliation, recommendation, and sponsorship, often through the patronage of existing (usually) male members. This was not dissimilar to membership rituals in other political cultures, but crucially for female communists, the rules of engagement were decoupled from traditional constraints of family, gender, and social status that governed women's participation in traditional politics and in the public sphere.

That Bolshevization signaled the end of internal chaos but also of autonomy for the KKE is widely understood; what remains obscured, which is pertinent to this study, is a central paradox whereby diminishing Party autonomy and the mission to bring it into alignment with Comintern principles laid the foundation for greater access to and integration of women into the KKE. There is little doubt that Comintern pressure accounted for the increase in the number of women cadres trained and employed by the Party between 1925 and 1936, a process of cultural change that would have been slower, perhaps impossible, under "organic" conditions. It was a challenging objective, nonetheless. In 1930, the Greek delegation of the Comintern reported that the inappropriate attitude of the Party to working with the masses was best encapsulated in its continued resistance to representation in the Central Committee. The delegation referred to the example of the most recent Plenum of the Central Committee, where both Politburo and the Central Committee members rejected the proposal to include one woman (a tobacco worker) in its ranks, a proposal that received all of two votes at the Plenum: "The comrades did not refuse to accept female comrades into the CC on principle, but rather claimed that they did not receive satisfactory proposals. Their entire attitude reflects the belief in the inferiority of women in a spirit that isn't communist. . . . The work of our Party—especially regarding farmers, trade unions, the unemployed, and women, will be corrected."[1] Chrysa Hatzivasiliou would become the first female appointment to the Central Committee of the Greek Communist Party in 1935, her eligibility impossible to deny after a decade of dedicated Party work. Christina Gilmartin notes a similar dynamic at play in relation to the changing status of women in the Chinese Communist Party (CCP). She argues, for example, that the main impetus for the establishment of a Women's Bureau in the CCP in 1922 came not from within the Party but from the Comintern, indicating that resistance to formalizing a women's program and legitimizing women's status in the organization, while unarticulated, was quite strong in the early Party.[2] As in the Greek case, the clearest manifestation of this shift was the inclusion of young women, often poor and semiliterate refugees, in the cadre education program starting in 1924, a pathway that had been open to the men of KKE since 1921.

I do not want to present Bolshevization as a feminist panacea. Historians rightly equate Bolshevization with Stalinization—the domination of national parties by the ECCI, itself coming under the power of Stalin. Stalinization did indeed have its impacts on the Russian Communist Party, the Comintern, and the "woman question." As Waters states, the events of the interwar dashed the Comintern's revolutionary optimism and eventually relegated the *Theses* to the shadows of the Comintern; the loss of the International Women's Secretariat's autonomy in 1926 and its reconstitution as a "women's department" in the Executive Committee of the Communist International signaled the final blow to the women's agenda ratified by the Third International.³ Bolshevization's focus on the emancipation of women, by the end of the 1920s, came to be understood entirely in terms of the workplace, and any "special subordination" of women in communist propaganda or campaigning, came to be regarded as a capitulation to bourgeois feminism, foreshadowing the well-documented reversion to more conventional Soviet understandings of women's place in the world in the 1930s and the curtailment of their liberation as women.⁴ The Comintern's shift away from the advancement of women to the "mobilization of women for the advancement of the Comintern" is conventionally understood as the combined effects of economic depression, an absence of working-class militancy, the rise of Stalinism, and the increasing centralization of the Comintern apparatus, although these factors only accentuated and institutionalized the already existing tendency to overlook gender as a source of conflict and a site of struggle. The infamous 1936 decree on the "Protection of Motherhood and Childhood" was the culmination of this shift, but as Krylova argues, the decree falls short of presenting the full spectrum of the Soviet state's policies and Soviet society's gender ideals. Pointing to the paradoxes of Stalinist gender policies—the situations where one state policy utilized the platform of traditional gender roles that another institution worked to overcome—Krylova underlines the futility of attempting to fit Soviet pre-war gender history into a coherent narrative.⁵

Similarly, the point I make relates to the paradoxes of Bolshevization, whereby deradicalization of the "woman question" and the women's movement at the Comintern coincided with new opportunities for women within national party structures and at the Comintern itself. As conceptions of women's emancipation shrank in scope, the Greek case shows that the restructuring and mobilizational practices of the KKE in line with the Comintern's agenda presented new and concrete opportunities for greater political involvement, integration, and advancement well into the 1930s, which were embraced by young communist women and men as opportunities that promised to be, and were, life changing. The biographical data and personal narratives of the female subjects examined here convey a path shaped by both circumstance and personal aspiration conditioned by migration, ethnic identity, gender, and class. All had enormous implications in Greek—and Soviet—society, and enormous resonance in everyday life, but as Fitzpatrick states in reference to Soviet women, class seems to have been a matter of more vital interest and anxiety than gender, which is hardly surprising given its salience in creating dangers and opportunities for families and individuals.⁶ The Comintern's and Soviet communism's shift away from gender and women qua women did not lessen the appeal of communism for the women who found refuge and purpose within the movement at this time.

The Historiography of Cadre Education at the Comintern

In the Soviet Union as much as in other countries where communist parties were founded, the need for capable cadres emerged very early, talented individuals who could rise to organizational, leadership, propaganda, and recruitment demands. The acceptance of the twenty-one binding laws of the Third International (Comintern) as articulated at the 2nd Congress of 1920, and the obligation of parties to organize on the basis of the principles of democratic centralism transformed the dynamics of national communist movements around the world by linking communist activists in various countries with Moscow, precipitating the development of an educational infrastructure that provided vital practical and theoretical training in Marxism-Leninism for the international movement. Cadres could undertake training in Central Party schools established in their home countries or could be selected to study in the purpose-built universities of the Soviet Union, or a combination of both. As Earl Browder said a decade later, reflecting upon the importance that communists attached to schooling, "there is no simple miracle by which workers become Marxists-Leninists by taking out a card in our Party. They will become Bolsheviks only to the extent that the Party organization sees to it that every Party member is interested in the study of this question as an essential part of the daily mass work."[7]

Likewise, when the SEKE accepted the "twenty-one conditions" of the Comintern at the Third Extraordinary Congress (November 26–December 2, 1924), after several failed attempts since 1920, and changed its name to Kommounistiko Komma Elladas (KKE; Greek Communist Party), it joined the swelling ranks of national parties painstakingly attempting to raise themselves to the Bolshevik standard. A month later the Party announced the educational aims of its Bolshevization program, in which three student categories were identified:

> The broad circle of sympathizers outside the Party, workers and farmers who needed a simple accessible analysis of the Party's program in order to understand that the Party is theirs and that they should join it.

Party candidates or trial members, as well as current members, who needed a basic communist education to recognize the foundations of the program and strategies of the Party.

Comrades who were flagged as potential cadres of the Party (organizers, editors, teachers, administrative cadres of the Party, professional leaders), the so-called professional revolutionaries who needed to acquire a Marxist education.[8]

The Comintern established three main universities for the training of foreign cadres, all of which opened Greek sectors.

Few men, and fewer women, attended the universities of the Comintern. One could not volunteer. Annie Kriegel stated that training at Central Party schools or in the universities of the Comintern was imposed rather than pursued by or offered to aspiring students. The students were not volunteers but promising militants who were simply "told to do the schools."[9] This is also the recollection of KKE leader Nikos Zachariadis, who "despite my resistance [to the decision of the Central Committee of the KKE], for which I was disciplined, I was sent to the Soviet Union to study in 1929."[10] In reference to the French Communist Party (PCF), Kivisaari states that "the selection process was supervised by both the national Party and the CPSU to ensure that 'only trustworthy people were sent,' as they were to become the political leaders needed by the Party, professional revolutionaries."[11]

The historiography of the British MLS sector generally classifies students as

(a) careerists who attended the MLS in the hope that the education and status of being a graduate would benefit them within their home parties or within the Comintern;
(b) dedicated functionaries;
(c) those who simply obeyed orders given by the national party, frequently as a means by which to fill Comintern quotas; and
(d) troublesome members temporarily "exiled" to the universities by their respective parties.

In fact, General Secretary Harry Pollitt struggled to fill the places in the MLS allotted to the CPGB partly because the School gave preference to bachelors to avoid supplementing the miserable allowance offered to dependents in Britain, but also because lower Party bodies were reluctant to release scarce cadres for a sojourn at the MLS.[12]

The personal records of former student and KKE cadre Markos Markovitis indicate that the push factor for Greek students was illegality and intensifying state anticommunism in Greece from 1925, from which the Soviet Union provided refuge from persecution. Upon arrival in the Soviet Union this group, categorized as political refugees (they held no passport and were thus illegals), were taken under the protective wing of the MOPR and issued residence permits that functioned as internal or domestic passports. They were then funneled into the communist universities after the residence permits were issued.[13] Former KKE leader Stavridis recalls that Greek communists suffering from tuberculosis who were sent by the KKE to recuperate in the sanatoria of the Soviet Union could also progress into the Comintern university system after the completion of their treatment. This applied, for example, in the cases of KKE leaders Kostas Theos and Yiannis Zevgos.[14]

Greek nationals at the Comintern universities were not necessarily officials or students. Twin sisters Evgenia and Elena Andreevna Dimitropoulou (pseud. Alexandra Vasilievna Kirova) had never been students of the Comintern university system but were employed as typists and clerks. Their story adds a necessary nuance to understanding the nature of the relationship between the Greek Party and the Comintern, as well as the paternal role of the Party for (some of) its members. Born in 1917 in Piraeus Athens, they were the daughters of a professional revolutionary of the KKE, presumably named Andreas Dimitropoulos. Unable to provide for his wife and children in Greece while working in the communist underground, he and his family were relocated to the Soviet Union in 1928 where they effectively became wards of the MOPR and the Comintern, beginning with the girls' placement in a sanitorium (for tuberculosis) and a MOPR children's home in Ivanovo till 1933, where they also received a basic education; they joined the Komsomol in 1932. A string of Party-sponsored roles and positions followed till 1941 when the file ends with "typist at the Comintern (1933–1934), typist at the MLS (1934) and KUNMZ (1934–1936)."

Following the father's death in Moscow in 1935 from tuberculosis, his family was placed in the care of the Soviet state. With the dissolution of the KUNMZ in 1936, on the eve of the Great Terror, Evgenia Dimitropoulou was seconded to the Greek Publishing Office in Mariupol after which she took maternity leave and became a dependent of the MOPR and the Comintern between 1937 and 1940. In 1941 she was assigned to work as a typist in the Foreign Languages Publishing House and in the Greek broadcasting editorial office. Dimitropoulou's references depict her as an

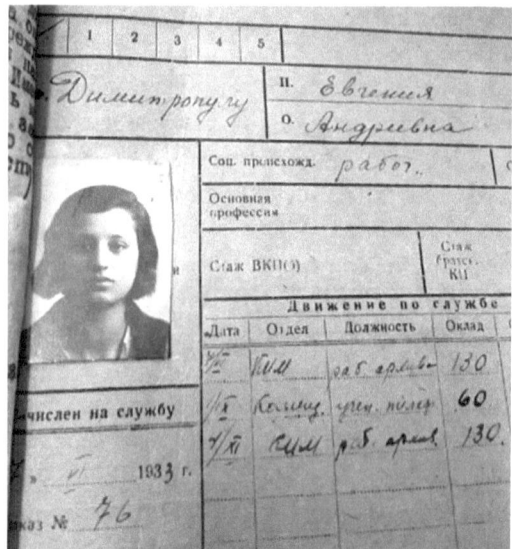

FIGURE 4. Yevgenia Andreevna Dimitropoulou. Photo courtesy of RGASPI.

experienced, hardworking, loyal, and deserving comrade, but the assistance she received—including special dietary requirements for her health condition and even firewood provisions—was clearly linked with her father's legacy, his "service to the Party."[15]

The files of the female students examined here show that that rather than falling into Comintern training by circumstance, they consciously sought it out, and it fulfilled a broad range of personal objectives. As for all national sectors, study in the Soviet Union for Greek communists was contingent on the recommendation of the KKE or the youth organization OKNE, and the final decision rested with the Greek representatives appointed to the ECCI. The majority of the female graduates who studied there became and aspired to become mid-ranking functionaries; most went on to work for the CPSU in the Greek settlements of the Soviet Union, became teachers and administrators in the universities, or became anonymous but critical cogs in the wheel of illegal KKE operations in Greece, underground operatives, "runners," or "conspirators," working across a broad range of activities as needs arose. And while Comintern education does not appear to have been essential to career progression per se, it held a degree of cultural capital in the Party and was especially valued by the graduates themselves as even a cursory examination of their autobiographies will attest.

The lives of the Greek "Cominternians," to borrow Brigitte Studer's term, have yet to receive the scholarly attention other national sections of these clandestine organizations have received since the opening of the Russian archives in the late 1990s. Very little is understood about the push factors and personal motivations of the vast majority of students who passed through these institutions, much less those of the female alumni. The only female students acknowledged by name in the historical record are Chrysa Hatzivasiliou and Olga Bakola (a.k.a. Aliki Kanda).[16] The heads and teachers of the Greek sectors, many of whom were women, often former students, have also faded from view. The heads of the Greek Sector of KUNMZ, such as Dimitris (Ivanovich) Makroyiannis (1929–1930); Lidiia Ivanovna Petrova, the head of the Greek Sector at MLS (1934–1936); Feodora Ignatievna Batman, the secretary of the Greek Sector of the MLS (1934–1936);[17] and Theodoros (Feodor) Varelopoulos who taught general history under Makroyiannis, have all disappeared from the historical record.

This obscurity is in no small part attributable to the dramatic events that followed and overshadowed the Bolshevization phase of the Party's social history—total war, Nazi occupation, the Resistance effort, and finally the collapse into bloody civil conflict—whose causes and particular outcomes have long dominated the historiography. Valuable memoirs of veteran communists like Kaiti Zevgou, Avra Partsalidou, and others convey that the professional revolutionary "type" entered the Greek Communist party largely through the youth wing. After the KKE entered the Comintern fold in 1924, a new generation of youth was formed, fanatical about the new principles and rules, who led lives defined by constant movement and absolute commitment to the Party. Socialist Party leader Stratos Someritis (1932) noted that these emerging elite cadres had abandoned the local—static—level of organization. Unlike other members, they were defined by their mobility and their exclusive preoccupation with Party activism.[18]

According to KKE cadre Kaiti Zevgou, this "type" was rare, or did not exist in Greece before 1924 when members of SEKE/KKE would simply catch up with their Party duties after work or university. After the 5th Congress, regular communist youth who enjoyed the small pleasures of daily life—rest and recreation, fashion, a nice house, friends, cinema, and theater—began to transform into "ideological crusaders, like those of religion, whose ascetic lifestyle and carriage marked them apart from other mortals."[19] Partsalidou recalled the long hours of conferencing, managing multiple tasks and responsibilities, after which "we would go home late at night, exhausted, having neglected our duties, our studies, our families."[20] Most endured negative consequences to which they seemed indifferent or resigned, or that they even invited. The greatest accolade for a communist was to be endowed with the quality of *kommatikitotita* (party-mindedness). The cadres of the Party regarded themselves as warriors or soldiers engaged in a struggle.[21] EAM leader and brother of ill-fated communist icon Electra Apostolou, Lefteris Apostolou also characterized the new generation of communists as absolutely committed to the commands of the 3rd International, with strict discipline and Party work, absolute opposition to every "liquidarist, factionalist, opportunist tendency."[22] According to Gonsa, the intellectual rigidity of the new generation and the wholesale acceptance of the role of the Comintern as legitimate was a response to the general state of the Party.[23] It was from this generation of Greek communist youth that the first elite cadres, the professional revolutionary cohorts, were drawn to enter what Studer calls the transnational world of the Comintern.[24]

A small number of communist memoirs offer some rare glimpses into the world of the cadres, the most probing of which is the recent biography of Markos Markovitis, a KUNMZ graduate, KKE cadre, and victim of Stalin's purges, an attempt by his son to piece together his father's political life and death using rare and invaluable materials from his father's archive.[25] Nikos Kazantzakis's highly publicized reports of his travels to the Soviet Union in the 1920s and 1930s were oddly silent on the activities of his own compatriots studying in the cadre universities of the Soviet Union at the time of his visits. Kazantzakis did however observe the "fanaticism" and "compromised femininity" of the young "Eastern" women who studied and taught at these institutions, which he found sad and odd, in his otherwise fawning admiration for the new "faith" transforming the East.[26]

The few scholars who have engaged with the Greek contingent of the Comintern university system, most notably Angelos Elefandis, Andrew Zapantis, and Heinz Richter, regard the growing influence of the "KUTVists" in the KKE primarily as a barometer for Moscow's increasing control of the Party, since none of the graduates, many of whom became leaders in the Party, had "roots in the Party." According to Zapantis, the reluctance of the SEKE/KKE to employ the KUTVists in Party work upon their arrival—as requested by the Soviet embassy—was entirely justified, as "these cadres felt loyalty only to their masters in Moscow. Soon they monopolized the contacts with the Soviet embassy and thus controlled the material aid flowing from Moscow to Athens."[27] Richter argues that the anticommunist campaigns of the Pangalos dictatorship in 1925/1926 "played into the hands of the KUTVists." As most of the old Party leaders had been arrested, the KUTVists' influence grew as they had been trained for illegality and thus many of them managed to escape the persecution of the police and soon controlled large sections of the Party. In a similar vein, former socialist leader Stratis Someritis wrote that "the conditions of illegality created a fertile ideal environment for the rapid expansion of the Party's network of professional cadres, which it put to full use."[28] The historiography however has not progressed beyond this standard interpretation to recognize the broader and contradictory, indeed democratizing, effects of Bolshevization policy, by which a proportionally smaller but steady stream of communist women found their way into the Greek sectors of the universities for the duration of the institutions' existence.[29]

The view of Greek KUTV alumni as servants of Moscow in the battle for control between the "center and the periphery" resonates with much of the English-language scholarship, which also interprets the emphasis on cadre education at the 5th Congress of the Comintern as symptomatic of the Kremlin's tightening grip on the Comintern. McIlroy and Campbell note that a shift in the 1924/1925 variant of Bolshevism "decisively replaced ideas of the party embodying openness and democratic decision-making, with conceptions of it as a military contingent with connotations of command closure and restricted democracy which had been gathering momentum since 1920."[30] All affiliates or sections were to follow the Soviet road that required no factions, tendencies, or groups, and which had to be fused in one mold. Organizationally, Bolshevization preached centralized leadership, organization based on workplace or locality, party-controlled mass work, an interventionist press, and customized education.[31] Cadre education was instrumental to the process by which parties could form, as Annie Kriegel states, "a nucleus that was solid, stable, and impervious to repression. Around it was a protective, more or less impenetrable . . . wall of militants, members, and sympathizers. The change, in effect, amounted to nothing less than the replacement of amateurs by professionals," and the replacement of the Party by a real organizational apparatus.[32] Professional revolutionaries were an important cog in the machinery of democratic centralism, acknowledged for their devotion to the cause and their unwavering loyalty.

This scholarship is generally captive to the objectives of the national parties for sending aspiring professional revolutionaries to study in Moscow, and in turn, the motives of the Comintern—and the Kremlin—for training them. In reference to the MLS, which took students from the Americas and Europe, McLoughlin states that cadre education for foreigners was less about "unifying the international communist movement along common ideological guidelines" than a long term investment by the Executive Committee of the Communist International (ECCI) to produce graduates who would return home "steeled" against all deviations from the Soviet *diktat* and ensure the fulfillment of the "line" by taking up leading positions in the pertinent "national sections" of the Communist International.[33] The influential work on the British sectors at the International Lenin School by Gidon Cohen and Kevin Morgan, likewise, views these institutions as "Stalin's sausage machines," also the title of one of their published articles.[34]

The nature of the relationship between Bolshevization, education, and the centralization of power lies at the center of the structuralist view: if Bolshevization signaled a trend toward Russian dominance of the Comintern, and if the Comintern's "unification" of the international communist movement indicated its subordination to the Center (Kremlin), it follows that the schools' singular mission was indoctrination, the molding of "Bolshevik clones," "spineless creatures of Moscow."[35] For Kivisaari, the political education system answered the problem of succession; by dovetailing the functions of democratic centralism and political education, leadership succeeded in adroitly securing power in their own hands and ensured their succession by ideologically reliable cadres.[36] The eminent historian of French communism Anne Kriegel underscored that the cadre universities were not research institutions per se, or even centers for the formulation of doctrine, but were intended purely for the cadres, unswervingly dedicated to the training and indoctrination of political leaders needed by the party.[37] Brigitte Studer refers to the process by which the inflexible militant of the proletarian cause would be created during the 1930s, the period of high Stalinism, and the goals and methods of the system of pedagogy deployed by the cadre schools to achieve this objective: "To become the 'true Bolshevik,' the student had not just to acquire a knowledge but an attitude. Hermetic, rigid, dogmatic, Bolshevik self-mastery called for a psychic economy organised around self-inspection . . . the communist cadre of the 1930s was expected to be, aspired to be, proved to be, a matter of self-cultivation, of self-perfection, a process of transformation that required one to learn a number of introspective and discursive techniques."[38] Berthold Unfried's examination of the behavior of German, Austrian, Swiss, French, and British CP militants when confronted by such rituals, especially the ritual of criticism and self-criticism, writes that these practices "perplexed and discomfited foreign communists for whom these practices seemed to violate Western notions of individuality and ignore the boundaries between private and public domains."³⁹

Drawing, perhaps erroneously, on Goffman's concept of "total institutions," Cohen and Morgan argue that as the MLS preached vigilance, discipline, and commitment as the highest party virtues, it ran counter to British Labor and Trade union traditions that molded the CPGB, and conclude that ultimately the effects of the school on the graduates, and in turn the influence of the graduates on the CPGB, were negligible.⁴⁰ A succession of counterarguments by Campbell, McIlroy, Loughlin, and Halstad argue that a proper reading of the data would make the *voluntary* nature of the MLS clear, that "the hegemony of the Russian-dominated Comintern hinged on consent—that is, the voluntary acceptance and commitment by British communists to its ideological and political pre-eminence."⁴¹ Thus the MLS legacy for and within the CPGB was nothing if not definitive. In their conclusion, the authors take issue with Cohen and Morgan's description of the students as "sausages"—given its origins as a simile used by CPGB leader Tom Bell that countenanced *against any possibility* that "we can turn out Leninists like sausages from a machine."⁴² Somewhat ironically, in a separate article on the British at the MLS, and the first English language study to broach the question of gender, McIlroy and Campbell resort to the very kind of oversimplifications of which they accused Cohen and Morgan. The section of the study dedicated to the background, university experience, and "destination" of the female students, and the extent to which they were distinct from or similar to those of their male counterparts, concludes in an outright dismissal of this history as a legitimate line of inquiry, as the female students' stay in Moscow did not seem to have transformed them or their Party. Indeed the category of the "woman cadre" ought to be contested, as the "main change in the role of women came about not because of the MLS, but because of the move from 1935 to popular front politics."⁴³ While there is no disputing the mobilizational successes of the popular front period, especially for women, to devalue the category and the history of the woman cadre for not delivering the "main change in the role of women" in the British Party and more broadly is not a standard by which the cadre category ought to be judged. In another study of the British at the MLS, McLoughlin and Campbell draw on Bruley's description of the "woman cadre category," that is, emulating the male political persona, usually single or in a liaison with a Party member, and childless, as further evidence of the dubious category of the woman cadre. They suggest that the term "aspirant cadre" might be better employed for many of the women, as more than half were in relationships with communist men, and their agency was thus inherently compromised.[44] This is a gendered rendering of a school of thought within Soviet historiography that doubts Soviet citizens' ability to develop any notion of individual subjectivity at all, as political initiative was monopolized by the revolutionary state, and revolutionary politics by their very nature undercut the production of stable identities.[45]

A more nuanced branch of Comintern scholarship forges a middle ground between the importance of institutional aims and that of individual agency to convey more complex, ambiguous, and reciprocal transactions among students, Party, and "system," as well as between center and periphery. It is in turn informed by a school of thought within the historiography of communism that sees the impact of Soviet revolutionary practice, including education, on individuals' sense of self as more productive than repressive. In Hellbeck's works, revolutionary politics was centered on making Soviet citizens think of themselves and act as conscious historical subjects.[46]

This perspective has the scope to acknowledge, on the one hand, that the Comintern and Comintern education were instrumental to the propagation of the Soviet disciplinary ethos and to the development of what Fitzpatrick has called the distinct *mentalite* that defined discipline and unity in almost mystical terms.[47] On the other hand, it also acknowledges that Comintern university outcomes were more complex and ambiguous than the ideal and reflected the highly variable internal dynamics and historical development of each national party.[48] This scholarship, of which the work of Lisa Kirschenbaum, Brigitte Studer, Irina Filatova, and Lana Ravandi-Fadai are among the most notable examples, acknowledges the human at the center of these institutions as complex, flawed, and aspirational as any other, and finds a far more complex exchange between student and institution, and center and periphery, than traditionally understood.[49]

Filatova's examination of the African experience at KUTV concludes that despite their many grievances—the limitations of education, Soviet realities within and outside the school, the stifling political atmosphere, and the increasingly threatening situation in the second half of the 1930s with the Great Terror—the majority of students were true believers in the ideals, ideas, and words of the Comintern. For them, tenure at the Comintern universities was a way to the holy of holies, to the center of their circle of absolute faith.[50] Ravandi-Fadai's examination of the Iranian students and teachers at KUTV reveals that the institution developed into one of the most important centers of "Soviet Orientalism," which sought to create a paradigm shift in the study of the East by redistributing the tools of Orientalist scholarship to Asians themselves, freed from imperialist prejudices and emphasizing a Marxist view of history over an idealized and nationalistic antiquity. Fadai notes that the KUTV illuminates the contradictions of the Soviet project itself in its aim to free the oppressed while projecting Soviet influence and rising above nationalist conceptions while simultaneously succumbing to them.[51]

Meredith Roman's study of black students at the MLS demonstrates how they negotiated the power, promise, and limitations of Soviet antiracist discourse in an effort to increase awareness and facilitate integration with their white fellow students "who were ready to condemn flagrant acts of racial injustice, but struggled to recognize that the same system of American racial apartheid structured their own attitudes and interactions with black people in subtle and not so subtle ways." Black American communists clearly derived a position of authority and a sense of dignity from Soviet antiracism; they saw it as having an intangible political value in the struggle for Black freedom.[52] In her study of international communism and the Spanish Civil War, Kirschenbaum sees the schools less as "agents of the center working to mold communists from the periphery," and more as a "point of connection between center and periphery, a site of everyday interactions among communists, both international and Soviet."[53] Drawing on totalitarianism theory, Kirschenbaum examines the relationships that constituted everyday life, life at the grassroots, acknowledging that even though students and teachers were in an unequal relationship as the Comintern built the structure and set the rules, nonetheless as they entered those structures and strove to live by those rules, students and teachers became to some degree co-constructors of the school.[54]

Far from an imposition, the growing Soviet influence or "Russification" of the Comintern answered the concerns of the foreign leaders in attendance at the 5th Congress, who recorded their lack of understanding of revolutionary politics, and in fact demanded a world party based on Russian politics and organization.[55] As McIlroy and Campbell state, affiliation with the Comintern "remained voluntary and self-willed, primarily ideological, and lubricated and reinforced by critical financial subsidies."[56] Under the Pouliopoulos leadership, the KKE embraced the Bolshevization drive emanating from Moscow and set forth to organize and to address its education deficits accordingly.[57] Access to Comintern universities in the Soviet Union was especially significant for the KKE as for other underground communist parties that could not readily establish Central Party schools.

Papastefanaki notes that a Marxist school for cadres was formed whose main teachers included Party intellectuals Serafim Maximos and Kostas Sklavos, both refugees from Eastern Thrace and Smyrna respectively. Educational centers were established in the refugee hubs of Kokkinia, Tambouria, Kastella, and Faliro-Moschato. More than one hundred students attended these educational centers (gender composition not noted), but most did not follow the lessons properly. The circulation of Party literature in Piraeus increased at a small but steady pace. *Rizospastis* reached a daily sale of 440 issues, although how this worked and what it meant is not straightforward given the low literacy rates. The conclusion was drawn that the working masses were "numbed" "as a result of incoherent tactics of trade union activism but also due to flaws in the very organization itself, the internal schism, and disappointment of the masses with us."[58] It was deemed that the isolation of the urban masses from the communist movement was mostly organizational, not ideological, and that mobilization of the working population would be only realized with hard persistent organizational work. This disconnection between the Party and its "natural constituents" was precisely what Bolshevization set out to address. As the KKE existed in a state of illegality or quasi-illegality from 1925 onward, while these underground educational efforts were made, they were haphazard by necessity, and lacked structure and continuity under the ever-present threat of discovery, disruption, and relocation. The Comintern universities answered many of the organizational and intellectual deficits of the Party for the next decade. The importance of Moscow-based cadre education followed the twists and turns of the policies of the VKP(b) and the Comintern in the 1920s and 1930s. The techniques cadres learned in Moscow for operating a party organization in conditions of illegality was of special value to Greek communists operating in increasingly repressive circumstances throughout the 1920s and 1930s, but they also proved their worth with the subsequent German invasion of Europe, and the emergence of mass resistance movements, most of which were led by communists.

The Cadre Universities

The KUTV was founded in Moscow in April 1921 under the auspices of the People's Commissariat for Nationalities (Narkomnats) for the purpose of educating communist cadres in the colonial world. In 1923 the KUTV was placed under the auspices of the Comintern, under the leadership of

Karl Radek, and proclaimed to have a dual aim: "creating cadres capable of serving the needs of the Soviet Republics of the East, and the other, to create cadres capable of serving the revolutionary requirements of the toiling masses in the colonial and dependent countries of the East."[59] The latter were trained in so-called "foreign sections" created in 1922. A separate Greek faculty or section started work in 1923.[60] The basis for delegating the first Greek student cohorts to the Eastern school, in the company of students from China, India, and Egypt, is unclear. As head of the Narkomnats, Stalin took a strong interest in the KUTV that came to bear his name after 1925 (J.V. Stalin Communist University for Toilers of the East). Stalin defined "the East" as consisting of two geographically and theoretically distinct regions: a Soviet East, "where imperialist oppression had been overthrown," and a foreign "colonial and dependent" East, to which Greece presumably belonged. But as Kirasirova argues, the construct was vague and flexible and indeed presented challenges for the KUTV community and scholars who had to work with it.[61] It was the case, however, that the Soviet conception of the East resonated with the KKE's view of Greece as a "semi-colonial" country that relied upon Anglo-American finance capital at this time, and indeed for most of the twentieth century.[62] Thus, sixteen young Greek men and women, both Greek nationals and Soviet Greeks, made their way to Moscow in 1924 and 1925 to enroll into the newly opened foreign Greek sector of the KUTV. A number of them had arrived in Soviet Union for training in March 1924, months *before* the KKE's official affiliation with the Comintern, suggesting that the Party was confident in its ambition to join the Comintern fold after several failed attempts.[63] Four of the students, or roughly 25 percent of the first Greek cohort, were women, consistent with the gender distribution across other national sectors of KUTV at this time.[64]

The Eastern allocation of Greek students was reassessed in 1927, following the intervention of the KKE representative at the Comintern, who argued that Greece ought to have its own sector at the Communist University for National Minorities of the West "like all the other Balkan countries," as the general political ignorance of people in Greece and the relative immaturity of the workers movement required professionals and trained leaders.[65] This accorded with the broader perception of the Communist University for National Minorities of the West (KUNMZ; Kommunistichesky Universitet Natsionalnykh Menshinstv Zapada) as a superior institution, but it was also the case that some of the most prominent Balkan communists like Josef Broz Tito, Ante Ciliga, and Edvard Kardelj had been both students and teachers at the KUNMZ by this time. If the KKE couldn't be equals in policy decisions made by the Balkan Communist Federation, of which it was a member, they could at least share in the same educational opportunities.[66]

The KUNMZ, also established in 1921, was originally intended for the training of political workers of Western nationalities living in the USSR, that is, from the Lithuanian-Jewish-Latvian, German, Polish, and Romanian higher party schools. These groups made up corresponding sectors of the KUNMZ, all of whom were to be trained for work outside of Russia, in their countries of ethnic origin.[67] Byelorussian, Bulgarian, Italian, Moldavian, Greek, and Yugoslavian sectors were subsequently organized.[68]

When the Greek sector of KUNMZ was opened in November 1928, fifteen students were waiting and ready to depart from Greece to Moscow.[69] Three out of the fifteen were women: Chrysa Hatzivasiliou, who enrolled under the pseudonym Alexandra Nikolai Armand; Elena/Lena (Dimitrieva) Anemelou; and Clio Dimitrievna Stai.[70] This marked the beginning of the Third Period (1928–1933), a term coined by communist theoretician and head of the Comintern Nikolai Bukharin to describe the new period of capitalist crisis that was fundamental, not cyclical, and was creating a revolutionary upsurge.[71] All forms of working-class struggles had to be elevated into assaults on the existing system, and all forms of collaboration with the organs of the capitalist system had to be opposed. This necessitated, in particular, an intensified struggle against social democracy, in view of its new, completely bourgeois and active imperialistic ideology. Coalitions with the reformist unions and social democratic parties were inadmissible; only united fronts "from below" were on the agenda for the Comintern parties.[72] It was in this context that the KUNMZ expanded to become a genuinely international institution with sixteen national sectors and more than nine hundred students for whom the courses were an important stage for becoming a real Bolshevik and rising through the ranks of their respective national communist parties. In 1931 the KUNMZ had one thousand student enrollments in its main Moscow location, in addition to a special branch for Baltic nationalities in Leningrad; the Stalin Communist University of the Toilers of the East (KUTV) had 1,200 students in 1931, although its Greek sector had shrunk as students flowed to the Greek sector of KUNMZ when it opened in 1928.[73]

The Third Period also coincided in Greece with a dramatic expansion of the KKE, whose numbers tripled between 1930 and 1936. The numbers of Greek students at the KUNMZ also reached a peak at this time; in 1929/1930,

Greek student enrollments had reached at least forty-three, peaking at fifty-nine in 1932/1933, of whom at least eighteen were women.[74] The rules of admission for the KUTV and the KUNMZ stated that students would be no younger than eighteen or older than thirty-two; would have a good command of their native language; would be numerate "at the level of whole numbers"; and would have received a basic education, ideally completing secondary school. The first-year course would be offered predominantly to workers and peasants recommended by the corresponding sections of the Executive Committee of the Communist International (ECCI); persons who had graduated from bourgeois universities were not eligible.[75] Greek students from Greece were selected on the initial recommendation of the KKE or the youth wing, OKNE, which could be accepted or rejected by the Greek representative members of the ECCI. Soviet Greek students were selected on the basis of their trade union or party links and service.

The third and most prestigious university, the Mezhdunarodnaia Leninskaia Shkola (MLS; International Lenin School), was founded in 1926. In the words of British communist John Murphy, it was conceptualized as "the highest Marxian educational institution for qualified Party workers," an "instrument for the Bolshevization of the Communist Parties in the capitalist countries."[76] It offered only two-year postgraduate courses for high-ranking members of foreign communist parties, and later added shorter nine-month courses to enable these much needed cadres to return to their parties as soon as possible.

According to the American communist Harry Haywood, who had attended both the MLS and the KUTV, MLS students were "mainly Party functionaries of district and section level as well as secondary national leaders who could be spared for the period of study, all of whom were generally at a higher level of political development than the students at KUTV."[77] Wanda Bronska-Pampuch (pseud. Alfred Burmeister), a virtually unknown yet prolific Cominternian, was a junior cadre who attended the KUNMZ. She is a rare exception among female comrades for writing an in-depth testimony about the organizational evolution of the Comintern from the time of the Great Terror until and beyond its dissolution in 1943. According to Bronska-Pampuch, the essential differences between the MLS and the other universities lay in the more intensive political training it offered, which matched the rank and experience of its elite foreign students, most if not all of whom already held an office in their Party. Pampuch noted, for example, that the higher officials among the emigres from Germany attended the Lenin school, while the lower ones attended the KUNMZ.

MLS students came to Moscow only for the period of their studies and were listed as foreign communists; they were expected to live in strict seclusion in the school and rarely left the vicinity to go into the city. The staff at the Lenin School were first-order instructors in comparison to the second-rank staff at the KUNMZ; Tito, Kardelj, and Stalin were among the leading communist figures who taught there. Prospective students who were suspected of deviation went to the KUNMZ rather than to the MLS.[78]

The gender ratios in the Greek sectors of KUTV and KUNMZ were never matched at the MLS due to a combination of its elite status and relatively rigid entry criteria, in conjunction with the waning of the Comintern ideal itself from 1934, which culminated in the closure of the schools in 1936. When the Greek sector of the MLS opened in 1932 it hosted between sixty and seventy-five Greek students out of a total student cohort of 3,500 over the twelve years that the MLS operated. This was a low figure relative to the size of other cohorts—the German, French, and Czech were the largest—but commensurate with the size of the Greek Communist Party in conjunction with the size of the Greek minorities of the Soviet Union. In terms of gender ratio, the Greek sector figures are elusive but student lists indicate that fewer than 5 percent were female. As a point of comparison, out of the 141 Finns who at one time or another attended the MLS, thirty-five (25.5 percent) were female; the Norwegian sector totaled forty-four MLS students of whom three (7 percent) were women.[79]

According to Markovitis, the appointment of a head of Greek Sector suggests that the size of the Greek cohort was regarded as substantial.[80] The head of the Greek sector was a Soviet Greek woman, Lidiia Ivanovna Petrova, a former student of the KUNMZ (1929–1931) and of the MLS (1932–1933), who was appointed to the position in 1934.[81] Feodora Ignatievna Batman, also a Soviet-Greek, was appointed secretary during the same period.[82]

Overall, the Greek sectors of universities sustained their female cohorts for as long as the Comintern cadre universities remained operational; their numbers remained low relative to male enrollments but consistent with the gender ratios across the other national sectors. The universities were overwhelmingly male environments, reflecting the fact that fewer women than men were willing to partake in a revolutionary lifestyle, as well as signaling communist men's unarticulated assumptions and ambivalence about sharing power and prestige in the Party with women, especially at higher levels. The most well-documented example involves the male Stalinist establishment's treatment of Romanian communist leader Ana Pauker. The Soviet rulers told the Romanian Politburo, "we don't need women in the hierarchy," and insisted on the immediate replacement of Pauker as a foreign minister (according to them, foreign "dignitaries" and ministry personnel were too embarrassed to work with her). She was purged from the Romanian Communist Party in 1953.[83] Nevertheless, and pertinent to this study, the small cohorts of Greek female students in these institutions dismantles conventional understandings of women's involvement in the pre-popular front phase of the Greek communist movement as negligible and wholly informal.

Students, Curricula, Challenges

As the main aim of cadre education was to produce ideologically reliable working-class leadership—functionaries and propagandists—for the national parties and their mass organizations, the curriculum consisted of political and ideological subjects with a focus on Marxist economic theory as well as Leninism and the history of the Comintern and the Communist Party of the Soviet Union. Kivisaari refers to the Comintern approach to cadre education—a synthesis of lectures, classes, group debates and discussions, practicals, communal meals, celebrations, periods of organized relaxation, sports, excursions, and teacher-student relations—as a "total school experience," an attempt to provide a "complete and final philosophy of the universe," alluding once again to the core aims of the universities, which were to mold students into loyal activists and to preserve communist unity and identity.[84]

The curriculum content of the KUTV and KUNMZ was similar. Both cohorts were required to undertake a three-year course comprising regular academic subjects, ideological/theoretical training in their native language, and practical work in factories, heavy industry, and *kolkhozes* (collective farms) to study Soviet production methods and the political activities of Soviet Party organizations such as factory cells, all the while benefiting from immersion in the "spiritual center" of international communism. The curriculum ranged from Russian language, mathematics, natural sciences (biology, physics, and chemistry), economic geography, political economy, the history of social forms, and Russian and world history to the history of the Russian Social Democratic Labor Party, Leninism and party-building, historical materialism, the Soviet system, economic policy, and party work, including clandestine work. There was also some (para)military training and strategy for the men, and summer holidays.[85]

The requirements in Russian language, history, and culture across both institutions left no doubt as to the direction in which the Comintern would develop under Stalin. But the curriculum during the Third Period (1928–1933), during which the KUNMZ expanded dramatically amid the conviction of imminent socialist revolution, also emphasized the importance of "nationalizing the curriculum," that is, focusing on the history and politics of students' own country of origin. This was an ambitious task given the chronic shortage of available and qualified teaching staff, and the ongoing need for the translation of teaching materials.[86] The KUTV and KUNMZ initially offered three- and four-year courses respectively, and eventually offered shorter courses to allow much-needed cadres to return to their countries as soon as possible. Irrespective of the length of study, all courses were study-intensive and included military camp, practicums in the countryside or industry, and a period of two and a half months a year for rest and excursions.[87]

The MLS curriculum contained far more ideological content than the other institutions, in line with the special mandate of the institution. Based on an assessment of the MLS data for 1933/1934, Krekola states that ideological subjects accounted for 63 percent of the total teaching time at the MLS, and lectures in practical party, trade union, and organizational work amounted to 30 percent, while the remaining time (7 percent) was used to discuss national issues. Training in clandestine party activities took up only a small amount of teaching time in practical party work—out of a total of 1,185 class hours, just 40 hours (approx. 3.5 percent) were dedicated to such purposes.[88]

According to the MLS's own stated requirements, prospective MLS students were to be party workers, either activists or functionaries, who had been active members of the party for no less than three years, or five years for those of nonworking or agricultural backgrounds, with preference given to factory workers, especially those working in heavy industry. MLS students were to be between twenty-three and thirty-five years old, in sound physical condition, and ideally single, that is, without dependents for whom the Comintern would have to provide financial support and medical treatment. Additionally, students were required to be proficient in at least one of the languages of instruction at the MLS: English, Russian, German, or French. Students who spoke little or no Russian were advised to undertake Russian language study prior to commencement, in order to "take active part in Party life" and to properly understand and engage with Leninist literature as soon as they arrived in Moscow; the minimum reading and knowledge expectation for MLS candidates included the works of Lenin, Marx, Engels, Bukharin, Kautsky, and Stalin.[89] These were very ambitious prerequisites, and if the Greek sector of the MLS is representative, were not always met in full or even in part.

The unique aspirations of the Comintern education system created special challenges for both students and teachers alike. Even though prospective instructors trained to teach the fundamental theoretical material at the Institute of Red Professors (IKP; Institut Krasnoi Professury), established in 1921, it was barely sufficient. These Institutes were established to provide redress to the "bourgeois stranglehold" on leadership positions in many of the special higher educational establishments (VUZy; vysshie uchebnye zavedenii) of the Soviet Union. The aim of these institutes was to produce as many communist professors as quickly as possible. According to instructions by the Central Committee to the Commissariat of Education, the teaching of social sciences had to be under the direction of Bolshevik professors, and noncommunist specialists had to work under the control of communists. In 1932 there were twelve Red Professors' Institutes in the Soviet Union with a total of more than three thousand students. Each Institute had its own specialization—for example, economy, general history, or Party history.[90]

This system, however, was certainly inadequate for the Greek sectors, whose human and educational resources were in chronic short supply. Qualified academic staff for Greece and the Balkan region were too few, as were the teaching resources; students had semi-regular access to Greek newspapers, which they were required to read for eight hours per week to keep abreast of the political and economic situation in the "country," in addition to and in the absence of other materials, while student newspapers provided an essential and popular avenue for students to develop critical writing skills.[91] Finding qualified bilingual speakers, that is Greek *and* Russian speakers, to teach courses in Greek and Russian language in the Greek sectors, was not simple or even possible at times, so the translation of lectures and other learning materials, as well as the search for translators, was constant and ongoing across all the Greek sectors. Inadequate academic training in combination with many students' basic knowledge deficit slowed the system down, resulting in repeated recommendations by "circle leaders" and heads of sector that the distribution of workload be commensurate with students' actual knowledge level to relieve pressure and address poor attendance and low participation in group discussion.[92] These pressures took their toll on both students and teachers. The written plea of KUNMZ teacher D. M. Kairofili, addressed to the head of the Greek sector, Makroyiannis, requesting permission to "resign from the job due to severe stress and loss of energy" due to inadequate qualifications, poor teaching ability, insufficient Russian or Greek to deliver lectures to the required standard, and general duty overload, was not unique to her or to the Greek sector.[93]

The standards that universities set for themselves were at best inconsistent; students *and* educators were unable to meet the exacting standards of entry to the MLS in particular at the time of enrollment unless they had received prior training at the KUNMZ or the KUTV. In his recollections of his encounter with the Greek students at the MLS during his visits to Moscow, KKE leader Vasilis Nefeloudis recalls that:

> The theoretical curriculum was overloaded, the students didn't have time to study, some were even illiterate, not having even completed primary school! Yet they would be called up to read the advanced texts of Marx and Engels and Stalin! None of this knowledge would have helped address the real problems of Party work in Greece. It seems that the high criteria for student acceptance did not apply to students that the KKE sent to the Soviet Union.[94]

The background of MLS students like Chrysanthi Kantzidou (Kaiti Vasiliou), show that the MLS did in fact offer places to students of limited education or political pedigree. Born in 1912, in Greek Thrace to a peasant family, Vasiliou left school at age eleven in 1923 and worked in tobacco till 1934. She joined the tobacco workers union in 1923, OKNE in 1928 at the age of sixteen, and the KKE in 1932. In 1934 she left tobacco and worked as a secretary for the district committee of the KKE in Serres (northern Greece) and became a member of the regional committee in Kavala. She'd never read Marx or Lenin. In 1935 she traveled to the Soviet Union to study at the MLS, returning in 1937. Kantzidou's references make clear that her general and political education were poor at that time; she worked very hard to make significant progress but her educational level needs further improvement.[95] This background was very typical for Comintern university recruits, including students of the MLS. In a different example, Clio Stai, a Greek refugee originally from Istanbul, became an instructor at the MLS possibly because, unlike most of her peers, she had completed secondary school (in Istanbul) and demonstrated competence and commitment. Stai joined the Communist Party of Greece in 1927 and traveled to the Soviet

Union in 1929 to enroll as a "volunteer" student at KUNMZ, which presumably meant that she did not receive a stipend from the Comintern.[96] Stai absorbed all the recommended literature for the second and third year of KUNMZ and became fluent in Russian in addition to having fluency in Greek, proficiency in French, and a basic command of English. But she had no formal political or party education and was described as self-taught. By the close of 1932 she was translating and teaching Greek language at the MLS.[97]

The MLS, thus, did not always satisfy the elite criteria conventionally ascribed to it in the historiography and in the entry requirements of the institution itself. But its prestigious status has endured, as has the perception of the KUTV as the least prestigious of the cadre training universities of the Comintern, and the one that has received the least scholarly attention, perhaps reflecting both Soviet and Western prejudices. Nevertheless, the KUTV had trained some of the most significant leaders of the international communist movement including Ho Chi Minh and Deng Xiao Ping, while Bukharin, Trotsky, Radek, and Zinovieff had taught at the KUNMZ.[98] Most members of the Central Committee of the KKE in the interwar period who had undertaken training in the Soviet Union were also overwhelmingly KUTV alumni: Kostas Eftichiadis/Korkozof, Andronikos Haitas, Kostas Theos, Kolozof, Paparigas, Sklavos, Nikolaidis, Nikos Zachariadis, Petros Roussos, Kostas Sklavainas, Vasilis Nefeloudis, Dimitris Partsalidis, Giorgos Konstantinidis, Yianis Michaelidis, Michalis Tyrimos. Nikos Zachariadis and Chrysa Hatzivasiliou constitute exceptions; Zachariadis is known to have studied at all three institutions, while Chrysa Hatzivasiliou was a graduate of the KUNMZ (1928–1931).[99]

The systemic challenges and shortcomings in the cadre university system and students' struggle with the "overly intellectual and academic" content of the courses was undeniable. It was also true that the myriad obstacles to teaching and learning were counterbalanced by the enormous effort students made to overcome their deficiencies. The fact that students could not "just volunteer" for party training did not mean that they were without motivation—quite the opposite. For the most part, "going to school" was considered a mission, an honor, and a responsibility. Political education was not seen "officially" as an avenue to a career, as careerism and promotion were considered dirty words. Nevertheless, attendance in party schools offered distinct rewards. Cadre education and the possibility of advancement in the school or in the party played the same role for communists as the social mobility of political elites in any society, through financial reward and patronage. As Offerle puts it, if the division of political work often seems to the outsider to be complete domination by the leaders of the led, it is possible only because those who are led are satisfied with the advantages they are drawing from the situation.[100] For most students, participation in Party training schools presented opportunities that were more satisfactory than those available outside. The nature of rewards was complex and variable, from the merely symbolic and psychological (security, purpose, affection, admiration, prestige, and belonging), to the material, such as employment, political participation, and education, as expressed vividly in the personal testimonies of teachers and students.

As the first-year curriculum shows (Appendix 1), students were taught several basic academic subjects in their native language, whenever possible, including mathematics, language, history, and physics, in parallel with ideological schooling, which made it possible for students with no formal education to join the courses. Despite the omnipresent communist prism, the students were getting vital exposure to Western science, social theory. and in some cases, to their own language and history for the first time. The majority of the students in the Greek sectors across the three institutions had completed all or some level of elementary school and a smaller number had attended secondary school; on rare occasions, the quality of a student's signature makes clear that the *anketa* and autobiography were written by a third party. Most, however, had basic literacy, could read and write in Greek or Russian or both. Filatova refers to the Comintern's "holistic" approach to education as wholly innovative, one that had not yet emerged in Russia or elsewhere in the world. That innovation extended to the political disciplines in which students were interactive and encouraged and taught to connect the content to the situation in their own countries by assembling and evaluating all the necessary materials to the extent possible.[101]

A Class Above

Despite the myriad challenges, the students of the Comintern's international cadre universities were aware that on the whole they lived in better conditions than did ordinary Greeks and Muscovites, including Soviet students who attended the regular Soviet Party schools, a large, highly integrated network of Party schools for ideological and political education was established in the 1920s. The most prestigious of these included the Sverdlov University established for the training of leading Party workers, like the Krupskaya Academy for Communist Education and the Red Professors Institute. The second tier included institutions like the Sovpartshkoly that trained middle-ranking Party workers, and finally there was the Politshkoly, which were elementary schools offering "political literacy" for ordinary members, candidates for membership, and so on. According to Katz, the material conditions of these schools were extremely hard, especially in the first years of their existence in the early 1920s. Students were supplied with a ration of a pound and a half of bread daily, lunch, supper, but no breakfast, and a small monthly stipend. Dormitories were overcrowded, classrooms were often without heating in the winter, and students generally had to be supported by the local Party committee that sent them to the VUZy.[102]

The sense of entitlement and relative privilege of Comintern students and teachers is clearly conveyed in Bourrinet's obituary of Croatian communist Ante Ciliga (1898–1992). In 1926 Ciliga, a member of the Central Committee of the Communist Party of Yugoslavia since 1924, was sent to Moscow in 1926, to teach in the Yugoslav sector of the KUNMZ and to take part in the Yugoslav section of the Comintern. Having obtained a doctorate in history from the University of Zagreb in 1924, Ciliga was chosen to teach history to his compatriots at the KUNMZ; each year twenty-five new pupils arrived in the Yugoslav sector created in 1925 to undertake a four-year course taught entirely in Serbo-Croatian (the official language of the Kingdom of Yugoslavia).[103]

When Ciliga first arrived in Moscow in October 1926, he was struck by the misery and backwardness of the "fatherland of socialism"; he arrived as the NEP debacle was ending, with an economy in paralysis and 2.2 million unemployed. Ciliga quickly realized that foreigners like him, members of the Comintern, were considered to be "living like lords" by Russian workers sunk in poverty.[104] Wolfgang Leonhard, a former student in the German sector of the Kuscharenko school, was similarly struck by the privilege of Comintern officials.[105] Irrespective of their position in the rigid Comintern hierarchy, the lives of bureaucrats from the most senior to mid-ranking officials, teachers, and students down to the Comintern "proletariat" was indescribably different to the life of an "ordinary" Russian.

These politically trained men and women had abandoned—for good in most cases—their original occupations (if they had any), and depended on the party, directly or indirectly, for their income, career prospects, standard of living, and promotion.[106] For the great majority of the Greek students, as for most students in the Comintern university system, the break with the past was a gift and a curse, presenting opportunities for further formal education, professional advancement, social security, a sense of purpose and belonging, but also great personal sacrifice under the pressures and demands of the communist life.

3

The Greek Sectors

The "KUTVists"

KKE members who were ambivalent about Comintern affiliation and the Bolshevization process were openly hostile toward the first arrivals, the parvenus from Moscow, whom they referred to pejoratively as "KUTVists," accusing them variously of incompetence, arrogance, or undue influence in the Party. Former KKE general secretary Eleftherios Stavridis, for example, had observed that the KUTVists treated other communists with contempt, "because they believed they knew everything and the others knew nothing. They were barely able to maintain basic courtesies toward the other members of the Party—which they did out of discipline rather than respect—whose actions, opinions, words, and even their private lives, they continuously criticized."[1] Upon arriving in Greece, Soviet Greek graduate Olga Papadopoulou (pseud. Vlasova) recalled being ridiculed by her Greek comrades, who "accused me of thinking that I came to Greece to start a revolution, as if it were not possible without my presence. . . . The young communists who came from Russia and who were not aware of the political situation in the country and did not speak the language as well were particularly distrusted."[2]

This ambivalence toward Soviet-trained professional revolutionaries was far from unique to the Greek Communist Party. In reference to Irish communists at the MLS, for example, McLoughlin observed a "polite scepticism" expressed by the Irish Communist Party about the ultimate value of the MLS, which seemed to produce graduates who were "often unfit for immediate Party duties on their return as they no longer spoke the language of the workers, were more inclined to parrot the Stalinist phraseology they had internalised, and showed themselves to be mentally and operationally inflexible."[3]

Others in the Greek Communist Party regarded the KUTVists as the personification of the Stalinization of the KKE, a process that began with the very passage of the Party into the orbit of the Comintern in 1924; developments in the KKE would thereafter echo developments in Moscow. Greek Trotskyist Loukas Karliaftis (pseud. Kostas Kastritis) noted, for example, that membership of the Comintern was immediately followed by a shift in the Party's position on Macedonian autonomy from opposition to wholesale acceptance—the most divisive and politically costly policy in the history of the KKE.[4] The great split between Stalin and Trotsky that resulted in Trotsky's expulsion from the Politburo in 1926 echoed immediately in Greece with the removal of Trotskyist and KKE general secretary Pandelis Pouliopoulos from the Central Committee in March 1927.[5]

The Comintern's appointment of a new leadership under Zachariadis in 1931, composed entirely of KUTV alumni, represented the completion of the Stalinization process. The consolidation of the Stalinist faction is also held accountable for increasing secrecy regarding student selection to the Comintern universities, especially after 1934. According to Nefeloudis, "the question of who and why somebody went to Moscow, or who would study at the cadre schools there, were questions that were never presented to the Politburo. They were dealt with exclusively by the three-member executive."[6]

Heinz Richter argues that the conditions of illegality and repression in Greece "played into the hands of the KUTVists," whose Soviet training in underground organization equipped them precisely for leadership under conditions of illegality, while scores of others were imprisoned and exiled.[7] Seen differently, the skills of the KUTVists were indispensable to the development and indeed survival of the Party between the Wars. These overlapping and contradictory effects, far from unique to the Greek case, suggest that the phenomenon of Bolshevization, at the very least, defies simple evaluation. As Mario Kessler states in relation to the German party (KPD), there is no doubt that Bolshevization drastically curtailed freedom of discussion in favor of creating a "monolithic party cast in a single bloc."[8] Once the KKE had been transformed along these lines, its leading members were no longer able to resist a full-fledged Stalinization, or subordination of the now monolithic Party to the needs of the Soviet state's oscillating foreign policy, a sectarian wing of the Stalinized Soviet state under Zachariadis.

Former KKE leader Eleftherios Stavridis had written that the KUTVists, who "periodically came to Greece from Russia, were ethnic Greeks who were born and raised outside Greek borders and were thus considered 'foreign' to mainland Greek communists." Stavridis makes a distinction between the "Hadjis" who were "persons *from* Greece who had on occasion visited the Soviet 'holy land,'" and the KUTVists who were "far worse":

> At least the Hadjis were persons from Greece, known within their country, of known origin and historical background. The KUTVists on the other hand, and especially the first arrivals, were all unknown, mysterious types, usually of unknown [foreign] origin and historical background, who lied continuously when approached for information about their place of birth, their background, profession, their revolutionary or other political activities. A general darkness hung over their entire pasts.[9]

But as Table 3 shows, the first Greek KUTVists and the subsequent cohorts of the KUNMZ and the MLS were not a monolithic group of foreign interlopers.

The majority of the students of the first KUTV cohort, as shown in Table 3, were Greek nationals (Brokas, Berkovskiy, Iliadis, Kritikou, Paterouli, Mensur, Midias, Zarres, Nikolaidis, and Aleksis), predominantly of Anatolian and Jewish background, including two students from Cyprus. The remaining six students were "Soviet citizens of Greek nationality," all of whom had Anatolian origins (Yiannis Michaelidis, Zanis, Pinakotas, Olga Papadopoulou, Stella Kerasidou, Kafafov, and Kimov).

Nationality was distinct from citizenship; not all Soviet Greeks had Soviet citizenship. The non-holders of Soviet passports belonged to two categories: those who had acquired Greek citizenship from the Greek consulates, and stateless people who had declared themselves Greeks to the Soviet authorities. The latter were registered as Greeks in the registers of the Greek consulate in Moscow yet remained people without official documentation. Some Pontic Greeks in the Soviet Union eventually gave up their Greek passports for Soviet ones, especially those who sought higher education for their children; significant numbers did not. As far as the populations were concerned, declaring themselves Greek was initially to their benefit. As foreign citizens, they were exempted from participation in the *kolkhoz* (collective farm) and allowed to keep their property. Moreover,

TABLE 3. STUDENT INFORMATION: GREEK STUDENTS, INTERNATIONAL GROUP, KUTV 1924/1925

Surname	Year of Birth	Place of Birth	Party Member	Social Origin	Date Entered KUTV
Emil Aleksis	1903	Limassol, Cyprus	Communist Party of Greece' (CPG) 1922; Russian Communist Party (RCP) 1926	Public service, office worker	Jan. 21, 1925
Kimov	1900	Banya, Bulgaria	RCP 1924	Peasant	March 26, 1924
Yiannis Mikhailidis	1899	Constantinople	RCP 1924; GCP 1931	Worker	Jan. 23, 1925
Giorgis Zanis	1898	Constantinople	RCP 1924	Worker	Jan. 23, 1925
Nikolas Nikolaidis (alias Gero, Pappou)	1907	Constantinople	Tomsk (Siberia) Communist Youth Union (TKSM) 1922; Russian Lenin Komsomol (RKSM); Greek Komsomol (OKNE) 1922	Public service, office worker, ship stoker	Dec. 16, 1924
Shan Zarres	1901	Thessaloniki (Salonika)	OKNE 1917; RKSM 1917	Public service	March 25, 1925
Leon Midias/Moutis	1900	Limassol, Cyprus	CPG 1922; RCP 1926	Public service	Jan. 22, 1925
Kostas Mensur	1908	Constantinople	TKSM 1921; GKSM 1921; RKSM	Worker	April 16, 1924

TABLE 3. STUDENT INFORMATION: GREEK STUDENTS, INTERNATIONAL GROUP, KUTV 1924/1925 (continued)

Surname	Year of Birth	Place of Birth	Party Member	Social Origin	Date Entered KUTV
Olga Paterouli	1901	Constantinople	non-party	Worker	Jan. 23, 1925
Smaro Kritikou	1900	Constantinople	non-party	Worker	Jan. 23, 1925
Iliadis	1905	Athens	GKSM 1920; RKSM 1920	Public service	March 25, 1925
Achilleas Kafafov	1905	Georgia	RKSM 1923	Intelligentsia	March 26, 1925
Anastasis Pinakotas	1899	Constantinople	RCP 1924	Worker	Jan. 23, 1925
Olga Papadopoulou (Vlasova)	1906	Batumi, Georgia (originally Anatolia)	RKSM 1924; CPG (1925–1930)	Worker	Sept. 25, 1925
Stella Kerasidou (Olga Nikolaevna Ivanova)	1901	Batumi, Georgia (originally Kerasund)	RKSM 1924; GKSM1925; CPG (1925–1930); RCP 1930	Worker	1923 (CM sector) 1924 (Greek sector)
Nikolas Berkovskiy	1906	Kalamata, Greece	GKSM 1924	Worker	Oct. 22, 1925
Nikolas Brokas	1907	Constantinople	GKSM 1923	Public service	Oct. 22, 1925

Source: Translated reproduction of table as it appears in the file "Student Information: Greek Students, International Group, KUTV," f. 532, op. 2, d. 83, 9, RGASPI. Istanbul is called Constantinople in all Comintern documents consulted.

they were exempted from conscription into the army. In the following decades, however, the situation changed drastically. Greek citizenship became a major constraint not only because it evoked suspicion about loyalties, but also because it meant exclusion from participation in several fields of social, political, and economic life. Students who were Greek nationals were not issued Soviet citizenship as they were expected to return to Greece, a plan thwarted by the Metaxas dictatorship, which made re-entering Greece increasingly difficult after 1936. These stateless persons marooned in the Soviet Union were among the victims of Stalin's purges; the lack of Soviet citizenship could result in expulsion from the CPSU, the confiscation of residential permits, unemployment, and worse as the purges against national minorities gained pace.[10]

Upon arrival in the Soviet Union, students who were KKE or OKNE members—not all students were—had their membership transferred from the home party to the All-Union Communist Party (CPSU; Communist Party of the Soviet Union), and thereby, like all students, became directly subject to its discipline and sworn to secrecy, conditions one assumes Greek students adjusted to relatively well as illegals in their own country.[11] Once selected, the students from Greece departed and returned—or arrived in the case of Soviet Greeks—to Greece clandestinely, often as stowaways on ships like the Soviet steamship *Chicherin*.[12] This was also the case for Soviet Greek graduates who were assigned to work in Greece, which was often referred to as "the country." There was a strong conspiratorial atmosphere in the Moscow schools, especially in the 1930s. The students were equipped with new identities, and to camouflage the real reason behind their presence in the Soviet Union, the Comintern could provide membership books for Russian trade unions, giving the impression that they had been employed in ordinary work during their stay. Due to security regulations from 1932, the students were not allowed to tell each other their real name, place of origin, or former occupation. No photographing of fellow students was allowed. Association with fellow nationals outside the school in national clubs in Moscow was prohibited, and the students were not allowed to make chance acquaintances or walk the streets of Moscow in groups of more than three. These regulations were often flouted, but were generally more easily accepted by students from countries like Greece where communism was illegal. Students who regularly and seriously contravened the rules were expelled from the school and transferred to industrial work before finally being sent back to their countries of origin. The secret culture permeating the schools led to the rise of rumors and intensified the whole mystery surrounding Soviet cadre education in Western countries.

The first KUTV cohort was comprised of individuals aged between sixteen and twenty-seven years old, most of whom were enrolled as "workers." The four women had Anatolian origins—both Greek nationals, Olga Paterouli and Smaro Kritikou, were Istanbul-born (noted as Constantinople), and both Soviet-Greeks, Stella Kerasidou and Olga Papadopoulou from Batumi (Batoum), Georgia, were originally from Kerasund, in the Black Sea region of northeastern Turkey (Pontos).[13] Papadopoulou was the only one of the four who held Party membership (Russian Communist Party or Russian Komsomol [All-Union Leninist Young Communist League]) at the time of enrollment. This was not anomalous in 1924/25 but gradually became less common by the second half of the decade as the gap between the Party and state institutions (communization) narrowed under Stalin and tightened the conditions of enrollment across all institutes of higher learning.[14] When Soviet-Greek students undertook missions in Greece, they became members of the Greek Communist Party, and likewise, Greek nationals became members of the CPSU for the duration of their studies in Moscow. All four female students of this KUTV cohort undertook missions in Greece upon the completion of their training.

Expansion of the Greek Sectors

Greek enrollments increased dramatically during the crisis of the Third Period (1928–1933), which saw a general expansion of the Comintern education system. It was the second spike since the death of Lenin in 1924, which witnessed a general surge of enrollments into the Komsomol and the CPSU. Greek students were no longer funneled into the KUTV but into the newly opened Greek sectors of the Communist University of the KUNMZ (from 1928) and the MLS (from 1932). Enrollments slowed but continued into the period of "high Stalinism," until the universities' final closure in the late 1930s.[15]

The KUNMZ became a genuinely international institution during the Third Period. It opened its Greek sector in November 1928, its numbers tripling between 1930 and the installation of the Metaxas dictatorship in 1936.[16] Among its first female students were future Politburo member Chrysa Hatzivasiliou, Elena (Dimitrieva) Anemelou, and Clio Dimitrievna Stai.[17] All three were refugees from Asia Minor and Istanbul (Constantinople)

TABLE 4. KUNMZ STUDENTS—GREEK SECTOR 1928–1936

Name and university pseudonym	Year of birth	Place of birth	Nationality	Education	Party	Language	Marital status	Employment and social origin
Koula Triantafyllidou (Theou)	1906	Kavala, Greece	Greek	Elementary school (Greece); one year of secondary school; KUNMZ	GCP 1926; RCP 1932	Greek	Married (Kostas Theos, GCP)	Worker, tobacco; Father, barber, deceased; mother, midwife
Feodora Ignatievna Batman	1903	Bolsh'aya Yanisol, Donbas, Ukraine, SSR	Greek nationality, Soviet citizenship	Elementary school; School for Protection of Motherhood and Childhood (OHMADET) 1928–30; KUNMZ 1932–34; head of MLS Greek sector 1934–36	RKSM 1923–28; RCP 1926	Greek, Ukrainian, Russian	Single	Peasants; * father deceased (famine 1921)
Clio Stylianou Christodoulidou (Nora Ivanovna Irman / Margarita Robopoulou)	1901	Limassol, Cyprus	Greek, Cypriot, and British	Elementary and two years secondary school (Cyprus); KUNMZ 1930–32	CCP 1926; KKE 1927–1930; RCP 1930	Greek, Russian	Single	Dressmaker; Parents – artisans

The Greek Sectors 89

TABLE 4. KUNMZ STUDENTS—GREEK SECTOR 1928–1936 (continued)

Name and university pseudonym	Year of birth	Place of birth	Nationality	Education	Party	Language	Marital status	Employment and social origin
Daria Mikhailovna Yarmosh	1908	Yalta, Mariupol, Donbas, Ukraine, SSR	Soviet-Greek	Elementary school (SU); Sovpartshkola 1931–33; KUNMZ 1935–36	RKSM 1926-1933; RCP 1931	Greek, Russian, Ukrainian	Divorced, one son	Well-to-do peasants
Anna Antonovna Todurova	1898	Yalta, Mariupol, Donbas, Ukraine, SSR	Soviet-Greek	Elementary school (SU); Sovpartshkola level 2, 1929–31; KUNMZ 1934–36	RCP 1926	Greek, Russian	Single	Peasant; parents deceased (famine 1921)
Olga Davidovna Abadzheva (Lisina)	1892	Allaverdy, Armenia, SSR	Soviet (Greek)	Secondary school (SU); KUNMZ 1933–36	RCP 1926	Greek, Russian, Turkish	Divorced, one daughter	Worker
Yelizaveta Kharalampovna Dardur	1897	Bolsh'aya Yanisol, Donbas, Ukraine, SSR	Soviet (Greek)	Elementary school (SU); KUNMZ 1932–34	RCP 1926	Greek, Turco-Tatar, Russian	Single	Peasant

TABLE 4. KUNMZ STUDENTS—GREEK SECTOR 1928–1936 (continued)

Name and university pseudonym	Year of birth	Place of birth	Nationality	Education	Party	Language	Marital status	Employment and social origin
Irini Solomonidou (Sonia Niku / Sofia Petrovna)	1906	Alexandria, Egypt	Cypriot/English citizenship; Greek	Elementary school (Cyprus); KUNMZ 1931–35	Cyprus Komsomol 1926; Cyprus CP 1928	Greek, Russian (poor)	Single	Typesetter; Father, rural laborer; Mother, factory worker
Maria Rodionovna Maksiuk	1905	Volnovakha district, Donbas, Ukraine	Soviet-Greek nationality	Elementary school (2 years, SU); Sovpartshkola 1932 (6 months); KUNMZ 1935–36	Komsomol (RKSM) 1923–31; RCP 1932	Greek, Ukrainian, Russian	Married	Peasant; Father deceased
Clio Dmitrievna Stai	1905	Constantinople, Turkey	Greek	(French) Elementary and secondary school (Constantinople); student and teacher of Greek at KUNMZ 1929–32; MLS teacher of Greek 1932–38	CPG 1927; RCP 1931	Greek, French, Russian, English	Married, one child	Petit bourgeois; Father, trader, deceased 1922; Mother, teacher

TABLE 4. KUNMZ STUDENTS—GREEK SECTOR 1928–1936 (continued)

Name and university pseudonym	Year of birth	Place of birth	Nationality	Education	Party	Language	Marital status	Employment and social origin
Lena Nikolaevna Dmitrieva (Anemelou)	1911	Panormou, Asia Minor	Greek	Elementary school (2 years, Greece); KUNMZ 1928–30; MLS 1930–32	OKNE 1927; RKSM 1929; GCP 1932	Greek, Russian	Single	Worker; Father, sailor, deceased 1912; Mother, tobacco worker
Alexandra Kuzminichna Apostolova	1905	Mariupol, Donbas, Ukraine, SSR	Soviet-Greek	Elementary school (SU, 2 years); Sovpartshkola 1931–33; KUNMZ 1935–36	RKSM 1924–32; RCP 1927	Russian, Turkish-Tatar	Single	Peasant; Father, deceased 1906; Mother, deceased 1922
Nina Dmitrievna Ashigova	1911	Opreti, Georgia, SSR	Soviet-Greek	(Greek) elementary and secondary school (SU); KUNMZ 1933–35	Komsomol 1927–36; RCP 1932	Russian, Turkish-Tatar		Peasants; Father, deceased
Chrysa Hatzivasiliou (Alexandra Nikolai Armand)	1903	Aidinio (Aydin), Turkey	Greek	(French) Elementary and secondary school (Constantinople); KUNMZ 1928–31	Greek Communist Youth / OKNE1924; GCP 1925; RCP 1928–31	Greek, French, Turkish, Russian	Married	Wealthy peasants

TABLE 4. KUNMZ STUDENTS—GREEK SECTOR 1928–1936 (continued)

Name and university pseudonym	Year of birth	Place of birth	Nationality	Education	Party	Language	Marital status	Employment and social origin
Yefrosinia Dmitrievna Diamantidou	1902	Trabzon, Turkey	Soviet-Greek	Elementary school (Trabzon); Sovpartshkola 1927–29; Institute of Socialist Studies 1932; KUNMZ 1934–36	RCP 1932	Greek, Russian, Turkish	Divorced	Office worker; Father, tailor (petit bourgeois); Parents, deceased 1914
Ksenia Dmitrievna Arnaoutova	1911	Yalta, Mariupol, Donbas, Ukraine, SSR	Soviet-Greek	No schooling; Sovpartshkola 1933; KUNMZ 1934–36	RKSM 1926; RCP 1931	Russian, Greek	Single	Peasants; Parents, deceased 1921
Ermofili Nikolaevna Venedekidou (Venetikova, Venedikova)	1894	Kvirike, Georgia, SSR	Soviet-Greek	(Greek) Elementary school (5 years, SU); KUNMZ 1931–34	RCP 1925	Greek, Russian		Artisan; Father, mason
Melania Alekseevna Shaganova	1907	Urzuf, Donbas, Ukraine	Soviet-Greek	Elementary school (one year, SU); Sovpartshkola 1929–32; KUNMZ 1935	RKSM 1925–26; RCP 1929;	Greek, Russian, Ukrainian	Single	Peasants, Father, deceased (famine 1921)

TABLE 4. KUNMZ STUDENTS—GREEK SECTOR 1928–1936 (continued)

Name and university pseudonym	Year of birth	Place of birth	Nationality	Education	Party	Language	Marital status	Employment and social origin
Olga Dimitrievna Kaloidou	1908	Maykop, Adygea, North Caucasus	Soviet-Greek	Elementary (one year, SU); Politshkoly (8 months)1927; KUNMZ 1928–31	RKSM 1927; RCP 1931; GCP 1933–35	Greek, Russian	Married	Peasant, unskilled, odd jobs, agricultural worker; Father, deserted 1925; Mother, deceased 1926
Yevgenia Andreevna Dimitropoulou (Aleksandra Vasilievna Kirova)	1917	Piraeus, Greece	Greek	Elementary school (Greece); secondary (SU) 1928–33; KUNMZ 1933–36	RKSM 1932	Greek, Russian	Divorced, one child	Workers
Lidiia Ivanovna Cherman (Petrova) (née Pino)	1897	Novo-Karakuba, Donbas region, Ukraine, SSR	Soviet-Greek citizenship	Elementary school (SU); Teachers' Training Institute 1917; Institute of Public Education 1925–26; KUNMZ 1929–31; head of MLS Greek sector 1934-37	RCP 1927	Russian, Greek (poor)	Married	Dressmaker, peasant background

Table based on data compiled by author.

TABLE 5. MLS FEMALE STUDENTS—GREEK SECTOR

Name and university pseudonym	Year of Birth	Place of Birth	Nationality	Education	Languages	Party	Marital status	Social origin
Olga Bakola (Aliki Kanda)	1917	Ipeiros, Greece	Greek nationality and citizenship	Elementary school; MLS 1935–38	Greek	OKNE 1933	Single	Workers
Chrysanthi Kantzidou (Kaiti Vasiliou)	1912	Drama-Macedonia, Greece	Greek nationality and citizenship	Elementary school (one year); MLS 1935–37	Greek	OKNE 1928–32; CPG 1934	Single	Peasants; Tobacco workers; Father deceased (Balkan Wars)
Lidiia Ivanovna Petrova	1897	Novo-Karakuba, Donetsk region, Ukraine, SSR	Greek nationality and citizenship	Elementary school (four years); KUNMZ 1929–31; MLS 1931–33; head of Greek sector 1934–37	Russian, Basic Greek	RCP 1927	Married	Poor peasants
Stella Vamniatzidou (Yiannoula Nikolaidi, Elena Arnova)	1910	Raedestos, Turkey	Greek	No schooling; MLS 1933–38	Greek, Turkish	GCP 1930	Married	Workers

TABLE 5. MLS FEMALE STUDENTS—GREEK SECTOR *(continued)*

Name and university pseudonym	Year of Birth	Place of Birth	Nationality	Education	Languages	Party	Marital status	Social origin
Stella Kerasidou (Olga Nikolaevna Ivanova)	1901	Batumi, Georgia, SSR	Greek; Soviet citizenship	Completed secondary school; KUTV 1923–25; MLS 1930–34; MLS teacher 1934–38	Greek, Russian, Basic Turkish	GCP 1925–30; RCP 1930	Divorced and remarried	Workers
Feodora Ignatievna Batman	1903	Bolsh'aya Yanisol, Donbas, Ukraine, SSR	Greek; Soviet citizenship	Elementary school; School for Protection of Motherhood and Childhood (OHMADET) 1928–30; KUNMZ 1932–34; head of MLS Greek sector 1934–36	Greek, Ukrainian, Russian	RKSM 1923–28; RCP 1926	Single	Peasants

TABLE 5. MLS FEMALE STUDENTS—GREEK SECTOR (continued)

Name and university pseudonym	Year of Birth	Place of Birth	Nationality	Education	Languages	Party	Marital status	Social origin
Clio Dimitrievna Stai	1905	Constantinople, Turkey	Greek nationality and citizenship	Elementary and secondary school (French / school in Constantinople); student and teacher of Greek at KUNMZ 1929–32; MLS teacher of Greek 1932–38	Greek, French, Russian, English	CPG 1927; RCP 1931	Married, one child	Petit-bourgeois
Lena Nikolaevna Anemelou (Dimitrieva)	1911	Panormou, Asia Minor	Greek nationality and citizenship	Elementary school (2–3 yrs); KUNMZ 1928–30; MLS 1930–32	Greek, Russian (poor)	OKNE 1925; RKSM 1929; GCP 1932	Single	Tobacco workers; Father, deceased 1912
Chrisoula Vagia (Alexandra Gromova)	1914	Raedestos, Anatolia	Greek	Elementary school; MLS 1933–35	Greek	OKNE 1930	Married	Tobacco worker; Family, tobacco workers

Sample only based on collected data

who were resettled in Greece after the population exchange of 1922. Of the twenty-two KUNMZ files of female students consulted in this study, fourteen belonged to Soviet Greeks (mainly of Pontic origin), six belonged to Greek nationals (four of whom were Anatolian refugees), and two to citizens of Cyprus (of Pontic origin).[18] The British occupation of Cyprus in 1878 and the freedom of political expression under the British regime created a basis for the further growth of Greek nationalism in Cyprus in ways that were unthinkable under Ottoman rule and ensured the survival of the island after the extinction of Greek communities in Asia Minor. This made the island of Cyprus an attractive yet relatively under-researched destination of Anatolian Greeks fleeing advancing Ottoman and Turkish armies in the late nineteenth and early twentieth century respectively.[19]

All students in this cohort were members of their respective parties or youth wings at the time of enrollment in the KUNMZ. At least ten of the total number of students undertook missions in Greece during or upon the completion of their training. They were Koula Theou (Greece), Chrysa Hatzivasiliou (Greece), Yevgenia Dimitropoulou (Greece), Eleni Anemelou (Greece), Clio Stai (Greece), Clio Christodoulidou (Cyprus), Olga Kaloidou (Soviet Greek), Olga Abadzheva (Soviet Greek), Feodora Ignatievna Batman (Soviet Greek), and Lidiia Petrova (Soviet Greek). Graduates worked as mid-ranking functionaries and underground operatives of the KKE, which encompassed a broad but ill-defined spectrum of activities ranging from propaganda work to liaisons/communications conduits (re)building Party organizations and networks that had fragmented or collapsed under the conditions of illegality. All students were expected to attend Comintern meetings and visit the offices of the organization to become familiarized with the central institutions of the international communist movement. Students could carry out work tasks in the Comintern bureaucracy or with other international communist organizations such as the International Trade Unions (Profintern) and especially International Red Aid (MOPR), in whose activities many of the Greek female Cominternians had been involved intermittently as it served as an important entry point into the Party, as observed in the previous chapter. All female communists, especially the graduates from Comintern universities dispatched to Greece, actively supported and were generally expected to contribute to the communist women's movement in Greece, which was understood in Comintern circles to have very few "politically literate" women in its ranks.[20]

An additional group of files belonged to Greek nationals who arrived at the universities not as students, but as employees of the KUNMZ, as ancillary staff, typists, translators, and clerks, on the request and recommendation of the KKE and its representatives in the ECCI. For example, Yevgenia Andreevna Dimitropoulou (Alexandra Vasilievna Kirova), born in Piraeus, Athens, in 1917, moved to the Soviet Union with her family after her father's death in 1936, where she and her mother became "dependents of the MOPR and the Comintern." This appears to be a gesture in memory of a valued comrade, "an active revolutionary and member of the KKE," and his contributions to the Party. Dimitropoulou went on to work as an archive clerk for the Comintern (1932–1933), and as a typist in the Greek sector of the MLS (1933–1934) and then at the KUNMZ (1934–1936).[21] This scenario was not uncommon. In addition to training its much-needed professional cadres, the Party utilized the Comintern relationship to solve a wide range of problems afflicting its rank and file—patronage offered relief from unemployment, sanctuary from political persecution, health care for tubercular communists (sanatoria), child welfare (MOPR/orphanages), underscored the far more nuanced character of the exchange between the periphery and the center than conventionally understood.

Finally, the sample of nine MLS student files consulted in this study belonged primarily to Greek nationals, most of whom were "proven" activists and militants in Greece, and most of whom returned to work for the Party in Greece. Stella Vamniatzidou, a Party member, tobacco worker, and political activist from Kavala, originally from Raedestos, Anatolia, was sent to Moscow in 1933 where she completed one year of basic studies at the MLS (1933–1934) followed by four years at the MLS Radio School. She became a Comintern employee, working as a radio operator at the Communications Services base of the ECCI, returning to Greece in 1940.[22] Chrysanthi Kantzidou (Kaiti Vasiliou) and Olga Bakola (Aliki Kanda) were sent to the MLS in 1935. Born in Ipeiros, Greece, in 1917, Bakola, a textile worker, joined the OKNE in Athens in 1933 at age sixteen and became a strike organizer, and a participant organizer of the National Antifascist Youth Congress of 1934. She was sent to the MLS in 1935 and completed her studies in 1938, returning to the Party in Athens via Paris with the outbreak of the War in 1939. Her trajectory was closely followed by Chrysanthi Kantzidou, born in Drama, Thrace, in 1912. An active OKNE and Party member, a tobacco worker and trade union activist in Kavala, she was also sent to the MLS in 1935 and returned to Greece via Paris where both women were tasked with helping reconstitute the KKE leadership that had been decimated by National Security during the Metaxas dictatorship. Bakola was fatally wounded by a German tank in occupied Athens in 1943 during

FIGURE 5. Lidiia Ivanovna Petrova, head of the MLS Greek sector, 1932–1936. Photo courtesy of RGASPI.

a demonstration.[23] Chrisoula Vagia, an unemployed tobacco worker from Kavala, Greece, born in Raedestos, Anatolia, was an active member of the Regional Committee of OKNE and a member of the Tobacco Workers Union since 1930. She was sent to the MLS in September 1933 and returned to Greece in June 1935.[24] Clio Stai, a teacher from Istanbul, joined the KKE in 1927 and then worked in the plenipotentiary representation of the USSR in Athens. Stai completed two years of training at KUNMZ (1929–1931) and became a teacher and translator at the MLS in 1932, returning to Greece in 1933. The two Soviet Greek students, Lidiia Ivanovna Petrova (Cherman) and Feodora Ignatievna Batman were from the Donbas region of Ukraine. Both had been students at the KUNMZ before joining the MLS, where they both became senior administrators in the Greek sector. Petrova was plucked out of the KUNMZ to staff the newly opened Greek sector of the MLS in September 1932, subject to two preparatory years at the MLS (1931–1933) to become well versed in Greek affairs before taking a teaching role and becoming the Head of the Greek sector of the MLS (1934–1937); Feodora Batman became Secretary of the Greek Sector (1934–1936) shortly after graduating from KUNMZ (1932–1934).[25] Of the two, only Petrova had undertaken assignments in Greece in 1933–1934, even though, unlike many of her peers, her Greek was elementary, and she was unable to read Greek newspapers. Petrova had never been to Greece and had no connections with "the country," but she was highly ambitious, "politically advanced and experienced in mass activism and Party work," her knowledge deficits

FIGURE 6. Feodora Batman, secretary of the Greek sector, 1934–1936. Photo courtesy of RGASPI.

compensated for by sheer hard work and commitment.[26] Indeed, Vasilis Nefeloudis, a former student of the MLS, recalls Comrade Ivanovna as an overzealous apparatchik, "coercive and autarchic" who routinely subjected her students to the ordeal of "criticism and self-criticism."[27]

Fundamentally, in terms of special qualifications, Party rank, or preparedness for study, there was not a great deal to differentiate the students of KUTV from those of the KUNMZ or the ILS. What bound them together was gender-inflected class disadvantage, the acquisition of a sense and language of social (in)justice, and an aspiration for a more meaningful life. The majority also shared a refugee background.

"Group A" and "Group B": Soviet Greeks and Greeks

Students of the Greek sectors shared an emigre and refugee status; they were predominantly Anatolian Greeks whose families were expelled or forced to flee from their homelands in the Eastern Mediterranean in the context of imperial competition and nation-building conflict. They are divided into two main groups: The Greek nationals (referred to within the universities as Group B) were predominantly Anatolian refugees, transplanted into Greece after the population exchange of 1923. Group B students began to arrive in 1924/1925, at the start of the Bolshevization drive when the KKE stepped up its recruitment efforts among female urban and agricultural workers, refugees, and students in an attempt to "align gender ideology with party practice." The Soviet Greek students (referred to as Group A) were also of Anatolian origin, in all likelihood Pontic Greeks, the most populous Greek subgroup residing within Russia, judging by the preponderance of surnames that end in -*idis* (masc.) and -*idou* (fem), a characteristic feature of Pontic Greek names.[28] Group A students were predominantly from "working" families and from the poorer segments of the peasantry, those who were landless, or who owned land that they could not afford to cultivate, and entered the ranks of hired labor on *kulak* land.²⁹ The Soviet-Greek students self-identified as Greeks—and were encouraged to do so—in line with the Soviet nationalities model that encouraged people of Greek descent to think of themselves as Greeks. Greek students presented as an undifferentiated group; Pontic origins, for example, were not noted by students in their *anketa* or autobiographical narratives and were of no political significance to the Soviet authorities. The students called themselves *Romioi* or *Urum*, depending on whether they spoke Turkic or Greek languages, or used *Greki*, their formal Russian ethnonym. According to Anton Popov, Pontic Greeks from the former Soviet Union only became familiar with the Pontic identity as a separate, albeit Greek identity when they immigrated to Greece after the collapse of the Soviet Union.³⁰

The strong presence of Greeks in Russia dates back to the seventh century BCE when they colonized many regions around the Black Sea, settling into communities whose first business was curing, packing, and exporting fish. These trading posts grew into towns with stone walls and then into maritime cities. Black Sea trade continued to grow through the Roman and Byzantine imperial periods but came to an end with the fall of Constantinople and Trebizond to the Ottoman Empire in 1453 and 1461 respectively. The cities of the coast were mostly abandoned, not to be revived until the eighteenth century when the Russian Empire reached the Black Sea.³¹ After the Russian annexation of Crimea in 1783, Catherine the Great made prodigious efforts to develop her vast new territories, recruiting colonists—primarily Greeks, as co-religionists, but also Germans and Armenians—and granting privileges to existing Crimean Greek populations, most likely descendants of Byzantine colonists, encouraging them to relocate to Mariupol, in the Azov Sea region. These colonists were soon joined by waves of Greek refugees migrating from Anatolia to the newly annexed Russian lands. The "Erzurum Greeks," for example, who originated from the Erzurum Vilayet of the Ottoman Empire in eastern Anatolia, fled their land and resettled in central Georgia at the end of the Russo-Turkish War of 1828–1829 following the withdrawal of the advance guard of the Tsarist troops. The third and most populous group comprises the Greeks of Pontos—derived from Éfxinos Póntos, the ancient Greek name for the Black Sea— a geographical area defined to a large extent by its Alps, located in the modern-day eastern Black Sea region of Turkey. Pontic Greeks immigrated or were forced by protracted conflict to leave their homeland in successive waves from the mid-nineteenth century, fleeing primarily to Russia to join earlier Pontic migrations, until their final expulsion to Greece as part of the forced population exchange that followed the Greco-Turkish War (1919–1922).[32]

Hasiotis states that before the Russian Revolution, 450,000 Greeks lived within the Russian Empire, of whom 250,000 were thought to be Pontic Greeks.[33] The size of the Greek population dropped to an estimated 250,000 in 1920 with the exodus after the Revolution, leaving a Pontic Greek majority living primarily in southern Russia, mainly in Krasnodar, a city of the fertile Kuban region; in the Crimea peninsula (Crimean Autonomous Soviet Socialist Republic); Mariupol in eastern Ukraine; and Batumi and Abkhazia in Georgia, all regions that align with the biographical data of the Soviet Greek students. The Greek diaspora in the former Soviet Union thus comprised a widespread population with diverse origins and interests. Surveying the character of the Greek populations of the Soviet Union in the 1930s, travel writer Ioannis Stogiannis observed that the Greeks of Moscow and St. Petersburg were indeed very different from the Greeks who lived in the south of Russia. The former were more or less fully assimilated and "served the status quo" as Russian nationals. The latter, those living on the Black Sea coast, lived "outside the status quo," as bourgeoisie or private agricultural workers, and were at war with the establishment, so one cannot simply "find the truth" about Greek life in the Soviet Union, as there were too many truths.[34]

Language Policy and Identity at the Comintern

A significant percentage of the Soviet Greek student cohort had attended Grecophone schools, first established in pre-revolutionary Russia by the Greek bourgeoisie, elite urban Greek communities who were concerned about the perpetuation of Greek culture.[35] Community leaders decided on standard Greek, rather than a version of Pontic Greek, as the language of instruction in order to unite a politically, culturally, and linguistically diverse minority. This meant that, until 1926 when the Soviet government introduced demotic Greek, Greek schools in Russia taught the purified *katharevousa* form of the language, which was used in Greek schools till the Venizelos reforms of 1929 that legislated demotic Greek for all elementary schools.

Reports on the situation of the Greek educational system across 115 Greek villages in the areas of Kutaisi and Tbilisi (Georgia), and Kars (an Armenian-dominated region in Eastern Anatolia under Russian rule

FIGURE 7. Areas of Greek settlement on the shores of the Black Sea. Google Maps, 2018. See Sam Topalidis, "The Relocation of Greeks from Pontos," PontosWorld, 2018, https://pontosworld.com/index.php/history/sam-topalidis/683-the-relocation-of-greeks-from-pontos.

1878–1917) describe the dramatic shortcomings of Greek school teachers and the system's impact on language preservation and national identity. Material collected by Puchner from the Russian and Greek newspapers in Odessa and reports from the wider area of the Black Sea on itinerant Greek professional and amateur theater troupes reveals that performances often took place in the Greek schools themselves in the effort to fill the gaps, commercialize the schools, and sustain ethnic identity.[36] School performances drew on Greek patriotic and nationalist themes in the effort to foster and cultivate ethnic identity. Even very small Greek communities, like the one in Sochi, with only thirty Greek families at the turn of the twentieth century, had functioning Greek schools and organized national events on New Year's Day that included the recitation of poems and the singing of the Greek national anthem by the pupils, expressions of nationalist sentiment that were mostly tolerated by the Russian educational system.[37]

The migration outflows of the late Ottoman period and the Russian Revolution took in the majority of these Greek urban and affluent populations that had had a leading position in the educational and ideological organization of the Greek diaspora, thus depriving it of its traditional elite. The cultural leadership vacuum left by migrating Greek elites was filled in the 1920s by a new elite of communist intellectuals and Party members.[38] Grecophone schools continued to be supported, indeed upgraded, after the Revolution, as "indigenization" (*korenizatsiia*) was seen at this stage as a means of preventing "ethnicism," disarming nationalism, cultivating socialist ideals among minority populations, and integrating them into the Soviet Union.[39] Stalin, the commissar of National Minorities in 1920, considered that the autonomization of national minorities and *korenizatsiia* proposed a form of nationhood that would not conflict with a unitary central state; it would foster national territories and languages and forge national elites who would in turn become invested in a Russia-dominated Soviet Union.[40] Thus, *korenizatsiia* was to play its part in the advance of the imperial Russian super-state or *derzhavnost* agenda, the forging of a centralized multinational state away from internationalism toward great power and status through "socialism in one country."[41] To prove the point, *korenizatsiia* began to be dismantled when it was perceived as undermining the unitary Soviet state. The policy ended with the Great Terror in the late 1930s with Stalin's violent assimilation of ethnic minorities and the elimination of ethnic minorities with foreign connections, who now appeared to the Soviet authorities as potential fifth columns, a process that lasted till 1949.

Until the Great Terror, the official language policy recognized the language of the dominant nationality in each region alongside Russian and the language of the particular people's democracy in which the minority was located, for example, Georgia.[42] The recognition of the Greek language as a dominant language happened first in Sokhumi and then gradually across all five recognized Greek regions in southern Ukraine, Donetsk, and Mariupol, and in Southern Russia—large parts of the Kuban region including Krasnodar and Krymsk. The establishment of demotic Greek as the official language of instruction in all Greek schools in 1926 was influenced in part by local cultural activists but primarily by communist Greek refugees who began to arrive in the Soviet Union in large numbers after 1924 with the entry of the KKE into the Comintern fold. They were considered experts in the language both by central Soviet authorities and by local Greek populations (*Rum/Romioi/Rumei*) who were Greek-speaking Greeks as opposed to Turkish-speaking Greeks (*Urum*). According to Baranova, in reference to the Mariupol Greeks, the discourse of Greek communists from Anatolia and Greece was all-powerful. Greek communists who worked as instructors in the summer training courses for teachers did not consider *Romeika*, the local Greek dialect of Mariupol (or any other local dialect), to be a fully fledged language but rather a poor dialect incapable of expressing great ideas, a view that was adopted by local cultural activists and spread among ordinary people.[43] From the Soviet central policy perspective, demotic Greek would unify the Greeks in the Soviet Union as the language of the unprivileged proletariat in Greece.

As Karpozilos states, although propagandistic in essence, the Soviet-Greek school network fostered the ethnic identity of the Greek minority, and at the same time reduced levels of illiteracy.[44] The students continued to be taught a language that was not spoken at home; standard modern Greek was a foreign language for the Pontic Greeks who constituted the Greek majority in Russia after the Revolution. Until 1926, the Greek schools in Russia taught the purified *katharevousa* form of the language, exactly as did the schools in Greece.

In 1926, the Soviet government introduced the demotic form in Greek schools, that is, three years before the same reforms were introduced by Venizelos in Greece.[45] Most of the adults were illiterate and spoke a Pontian dialect; apart from those who spoke the dialect of Mariupol (*Romeika*), there were only a few thousand who spoke standard Greek, living mainly in Odessa and the surrounding region.[46] Indeed, records of summer internship programs kept by the KUTV and KUNMZ attest to the fact that demotic Greek was not spoken by most of the adult population in many areas of Greek settlement, whether of Pontic origin or otherwise. These records alluded to the need for "better language preparation for the students who, in the face of multiple local Greek dialects they didn't recognize, resorted to Russian language. For example, Ukrainian Greeks spoke two dialects: Tartar and Greek-Tartar. In Armenia, local Greeks spoke Armenian. In the Tsalka region, several Turkic languages were spoken. There were places where Turkish was the only language spoken."[47]

The fact that a significant number of the young Soviet Greek students examined here had attended Greek schools before and after the Revolution was thus of crucial significance to their respective trajectories and to this history. It enabled their identification and integration into the Greek sectors of the Comintern universities, the relationships they cultivated within them, and ultimately the links they were able to establish with Greek communists and the Greek Communist Party.

Soviet-Greek (Group A) students, as Soviet nationals, originally began their training in the KUTV's General or Community Minority Sectors, as decreed by the National Minorities Central Committee of the CPSU.[48] Soviet Greek students were eventually admitted to the newly opened "international" or "foreign" Greek sectors in the KUTV and the KUNMZ or transferred at individual students' own request. Yefrosinia Diamantidou, a Soviet Greek student (originally from Trabzon), for example, agitated to be transferred from the Institute of Socialist Studies to the Greek Sector of KUNMZ because "there were no Greeks there and she wished to study in her native language."[49] Daria Yarmosh, born in 1908 to a "middle" peasant family from Yalta, Mariupol, had made the most of the Soviet opportunity structure. She had only completed seven years of school but went on to study at the *Sovpartshkola* of Mariupol, then worked as a teacher at a local secondary school and as a propagandist at a local factory. In 1935 she inquired into the KUNMZ admittance policy and procedures as she was Greek and wanted an opportunity to go to university and to study in her native language. She could speak in her native language but wanted to raise the level as she had received no formal education.[50] KUTV graduate Papadopoulou worked very hard to demonstrate her eligibility for transfer from the "general" sector of KUTV to the Greek sector (International), as she desired to be with her "Greek comrades who were being prepared to be sent to Greece" and to work in her "native country Greece after graduating from the University" even though she had never been there.[51]

If for Greek mainland students the universities presented the first opportunity to visit the "holy land," for many Soviet Greeks it would be the first opportunity to connect with the "mother country." The Comintern universities were instrumental in forging links between Soviet Greeks and mainland Greeks, between Soviet communists and the Greek communist movement, between Soviet Greeks and the "country" or the motherland, an emotional and psychic bond that in many cases cited in this study already existed. According to Pratsinakis, although rather insignificant at the political level and situated far from Pontos itself, the small Greek Kingdom proved to be very influential at the ideological level. The Greek state's export of new ideas such as national identification and historical determinism, and the internalization of these ideas by Pontic Orthodox populations, gradually drew them into the larger community of the Greek nation.[52] Ethnic solidarity was such that it raised concerns about the paradox of "nationalist behavior" among the students in the international sectors who spent most of their time with their Greek compatriots and generally avoided foreign students, although a lack of money or understanding of foreign languages must also have been a factor.[53]

In a 1932/1933 report, then Head of the Greek sector of KUNMZ Comrade "Georgiadis" commented on the mutually beneficial educational outcomes of merging the two groups:

Authentic [sic] Greeks help Soviet students of Greek origin to learn about life in Greece, the class struggle, and the role of the Communist Party in the development of the country.... The reverse influence of Soviet Greeks on their Greek comrades was also favorable and should be noted. Students socialize, help each other with studies and language learning, do field work together and exchange experience.... Co-education between the two groups has other advantages. Soviet Greeks are trained as a reserve for Communist Party of Greece that can be used in future for the taking of power by the proletariat and building socialism in Greece.[54]

Assessing university records and the files of students many decades later, Georgiadis' statement rings true; the Comintern system did indeed bring both groups together and fostered the formation of substantial and long-standing relationships between students of both groups and with both countries; both contributed to the development of the Soviet and the Greek communist projects. Soviet-Greek communists who were competent or fluent in Greek language were indispensable to the Greek sectors as the Comintern education system expanded, often being transferred from other departments of the Comintern to take administrative or teaching positions in the KUNMZ and the MLS. The KUNMZ records, where the great majority of Greek students appear to have studied after the opening of its Greek sector in 1928, make repeated references to the ongoing shortages of teaching staff and translators, a void filled largely by Soviet Greeks.[55] A communication from the KUNMZ administration to the Department of Cultural and Educational Propaganda (Kultprop), as late as 1934, reiterated the impact of the acute shortage of national teachers on the "serious academic underperformance" of the Greek sector, especially in the subjects of politics, current affairs, and national issues. Soviet Greeks were procedurally discharged from other duties and seconded to KUNMZ to work as lecturers. Yanis Georgiadis, member of the CPSU since 1918, who was transferred from his position as Head of Records at OGIZ (Unified State Publishing House) at the All-Union Association of State Publishing Houses, became a teacher of Leninism and the history of the Comintern. Kharitina Vasilieva (Vasiliadiou), a member of the CPSU since 1925, was transferred from her position at Kultprop to teach political economy at KUNMZ. Fiodor Ivanovich Gavrilidis, a member of the CPSU since 1919, was a postgraduate student studying Marxism-Leninism in Tiflis (Tbilisi), Georgia, who spoke "perfect Greek" and became a teacher of "national subjects."[56] Pandelis Koundouris, a member of the CPSU since 1920, a former editor of the

Greek newspaper "Kommunistis," and Head of the Political Division at the Ust-Labinsk Machine and Tractor Station, was "highly politically educated" and a fluent Greek speaker who was seconded to KUNMZ to teach "national subjects" including history. N. Kiriakidou, a history teacher at KUTV, was also transferred to KUNMZ.[57]

To be sure, the Soviet-Greek communists came to inhabit a more precarious position; a desire for ethnic connection that drew them to the Greek foreign sectors of the Comintern and to the KKE would put them at great odds with the Greek nation and even with members of the Greek Communist Party; the very same ethnic identification made them vulnerable to "liquidation" and deportation during the years of the Great Terror and after the War.

Outcomes after the Comintern

If as Kriegel suggests, election to the Central Committee represented the crowning achievement of a communist's career, it would be useful to scrutinize the correlation between election to the Central Committee of the KKE, at least in the heyday of the 1920s, and study at the Comintern.[58] As mentioned in the previous chapter, most members of the Central Committee of the KKE in the interwar period who had undertaken training in the Soviet Union were also overwhelmingly KUTV alumni: Kostas Eftichiadis/Korkozof, Andronikos Haitas, Kostas Theos, Yiorgos Kolozof, Dimitris Paparigas, Kostas Sklavos, Yiorgos Nikolaidis, Nikos Zachariadis, Petros Roussos, Kostas Sklavainas, Vasilis Nefeloudis, Dimitris Partsalidis, Yiorgos Konstantinidis, Yiannis Michaelidis, and Michalis Tyrimos. Nikos Zachariadis and Chrysa Hatzivasiliou constitute exceptions; Zachariadis studied at all three institutions, while Chrysa Hatzivasiliou was a graduate of the KUNMZ (1928–1931).[59] Eight of the fifteen individuals elected to the Central Committee at the Greek Communist Party's Third Extraordinary Congress in 1924—Pandelis Pouliopoulos (general secretary), Thomas Apostolidis, Serafim Maximos, K. Sklavos, N. Nikolaidis, K. Theos, A. Haitas, and Y. Konstandinidis, commenced their studies at the KUTV after their election to the Central Committee. After the completion of his studies at KUTV, Russian-born Kostas Eftichiadis (Korkozof, Karakazof) set sail for Greece in 1925 to "help the KKE get organized"; he was elected to the Central Committee of the KKE in 1927.[60] Georgian-born (Pontic Greek) Andronikos Haitas (KUTV years unknown) became the secretary of the Central Committee in 1927; Kostas Theos was elected to the Central Committee in 1924 on the eve of his departure to a Soviet sanatorium for tuberculosis therapy, after which he enrolled in KUTV and returned to Greece in 1926. Yiorgos Kolozof (b. 1901) was elected to the Central Committee in 1928 (KUTV years unknown). Party chief Nikos Zachariadis, born in 1903 in Eastern Thrace (present day Turkey), studied at the KUTV before going to Greece in 1924 and the MLS from 1929 to 1931, and was installed as the leader of the KKE by the Comintern on his return in 1931. Stelios Sklavainas (b. 1907) pursued studies at the KUNMZ or KUTV after being elected to the Politburo in 1931, returning in 1932; Asia Minor–born Vasilis Nefeloudis (b. 1906) was elected to the Central Committee in 1931 under Zachariadis (KUTV years unknown). Trabzon-born Dimitris Partsalidis (b. 1903, KUTV years unknown) was elected to the CC in 1934; Yiorgos Konstantinidis (b. 1907) studied 1930 to 1931, and was elected to the CC on his return in 1931 under Zachariadis; and Istanbul-born Yiannis Michaelidis (b. 1899) studied at the KUTV from 1924 to 1926 and returned in 1931 to join the KKE leadership under Zachariadis. Tyrimos (b. 1908) studied at the KUTV or KUNMZ (years unknown), and was elected to the Central Committee at the Party's 5th Plenum in 1934. Thus, while the correlation between senior leadership and Comintern education seems self-evident, these data indicate that it was more likely that formal qualifications served the purpose of consolidating rather than establishing status and a leadership position in the Party. That is, a critical number of "top-tier" communists were already "part of the apparatus" before they undertook studies. In their study of the British students at the MLS, Halstead, and McLoughlin note that of thirty to forty members of the Central Committee of the Communist Party of Great Britain in the 1930s and 1940s, about sixteen were MLS alumni. Ex-students were most heavily represented in the Central Committee at 20 percent from 1929 to 1935.[61]

The example of Chrysa Hatzivasiliou (b. 1904?) represents an exception. Hatzivasiliou was elected to the Central Committee of the KKE as a full member in 1935, four years after having graduated from the KUNMZ (1928–1931)— not necessarily because of it—and then to the Politburo in 1942. Hatzivasiliou's advancement through the ranks to the leadership therefore took significantly longer than it did for many if not all her male counterparts who joined the Party at roughly the same time, and who undertook similar studies or no studies at all. The election of her husband, Petros Roussos (b. 1908 in Eastern Thrace), to the Central Committee in the same year, a less accomplished functionary and revolutionary by all accounts, is likely to have been a matter of honor between men. Like her male comrades however, Hatzivasiliou was regarded as a formidable functionary, respected for her learnedness (unusual for a Greek communist—male or female—of her generation), organizational ability, discipline, and dogged commitment to the Party rather than for her Comintern qualifications. To be sure, her "exceptionality" quietly disrupted and simultaneously confirmed the patriarchal core of the Party at least within its higher levels.

The three women who were elected to the Central Committee of the Greek Communist Party *after* the War—Allegra Felous, Avra Partsalidou, and Rodi Katou—had not attended Comintern schools. Their election was symbolic of a world transformed by the trials of the War and the unprecedented contribution of women to the communist-led Resistance effort in Greece. Notably, in a lengthy autobiographical report (1953) to the Party in exile, Allegra Felous (Kapeta) reflected on her election to the Central Committee at the 7th Plenum in 1945 as "very unexpected." Felous, who had not attended a Party school, disdained her knowledge deficit in Marxism, which she considered to be vital for a cadre and one of her greatest weaknesses.[62]

For the vast majority of the cadres of the KUTV, KUNMZ, and the MLS between the Wars, the universities were without a doubt a vehicle for upward mobility, perhaps the only vehicle available to them. Most became low to mid-level functionaries who moved between Greece and the Soviet Union and beyond, working as underground operatives for the KKE, as Party consultants, propagandists, and organizers among Greek-Russian refugees in Greece. Some served in the Greek minority zones of the Soviet Union as organizers and propagandists among "low-performing Greek collective farms," described by Comintern authorities as an entrenched problem in the more prosperous, "inherently individualist" Pontic Greek agrarian communities whose well-rooted traditions of free enterprise and strong religiousness made them generally resistant to collectivization and Soviet policy in general.[63] Lingering bourgeois attitudes, very low party membership, and an inclination to emigrate to Greece were reportedly strongest among the Greeks of the North Caucasus. Students from the universities were tasked with strengthening cooperation toward collective farms; preparing the grounds for the organization of new production associations; and discouraging emigration sentiments by organizing lectures on the current situation in Greece and the plight of refugees.[64] Graduates also became teachers and administrators in the Comintern university system and the ECCI. As the political winds turned against the Comintern in the late 1930s, the Comintern's most symbolic institutions came to a close.

Greek Nationality during the Great Terror

In the years before the Great Terror, the Greek sectors were generally characterized as "politically stable, without deviations or irregularities," helped along by the periodic reviews of the Purge Commissions that were renowned for reinvigorating the "political awareness" of students. Those who "deviated" from the Party or exhibited "politically unhealthy" behavior were reprimanded, could have their VKP(b) (CPSU) membership canceled, be expelled from the Party, downgraded to candidate level membership of the Party, or have their membership put on hold.[65] In 1936 the Comintern decided to disband all Soviet-based education for legal Western European communist parties. Instead, they were instructed to establish central Party schools in their own countries, where the students, still following Comintern guidance, would be more in touch with national politics. According to the new Comintern popular front tactics (the Fourth Period, beginning in 1934), the ideological education in the Soviet Union was accused of producing sectarian attitudes among the students and isolating them from the actual political situations in their home counties. More importantly, the increasing fear of espionage and terrorism in the Soviet Union had raised suspicions against the foreign students and many of the nationalities that had long resided within the Soviet Union's borders. The fate of many Greek students at the KUNMZ and the MLS during Stalin's purges in 1937/1938 followed the fate of other national minorities that were deemed "suspicious" amid growing paranoia about foreign infiltration, espionage, encirclement, and internal wreckers. Despite the decision to keep the Greek sectors operational, in line with the Executive Committee of the Communist International policy to continue training foreign cadres from illegal parties, Greek students too were regarded as suspicious and unreliable national minorities, as their true "motherland" was located outside Soviet borders, in the capitalist world. Progressive policies of national delimitation and nation-building within the Soviet Union began to implode under the pressure of the grain requisition crises, famines, troubled economic conditions, international destabilization, and the reversal of the immigration flow in the early 1930s; the Soviet Union became increasingly worried about the possible disloyalty of diaspora ethnic groups with cross-border ties (especially Finns, Germans, and Poles), residing along its western borders. This eventually led to the start of Stalin's repressive policy toward them. Stalin's "Greek Operation" (Gretseskayia Operatsia) began in 1937/1938 when at least 3,029 Poles, 3,608 Germans, and 3,470 Greeks were shot in the Donbas alone.[66] It ended in 1949 with the last wave of deportations or "transfers" of the remaining Greeks who lived on the Black Sea coast (about 27,000, mainly from Georgia and Armenia) to Kazakhstan as *special settlers*.[67] Sources estimate that there were between twenty and fifty thousand casualties by the end of the campaign, including the heads of the Greek Sectors of KUNMZ and the MLS, Dimitris Makroyiannis and Lidiia Ivanovna Petrova.[68] The fate of Ivanovna, among the most zealous and loyal of cadres, encapsulates the shift in 1937 whereby political enemies were rounded up in groups of kin, family ties marked people as disloyal, and "counterrevolutionary" charges against one person threatened also his or her relatives. Ivanovna was purged following the arrest of her sister's husband and her husband's brother by the NKVD in 1937, even though she had dutifully informed the Party immediately of the event in accordance with Party protocols.[69] The students and staff of the Greek sectors were thus not spared the fate of expulsion, deportation to Central Asia, loss of employment, arrest, and death by firing squad or exile to the Gulag.

With the closure of the universities, those who had escaped unscathed continued their work in the Greek settlements of the Soviet Union until Stalin's deportation policies properly caught up with the Soviet-Greek communities, uprooting from their homeland on the Black Sea Coast. Others found their way back to Greece to help reconstitute the KKE that had been decimated by the repressive measures of the Metaxas regime, later to be drawn into war and antifascist resistance. The next chapter takes a closer look into the individual lives of communism's most obscured revolutionaries.

4

Professional Revolutionaries
Interwar Trajectories

Gendering Poverty

This chapter examines the lives of individual communists as presented in their *anketa* and as narrated in their *autobiografia*. Autobiographical narratives became a genre only after the Revolution and the "alphabetization" of the population. The ability to write an autobiography was itself political. The spread of literacy went hand in hand with the expansion of autobiography and diary writing as new authors groped for a language of self-expression at the same time as they learned to read and write.[1] The biographical data and personal narratives of the female subjects examined here convey a path shaped by both circumstance and fate; students present themselves as both agents and victims, primarily on account of their class. Yet the collusion of gender, class, and ethnicity (many were refugees) is ever-present, as the authors narrate their struggles and triumphs in the quest to reconstitute the self, or in Hellbeck's words, "to lay out the path of their journeys toward the communist light."[2]

The students in the Greek sectors across all three institutions were typical candidates of the Comintern cadre education system—Greek nationals were mostly urban refugee industrial workers, often tobacco workers, while the Soviet Greek students belonged to the poorer segments of the Greek agricultural or peasant communities.

The students were young, rarely beyond their thirties, and had already been socialized into the Party, demonstrated leadership capacity, and gained considerable experience in organizational work including serving in elected positions, all consistent with the selection process. Many had distinguished themselves by having been subjected to imprisonment, beatings, and torture and not succumbing to signing *diloseis*, or betraying comrades under pressure. A small percentage of students were of relatively privileged backgrounds—prosperous peasants or those designated as *kulaks*, petit-bourgeois teachers and traders or artisans.[3] A number of these received reprimands for attempting to conceal their class origins upon enrollment, reflecting an ongoing Bolshevik ambivalence about the nature of revolutionary identity and the extent to which an "acquired" class consciousness was sufficient basis for the development of the communist personality and the professional revolutionary.[4] The students were all aspirational and pragmatic, expressed varying degrees of ideological conviction, and were surely less certain of the path they had taken than they were that their former lives, the good and the bad, had been irrevocably left behind.

The earliest cohort of Greek students identified attended the KUTV; of the four female students listed only two individual files were located, those of Stella Kerasidou (pseud. Olga Nikolaevna Ivanova) and Olga Papadopoulou (pseud. Olga Vlasova). Not much is known of the other two students, Olga Paterouli and Smaro Kritikou, beyond their basic biographical details and the brief and generic descriptions of their performance in the student progress reports, written in "Bolshevik" shorthand.[5] Both were born in Istanbul in 1901 and 1900 respectively, and had arrived in Greece as refugees with the population exchange, entering KUTV in 1925 as "non-Party" workers, a category that had disappeared by the rigid conditions of membership that characterized the Third Period. While their non-Party status was not so unusual in 1925, it is hard to reconcile with their relatively good command of communist literature and understanding of the Greek political scene. Kritikou was "well-versed in Greek issues" with "sufficient" theoretical knowledge and showed "good ideological development" throughout the period of study at the University.[6] Similarly, Paterouli was "well-versed in Leninism and the history of the Communist Party of Greece, took an active interest in Greek politics. Both performed well during their practicals in regional industrial plants; both contributed to Red Aid and did their part for the 'special work with women' as was expected of female students."[7] Paterouli left no traces of her life after KUTV; Kritikou left very few. She returned to Greece upon completing her studies and disappeared into the communist underground, resurfacing during stints of imprisonment between 1930 and 1935. Her release from exile on Ai Strati in 1935 under the general amnesty is the last trace.[8]

Much more can be gleaned from the files of Olga Papadopoulou and Stella Kerasidou, both of which were located in full. Both were Soviet Greeks of refugee background. Papadopoulou was born in 1906 in the ancient port city of Batumi, Georgia, to a Greek family originally from Eastern Anatolia who had fled to Batumi during the Armenian massacre. Her mother tongue was Greek, and also spoke Turkish, Armenian, and Russian.[9] Stella Kerasidou was also born Batumi, in 1901, to a working-class Greek family originally from Kerasund (in eastern Anatolia) that had relocated to Russia in the course of the Russo-Turkish Wars. She spoke Greek and Russian fluently and had basic French and Turkish.[10] The year of her family's migration is not recorded, but the frontier between the Russian Tsarist and Ottoman empires was in constant flux according to the power relationship between the two armies. The Pontic Greeks always welcomed the Russian troops as co-religionist liberators and often went off with them into the Caucasus to avoid reprisals from the Ottoman troops when the Russian troops had to retreat and return to their homeland. The Caucasus thus became an area of retreat and then settlement for Pontic Greeks, starting in the nineteenth century (indeed since the fall of Trabzon to the Ottomans in the fifteenth century). At the end of the First World War, following the Russian revolution, many pro-Russian Pontic Greeks were forced to flee by advancing Ottoman troops and took refuge around Tbilisi and in the north of the Caucasus, then in Batumi where ships sent by the Greek government came to pick them up in 1920 and 1921. The Kerasidou clan, having lost the patriarch/head of household in 1916, remained in Batumi. Both Papadopoulou and Kerasidou were very likely to have been Pontic Greeks although, as discussed in the previous chapter, this biographical detail was not noted in the *anketa* of Greek students or referenced in their autobiographies.

Papadopoulou and Kerasidou describe themselves as poor, a poverty linked in their narratives, and in the narratives of many other students, to war, migration and displacement, unemployment, ill health and disability, the loss of parents to war or famine, family neglect, or a combination thereof. The absence of fathers was especially common, often victims of the famine (*Povolzhye*) of 1921 and 1922, a result of the combined effects of economic disturbance caused by the Russian Revolution and the civil war, rail systems that could not distribute food efficiently, and intermittent drought, which killed an estimated five million people. The man-made, or politically engineered, famine of the 1930s (*Holodomor*) in Ukraine did not discriminate between Greek, German, and Russian peasants, all of whom suffered equally to Ukrainian peasants, but the Donbas where most Greeks lived saw a much lower mortality rate. As a showcase region of the Stalinist industrialization project, even during the famine years inhabitants of Donbas received the highest food rations. Moreover, the rural population in the Donbas generally profited from the higher bread rations given to urban workers, as many peasant families had relatives working in the coal mines.[11] As mentioned in the introduction, Anatolian refugees had also lost their menfolk in the Greco-Turkish War (1919–1922), when they were killed or deported to various inland regions of Asia Minor to perform lethal labors as so-called labor battalion conscripts.

The loss of parents, especially fathers, created both an economic imperative and a shift in family dynamics already tipped against female children and women. If gender is not explicitly articulated, it hovers between the lines of most student narratives. One can take inadequate food (calorific intake) and money as measures of economic deprivation, and see that the girls and women of impoverished Greek families in Greece and in Russia lived in a world where they generally ate the smallest portions, received the least amount of protein, and generally ate *after* their male kin, despite being the tillers of the fields and the stevedores of the village, bearing the children, maintaining the home, and often times serving as beasts of burden when the "mule supply was insufficient or the weather was bad."[12] In the cities women had less money as a result of poorer paying and less secure jobs, were more vulnerable to unemployment, and generally occupied the lowest social rungs in both countries.

Papadopoulou's life began as an unwanted child in a poor family of many children:

> It is bad when a person is born to be unwanted by everyone in the world. When I was born there were many children in the family and my relatives did not particularly want me to live. They used to leave me hungry. And my mother was at her deathbed then. Luckily there was a person who gave me a lump of sugar wrapped in a handkerchief almost every day and thanks to that I stayed alive. When the Armenian-Turkish massacre happened, I was left under a bench at a railway station. Shards of glass were falling on me all the time and I survived only by a miracle. The Turks tortured Father

Gyaur so much that there was some wild meat growing on his neck and he was nicknamed "two-headed." Our family with children, barefoot and hungry, fled from Gengi to Batumi and were hidden in a Greek church. Then we moved to the city. My mother and my elder sister laundered Circassian coats. And my younger brother and I sold boiled corncobs. In the evening we would go to the Batumi Port to collect planks, coals, and whatever we could find. As a child my nickname was "Yellow Skeleton."[13]

According to the work of Tapia and Raftakis, gender discrimination through female infanticide and mortal neglect was linked to very high sex ratios. Greek families prioritized boys' well-being and, in a context characterized by widespread poverty and high mortality, discrimination in terms of food, childcare, and/or workload impaired girls' net nutritional status and increased their mortality due to the combined effect of malnutrition and diseases. In addition to the perils of war and displacement, the status of Greek girls and women, living within and outside the borders of the Greek state in Ottoman and Russian lands, was negatively shaped by patrilineality and the obligation that the dowry pattern of marriage and wealth transfer imposed on families, a practice that persisted well into the twentieth century. The prevalence of conflict in the late Ottoman period, the fear of war and of blood feuds, may also have contributed to a strong son preference due to the perception that males were defenders while females needed to be defended. These cultural beliefs and practices, like the cultural beliefs of any community, continued to have currency in the adoptive homeland, in this case, Greece and Russia.[14] It is not then surprising that a significant number of students were evaluated as weak, unwell, or suffering chronic health conditions during examinations carried out by university medical directors to determine fitness for study. These conditions, for which they could receive treatment in the sanatoria of the Soviet Union, ranged from basic undernourishment-induced anemia and fatigue to more chronic illnesses like tuberculosis, malaria, syphilis, unspecified bouts of "neurasthenia" and "cardioneurosis," and, as in the case of Chrysa Hatzivasiliou, leukemia. Papadopoulou, for example, was assessed as generally exhausted and undernourished, but fit to attend classes. She was also diagnosed with hereditary syphilis.[15] In Greece, the lack of welfare infrastructure for social relief and the country's general unpreparedness for the arrival of more than a million refugees, many of whom lived in overcrowded and unsanitary conditions in the newly industrializing center of Athens, accounted for multiple outbreaks of tuberculosis, especially among young people aged between ten and thirty.[16] In northern Greece, the communist Tobacco Workers' Union lobbied local authorities relentlessly for proper medical care of the large numbers of men and women struck with tuberculosis after prolonged exposure to the small, dark, humid working conditions required for the protection of the tobacco leaves. In one petition issued in 1925 the union referred to the sanatorium of the region as a *tafos ton zondanon* (tomb of the living dead).[17] It's of little surprise that the KKE sent so many of its tubercular cadres to the sanatoria of the Soviet Union.

Stella Kerasidou draws a distinction between her life before and after joining her trade union and the CPSU, on the basis of gender. Her autobiographical narrative infers an early awareness of gender-based social injustice within the private domain of the conservative Greek community in Batumi that increasingly frustrated her ambitions. It was the politicized environment of union work and subsequent communist activism that equipped Kerasidou with the necessary language and emboldened her to leave the family circumstances that obstructed her "new life." In her words, "despite my active participation in my new life, my family, and the outdated Greek cultural environment full of eastern prejudices, pressured me. I wanted to escape this environment and continue my education."[18]

To be sure, the communist movement did not engender feminist consciousness, but as Gilmartin notes in relation to the Chinese Communist Party, as a vigorous proponent of women's equality it at least presented the possibility of an alternative lifestyle to those, like Kerasidou, who resisted conventional gender roles and relations.[19] To be sure, very few Comintern graduates would advance to the highest levels of the Party, far fewer than their male counterparts; Hatzivasiliou was the famous exception that proved the rule. The relative achievements of female and male graduates reflected the masculine character of the KKE and the Comintern but also the different ambitions of male and female students. It is not especially meaningful to assess the emancipatory aspects of interwar communist involvement only in terms of gender representation at the executive levels of Party leadership, however.

Graduate cadres were trained to perform diverse tasks in the movement—organizational, technical, political, and social (group leadership, ideological training for workers, networking, strike organization, public presentations, etc.); they experienced promotion and recognition. In other words, their gendered lives as communists bore no resemblance to the gendered lives they left behind.

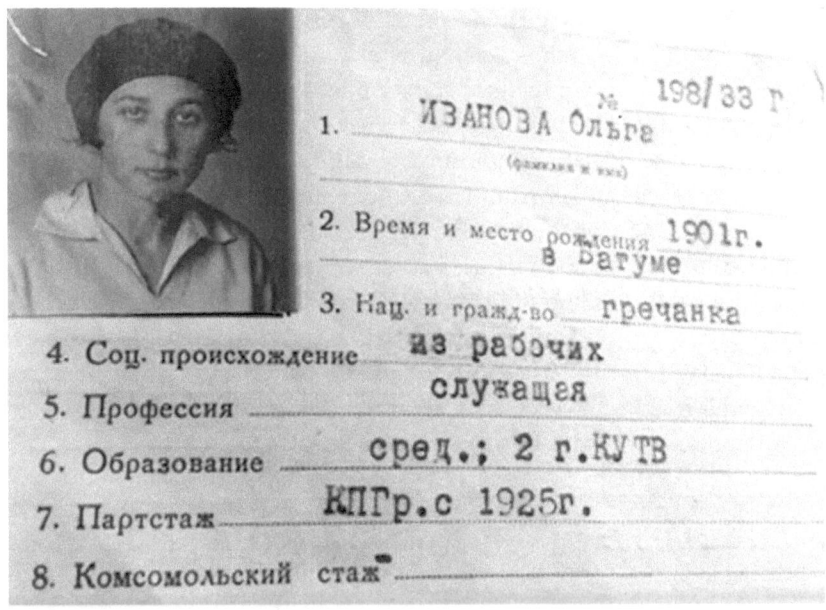

FIGURE 8. Stella Kerasidou. Photo courtesy of RGASPI.

The KKE, like other illegal parties, was less inclined to cast its committed, trained women as "adjunct revolutionaries." The conditions of illegality mitigated the common trajectory of ambitious young communist women elsewhere in interwar Europe, who often undertook party positions in the "natural" feminine domains of children's welfare, safety, education, and Red Aid work. As Sewell puts it, resilient gender patterns of work and service fused with an underlying Soviet/communist ambivalence about women's emancipation and citizenship and the need to rally and maintain a broad feminine audience.[20] This pertained equally well to Greek communist women, many of whom came to the movement through service in EBE and retained links with the organization throughout. But in the ever-worsening conditions of illegality and persecution, because women were regarded as less suspicious, the KKE valued them, trained them, and relied upon them to work as high-risk underground operatives. In turn, the risk of capture and imprisonment, with its attendant, often sexualized violence, also contributed to the revolutionary credibility and identity of communist women.[21]

Underground work could also involve the most mundane of roles; communist women were often charged with the responsibility for scouting and leasing prospective safe houses that the KKE used extensively to hold its meetings, store its archives, and provide refuge to its fugitive members. This role entailed the immediate cessation of all links with the Party and involvement in its activities for the duration of the lease and was a source of frustration for those communists who desired a more active role. Koula Theou, a tobacco worker from Kavala, joined the KKE in late 1926, after serving as secretary of the Kavala branch of EBE. By the decision of the Politburo in 1928, Theou was used as a cover for the apartments that the KKE utilized, forbidding her from talking to anyone or engaging in any other activity for indefinite periods of time.[22] As critical as the work of these mid-level functionaries was, it was also by design invisible, hard to trace, and it received no accolades, all of which also contributed to the virtual disappearance of this history from the record.

Fashioning Male Normativity

The profile photos of the Greek female students show a style that conformed with the style and comportment of their other European counterparts, especially the influential German Communist Party (KPD), whose feminine ideal Sewell describes as "healthy and simple, modern and serious, with short hair, preferably bobbed," much like the style sported by Kerasidou and many others.[23] Sewell draws links between interwar communist femininity and the image of the New Woman—the communist woman was a working-class rendering of the New Woman who was youthful, slender, healthy, and athletic. This styling, according to Weitz, was symptomatic of communism's conceptualization of gender equality as a "defeminization" or "masculinization" of women that in turn chimed with the ethos of discipline, conformity, and asceticism that became synonymous with communist culture.[24] Greek Bolshevik style sits very well within this characterization.

Some students were married; some bore children; some were divorced and remarried. As Murphy states, communists married communists. The party was a small, rather narrow circle within a hostile world, a circle in which party men and women loved, married, dined, and argued; they were, of course, engaged outside the party, often with extensive experience of travel and international contacts, but such intense activism meant that loyalty to the party was also about self-identity. Habit, friendship, group allegiance, and intermarriage were inevitable and bound activists to each other.

FIGURE 9. From left: Anna Todurova, Vera Karagianni, Olga Kaloidou, Olga Bakola, Nina Ashigova, Ksenia Arnautova, Ermofili Venedekidou, Chrisoula Vagia. Photos courtesy of RGASPI.

Friendships reveal themselves occasionally when party members vouched for each other and signed off on their comrades' behalf when authorities sought proof of identity, history, and party affiliation across the transnational divide. The self-identity of being engaged in struggle meant that members were often tightly bound to the party's interests, reinforced by the Leninist tradition of unchallengeable authority.

Kerasidou and Papadopoulou were among several Soviet Greek communist women who became involved with Greek Communist Party men, a factor that consolidated their Greek identity and sealed their relations with Greece and the KKE. Kerasidou met her future husband, one-time General Secretary of the KKE Andronikos Haitas (pseud. Sifnaios), during his visit to the Greek sector of the KUTV as representative of the Greek Communist Party at the fifth plenum of the ECCI in March and April 1925. When it ended in divorce in 1932, Kerasidou cited Haitas's "non-Party" conduct toward her as his wife, as well as his leading role in the factional infighting between his own Stalinist faction and the Trotskyists represented by Pouliopoulos/Maximos, a dispute in which Kerasidou, in the customary manner of communists terrified of ostracism and "excommunication," emphasized her support of the Comintern line.[25] Kerasidou later married another KKE cadre and KUTV alumnus referred to only as "Kimov," who languished in the Greek prison system long after she returned to the Soviet Union in 1930.[26]

Sexual "irregularity," namely divorce and remarriage, were common among Greek communist men and women relative to the rate of divorce and remarriage in Greece—and pre-Revolutionary Russia—especially among women, across the classes.[27] On occasion, perhaps depending on the status of the couple and broader circumstances, the petition for divorce had to be sanctioned by the Party leadership.[28] But, as is well known, the conservative turn that took hold in 1936 not only unleashed the Great Terror but also witnessed a giant step back from the great socialist experiment to the promotion of very traditional (bourgeois) family values, beginning with the reversal of the family codes of 1918 and 1927 to make divorce more difficult and to outlaw abortion. The new law required that both spouses appear in court to file for divorce. It also raised the fee for divorce from three to fifty rubles (with a fee of 150 rubles for a person's second divorce and 300 rubles for the third).[29] In Greece, divorce rates were at very low levels until the 1980s. In the first half of the twentieth century, in particular, a marital union usually ended with the death of one of the spouses. As elsewhere in Europe remarriage was not uncommon in populations that experienced high mortality, but it was usually males who remarried; women tended to remain widows, at least till the 1960s.

The Soviet shift toward pro-family and pro-natalist policies and an essentialized notion of women's "natural role" as mothers was consistent with broader European trends toward state control of reproduction in the interwar period. Several scholars have explored the causes of this shift in Soviet policy. Richard Stites noted that many of the original Bolshevik leaders, including Lenin, held conservative views regarding morality and the family.[30] Wendy Goldman's work revealed that many peasants and workers opposed policies that facilitated divorce or in other ways weakened the family. She also described the social and material realities (millions of homeless children, a badly underfunded orphanage system, rising juvenile crime, and widespread male irresponsibility) that prompted Soviet leaders to promote a more traditional model of family and motherhood.[31]

But, as Hoffman points out, even though the Soviet government encouraged marriage, discouraged divorce, and promoted parental responsibility, at no time during the campaign to bolster the family did Soviet officials suggest that a woman's place was in the home. To ensure that pregnant women could continue working, the Politburo approved a decree in October 1936 that made it a criminal offense to refuse to hire or to lower the pay of women during pregnancy. Soviet propaganda constructed gender in a way that stressed both women's economic contribution and their role in raising the next generation, the so-called double burden.[32]

If communist counterculture helped loosen traditional gender relations and questioned the basis of the traditional marital bond—at least till the 1930s—it drew a line at promiscuity, real or perceived, especially regarding women. Olga Papadopoulou, for instance, attributed her struggles for advancement within the KKE to the rumors of her inherited syphilis spread around "with the speed of lightning" that reached the Central Committee of the KKE and Zachariadis, in particular, who "believed the lies and rumors about my illness and considered me a loose woman."[33] Congenital syphilis was a known phenomenon in the twentieth century; Papadopoulou's reference to her mother's worsening health and paralysis may indeed have been an indicator of her own illness and maternofetal transmission. Whether inherited or not, its sexually transmitted origins would have been stigmatizing for Papadopoulou.

Equally common was family estrangement. Once inducted into the communist life, the relentless pressures and risks necessitated rupture with the past. When Olga Kaloidou, a Soviet-Greek woman, joined the Greek sector of KUNMZ, a flurry of letters addressed to the Comintern authorities followed. Letters written by her brother, Ivan Dimitrievich Kaloidis, to the director of KUNMZ in 1936 make clear that his sister, like so many students who were sworn to secrecy as a condition of study, simply vanished after entering the KUNMZ:

> I know that on graduating from the university she went to Greece. We didn't write to each other. She was supposed to come back to Moscow in two years' time, but it's been four years since she left, and I haven't heard from her since then. She is my only family left and I would like to find her. Maybe you know something about her whereabouts. I fear to think that she might have passed away or is in danger. I hope you know at least whether she is still alive. Also, I know that she had a child. What happened to the child? I really look forward to your reply as I worry about my only sister and seek any information about her.[34]

Kaloidis eventually received a brief reply from the Comintern assuring him that his sister was working in the USSR, which was in fact the case according to her own file entries. Thrust into an environment that was averse to the preservation of external biological bonds, inductees formed strong emotional attachments to the Party—and to each other. The Party stepped in for family and faith; it was a covenant that anchored those who were adrift. In Fitzpatrick's words, "if there was a significant other, it was the Party—or fate itself."[35]

Estrangement between parents and children was the most difficult, often resulting in the long-term displacement of children as a result of parents, especially mothers, who were constantly on the move. The children left behind become spectral presences that haunt many of the autobiographical narratives and *ankety* that feature in this book. In reference to Romanian communist leader Ana Pauker, who also studied at the KUTV and who had several children, Brigitte Studer states that political activity took precedence over childcare, or in a more abstract way, took precedence over gender's role as a structuring social category. At least in the early phase of Stalinism, the early 1930s, the traditional family that many communist parties would later defend did not necessarily have sway in communist circles. In practice, the notion of family adopted a broader meaning that included Party members.[36] To be sure, the risks and commitments of communist involvement fostered such a bond.

Papadopoulou married three times and bore two children who appear to have been lost in the chaos of international communist life. Divorced at the time of enrollment at KUTV, she met her second husband, a Greek communist, at the Communist University of the Workers of the East (KUTV), to whom she bore a daughter. After graduating in 1927 the couple left for Greece, leaving the infant daughter in the care of the state and eventually losing all contact with her, because "for me the cause of Lenin was greater than the care for my child."[37] While recounting the cold reception she had received from her Greek comrades in Athens, Papadopoulou recalled past miseries, that "no one cared that I could hear my [abandoned] daughter crying and moaning at night and I could not go to sleep."[38] After returning to the Soviet Union in 1940, Papadopoulou remarried and gave birth to a son but could not find her daughter. "Some were saying that she was dead, some that she was alive, but at the Balkan Sector of the IKKI [ECCI], I was told that I was young and could still give birth to four more," a harsh statement on the brutal militarized masculinity that came to be equated with real Bolshevism, reflected in the "masculine" appearances that were adopted by women cadres.[39]

Strivers

Education—inadequate, sacrificed, bypassed, and yearned for—is a common theme in autobiographies across the Greek and Soviet-Greek cohorts, determined by class and gender, given the prevalence of gender-based discrimination in family determinations on the education of their children. In Greece, as in the Pontic Greek communities of pre-revolutionary Russia and the Soviet Union, the literacy level was especially low among females. The Greek census data for 1928 reported a sharp contrast in the literacy rates between men (77 percent) and women (42 percent) and an overall literacy rate of 59 percent for persons aged eight and over.[40] The education reforms of 1929, as discussed in the first chapter, were poised to worsen the situation, especially for the refugees who had few outlets for upward mobility.

In Russia, the success of the Revolution in 1920 was a clear turning point in the expansion of education, which became freely available. The importance of education resonates with Christian Gonsa's study of published Greek communist autobiographies, which, although entirely overlooking communist women and gender, notes that the opportunity for education or lack thereof, poverty and deprivation, and class hatred dominate authors' reflections on joining the communist movement in Greece. Most of the authors of these autobiographies were of agricultural or petit bourgeois families; access to education depended upon the resources of the family and on "family strategy." Citing from the autobiography of Cretan communist Manolis Roumeliotakis, Gonsa writes:

> In terms of learning, the children of the boss had all the privilege of high school university, positions in the public service, in political life. The children of smaller householders [*mikronoikokirides*] would at best complete high school or learn a trade, and that only if there were enough family members available to work while they studied. The children of hired laborers [*exartimenon*] mostly didn't even complete elementary school and generally followed the fortunes of their family.[41]

Sometimes even the poorest families could send their children to high school and university, but not all of them; it was generally the younger children who would go to school if they showed any ability, while the oldest son would learn a trade or help his father in the fields. Former KKE Yiannis Manousakas, an eldest son, recalled the humiliation he felt when he was unable to understand his younger brother's teacher who spoke to him in *katharevousa*.[42] Dimitris Vlandas's education was cut short by the First World War, which he spent carrying wood to Heraklion from his village in Crete in exchange for food. He learned to read and write many years later with the help of the secretary of the local Party cell.[43]

The writers express the consequences and indignities of poverty very clearly, the hunger and of exclusion from education, and a hatred toward rich people and the ruling classes. Leader of the communist Greek Democratic Army Markos Vapheiades explained his attraction to communism as the natural outcome of his identification with the downtrodden and with social injustice:

> In this context, I heard the first Marxist teachings, I got familiar with simple brochures like those by Kropotkin etc. I understood some parts, did not understand other parts, but that which pulled me in deeper was the idea that things were set up in such a way that some people lived in wealth without working, while others labored but lived hand to mouth. The KKE above and beyond everything else was a party for everyone.[44]

Most of the students examined here were literate (able to read and write) or semiliterate (able to read) in at least one language, having completed elementary school in most cases, and secondary school in fewer cases, invoking the links made by some scholars between poverty, high literacy, and radical politics, to which I would add gender status. In studies focused primarily on the communist vote in India, social scientist Donald Zagoria argued that poverty—though exclusively a peasant or agrarian poverty—in conjunction with high levels of literacy made for an explosive combination implicit in a high communist vote. Paul Brass has since argued that communists tend to be more successful in regional environments where the composition of the working force has begun to change from a predominantly agricultural basis and where literacy rates and newspaper circulation are relatively higher. This bears some relevance to both the Soviet and Greek economic landscape in the period under study; poverty and literacy are joined by the additional pressures of displacement in the case of the Anatolian refugees in Greece.[45]

"Group B" Students

As mentioned, Greek nationals (Group B), were predominantly Anatolian refugees who had fled during the Greco-Turkish War or were "exchanged" afterward in accordance with the Treaty of Lausanne, or were refugees from earlier conflicts in the region. Many worked in the Greek tobacco industry that was female dominated and run by the most militant and highly organized union in Greece, the "Red" Union of Tobacco Workers.

Chrysanthi Kantzidou (pseud. Kaiti Vasiliou), an MLS student, was born in Drama in 1912 to a "middling" Greek peasant family from Eastern Thrace who fled westward to Drama during the Balkan Wars (1912–1913). Less given to personal disclosures than others, her file nevertheless conveys a life of similar adversities on the one hand, and a formidable determination to prevail on the other. Having lost her father and the family landholdings in the war, and with a mortgage in arrears, Kantzidou completed only one year of elementary school. She became a tobacco worker in Kavala in 1923, at age eleven; her brother was a blacksmith, one sister a dressmaker, and the other a housewife—only Kantzidou joined the communist movement. She was the only member of her family to do so and the only one not to marry or have children. Her unique trajectory would

FIGURE 10. Chrysanthi Kantzidou (pseud., Kaiti Vasiliou). Photo courtesy of RGASPI.

be attributable, at least in part, to her work in EBE and her membership in the militant tobacco workers union, which set her on a path of intense political activism—street protests, strike action, community mobilization, and nine imprisonments—and ultimately membership in OKNE (1928) and KKE (1934). Her elections to the OKNE district committee of Kavala, the district Party committee, and the trade union executive committee stood her in good stead for a Party recommendation to study at the MLS in 1935. Like so many of the students, Kantzidou's very poor general education was countered by serious-mindedness, discipline, engagement, and hard work. The challenges and adversities of communist life—arrests and beatings, estrangement from family (she had not communicated with her family for two and a half years)—never caused her "revolutionary attitude to falter." She completed her studies successfully and returned to Greece and the KKE in September 1939, shortly after the War broke out, after which all traces disappear.[46]

Greek communists Stella Vamniatzidou (pseud., Elena Agneva, Stella Vudanya, Yiannoula Nikolaidou, and Elena Arnova) and Lena Anemelou (pseud., Nikolaevna Dimitrieva), introduced in the first chapter, were also refugees from Asia Minor who worked in tobacco. Vamniatzidou is perhaps the most outstanding example of the gap between the MLS's target student and the reality. Vamniatzidou was an MLS graduate who had not attended school at all, claiming in her *anketa*, with some exaggeration, that she had

FIGURE 11. Stella Vamniatzidou (pseud., Yiannoula Nikolaidou). Photo courtesy of RGASPI.

"eliminated her illiteracy" when she joined the Party.[47] Born to a poor peasant family from Raedestos, Anatolia, who settled in Kavala, Greece, as refugees in 1922, she began working in tobacco on arrival at age twelve. She joined the Red Tobacco Workers Union in 1924, a common precursor to communist involvement; her sisters and husband were also in the movement. Vamniatzidou became a member of EBE in 1929, a common pathway to the KKE, and thereafter held various elected positions, the most senior of which was member of the regional committee of the MOPR (Kavala). At the instruction of the Party, she organized meetings, rallies, and strike actions among the tobacco workers and endured beatings and a month in prison, all of which culminated in a Party recommendation for study in the USSR in 1933. Compensating for the lack of formal education with hard work and determination, Vamniatzidou departed for Moscow to train at the radio school of the International Lenin School (MLS) in 1933. Vamniatzidou's very "poor general training," as her (il)literacy level was referred to, was atypical among Comintern students, but she possessed attributes that were prized by the institution—"politically developed," active in the political and social life of her group, and a respected and devoted comrade. Her limitations, in turn, were dealt with by employing her in "simple technical work after the completion of her training in 1938."[48] She was employed as a radio operator at the Communication Services station of the Executive Committee of the Communist International (ECCI), for which she received 450 rubles a month. This wage was significantly above average; Soviet workers and employees (outside agriculture) earned an average annual wage in 1937 of 3,140 rubles.[49] Vamniatzidou returned to Greece and the KKE in 1940, on the eve of the Axis occupation.

Lena Anemelou (pseud., Nikolaevna Dimitrieva/Dimitrova) and her mother settled in the tobacco town of Kavala, Greece, in 1922, as refugees from Panormou, Asia Minor; her father had died in 1912 during the first Balkan War. Mother and daughter both worked in tobacco on arrival in Kavala; Anemelou had only three years of elementary education behind her when she began work in 1923. She joined the Tobacco Workers' Union in 1924 and thus began her activism in the labor movement, which crossed over into the communist movement when she joined the OKNE in 1927. The following year she received a study recommendation from the Politburo and departed for the KUNMZ where she remained until 1932, one year longer due to illness. Her four years at KUNMZ were characterized by low participation in the core activities of organizational work in the factory environment and in group discussion, probably due to linguistic disadvantage as she had no Russian and didn't acquire it. On the other hand, Anemelou displayed the highly prized values of sincerity, perseverance, consistency, and discipline toward her learning and her duties. She worked as a trainee in the International Women's Secretariat of the Comintern, earning a recommendation as "useful for trade union work and 'work among youth and women'" on the completion of her studies.[50] Anemelou commenced "technical work." the nature of which is not documented, when she returned to the Piraeus district of the Party in Greece in 1932.

Not all Greek communist women came to the movement through tobacco union channels. The background and (early) trajectory of Clio Stai was very similar to that of Chrysa Hatzivasiliou. She was born in Istanbul in 1905 to an impoverished petit bourgeois family. Her father was a trader who died in 1922, and her mother a teacher; Stai was able to complete her secondary education in a French high school despite the adverse circumstances of war and family loss. The family relocated to Greece in 1925 as part of the population exchange; Stai found work as a teacher in an Athens private school until she joined the KKE in 1927 on the recommendation of a fellow teacher, thereafter becoming an activist in the Athens women's committee (*gynaikia periferiaki epitropi*) and a propagandist in the domain of antimilitary activism, that is, "as a liaison between the Central Committee and the soldiers."[51] All Party activities ceased when she commenced work

FIGURE 12. Clio Dimitrievna Stai, Photo courtesy of RGASPI.

in the Press office of the Soviet Embassy in Athens, tasked with the transcription of all the documentation of the Athens organization.[52]

As she was fluent in Greek and French, and trained as a teacher, Stai became a compelling candidate for translating and teaching at the chronically understaffed Greek sectors of the KUNMZ and the MLS. She departed for the Soviet Union in 1929 where she voluntarily taught herself the second and third year curriculum of KUNMZ, learned Russian, and took up the role of translator, typist, and teacher of Greek and Labor history at the KUNMZ and the MLS. In 1932 she became a member of the CPSU and one year later made a request to work in public outreach activities so that her "political [in] experience would match her theoretical development." She became a Party educator for Greek women workers of the Markov cotton mill in Moscow in 1933.[53] Stai, not atypically, was the only member of her family to join the communist movement and eventually married a communist (Stais), with whom she had one child. She was still in the Soviet Union when the war broke out in 1939, where the file record ends.

Clio Stylianou Christodoulidou was born in Limassol, Cyprus, in 1901, to a family of artisans (carpenters), also probably of Pontic Greek origin. She completed eight years of school (probably till the age of fourteen) after which she worked as a hired dressmaker for wealthy ladies, working from home because she suffered from tuberculosis. She "took an interest" in the

Communist Party of Cyprus (CCP) in 1924 and joined in 1926, working with women and youth as a Komsomol and trade union organizer. Most of her work thereafter was focused on the mobilization and organization of women. Her move to Greece and the KKE in 1927 was in the context of a CCP assignment, but she did not return to Cyprus, at least during this period. Christodoulidou settled in the cotton mill precinct of Podarades in Athens and steadily rose through the ranks. In 1928 she became a member of the editorial board of *Ergatria* (a press organ for the Central Committee of the KKE aimed at working women) and was elected to the Central Executive Committee of the newly formed communist-controlled Unitary General Workers' Confederation (EGSEE), or Enotiki, in 1929, to organize cultural and propaganda work among women. The organization of numerous strike actions and arrests followed, culminating in a Party recommendation for study at the KUNMZ (1930–1932), including a traineeship in the International Women's Secretariat. Her "practical" assignments in the Soviet countryside comprised "cultural work," or propaganda work, among women in the Greek districts of the Northern Caucasus (Sokhum, Abkhazia); various teaching positions in the Greek sectors of the teacher's colleges in Sokhum (1932–33) and Mariupol, Ukraine (1933–34); and eventually propaganda work on the factory floor. While KKE evaluations of her performance emphasize her loyalty and enthusiasm, good knowledge of theory, and "no deviations from the party line," her poor health and lack of Russian language affected her academic progress and her "standing in the community." Her character reference upon graduating from the KUNMZ advised that "in the USSR she could be useful in propaganda work under the guidance of more experienced comrades" and could teach political subjects in Greek schools.[54]

In a letter written in October 1932 from Abkhazia to a Greek comrade, Christodoulidou conveys the pros and cons of her role in the countryside, such as social isolation, surrounded as she was by Greeks whose dialect was unintelligible to her. Her earnest request for Greek newspapers offers insights into the linguistic challenges and the importance of Greek schools, which had enabled Soviet Greeks to join the Greek sectors and cultivate links with the "motherland":

[Comrade Panov],
    I think I have a duty to write to you to let you know how my work and my life are going. I've been in Sokhum since September, and I've been working among the Greeks [*Greki*] as an instructor for 300 roubles

FIGURE 13. Clio Christodoulidou (pseud., Nora Irman). Photo courtesy of RGASPI.

a month. My work is very interesting, and the responsibility is great, my only difficulty is their language which I don't understand, and the villagers do not even speak Russian. . . . Please arrange for permission to be given to have Greek newspapers sent to me from time to time, and I will send them right back as soon as I've read them. I'm so far away down here and I don't want to become estranged from the movement [in Greece]; the newspapers will also help me in my work here.[55]

When the KKE issued a request for Christodoulidou's return to Greece in 1934 it was denied by Comintern boss Dimitrov, for reasons not stated; her fate after 1935 is unknown.[56]

The final profile from Group B included in this section belongs to Olga Bakola (pseud., Aliki Kanda) who shares a special status with Chrysa Hatzivasiliou as one of only two KKE women whose sojourn at the Comintern universities has been acknowledged in the historiography, the former by virtue of her singular status in the Party, the latter perhaps due to her publicized death during the Axis occupation.[57] Bakola was born in Ipeiros in 1917, one of six children; her mother was a housewife, and her father was a baker, though debilitated by consumption and unable to work. The family owned a small parcel of land but could not afford to work it. Bakola's father and one sister were also members of the KKE.

Bakola managed to complete five years of elementary school. Upon moving to Athens in 1933 and finding employment in a cotton mill as a weaver, she joined the textile workers union, worked for the EBE, and became a correspondent for the communist newspaper *Rizospastis* and a member of the OKNE, all in the same year. Numerous arrests for strike actions followed, as well as election to positions in the local OKNE cell and in the District Committee (Larissa, Thessalia). Her subsequent involvement in the emerging antifascist movement, specifically in the Panhellenic and Anti-Military Youth Committee and the National Antifascist Youth Congress of 1934, drew greater Party attention and culminated in a recommendation from the Central Committee of OKNE in 1934 to undertake studies at the MLS.

Once again, MLS reports cite Bakola's poor political education trumped by sheer will; she passed with good marks because she was "smart and diligent, took an active interest in learning, and showed good discipline."[58] Bakola's admission papers noted that she was fond of declaring her communist credentials to the arresting police, as she wanted to show fearlessness.[59] With the closure of the MLS in 1938 she returned to Greece via Paris with several other Greek graduates, including Stella Kantzidou. They arrived in September 1939, tasked with helping reconstitute the KKE leadership that had been decimated by security services. She joined the communist-led Greek Resistance movement in 1943 and became a member of its youth wing, EPON, but her life was cut short when she was mowed down by a German tank during the July 22 protest against the ceding of Eastern Macedonia and Thrace to Bulgaria. She died in a hospital five days later.[60]

As communism traditionally recruited from the disadvantaged social categories, the party functioned as an important and even irreplaceable agent of political socialization, compensating for social, educational, and cultural handicaps. Access to revolutionary training or education in Moscow for generally underprivileged and uneducated "ordinary workers" like Vamniatzidou, Kerasidou, and Papadopoulou has been taken as evidence of the illegitimate character or sinister purpose of the Comintern universities. Historians of the Comintern universities have been more inclined to recognize their function as "product manufacturers" than as disrupters of working-class fate. The Comintern education system also drew criticism from communists themselves. For former KKE leader Eleftherios Stavridis, the admission of "illiterates" demonstrated that the Kremlin sought merely to "manufacture" cadres for the communist parties, not to educate people for their own benefit.

FIGURE 14. Olga Bakola (pseud., Aliki Kanda). Photo courtesy of RGASPI.

[The KUTV] called itself a university but it was anything but a university. As communism ridiculed all moral values, so too did it ridicule the meaning of the university. First in line were students from across all those countries of the east who were bereft of any education. How was it possible to enter "university" for students who had merely graduated from elementary school of their respective countries, and sometimes had not even completed elementary school, but who simply had an introductory letter from the Party of their country?[61]

The fact that trained militants had a chance to succeed socially on the basis of "unconventional" criteria that required no particular technical proficiency or scholarly attainment was of course precisely the point. Many if not most of the students came to owe their entire political educational and cultural progress to the party and its teachings.[62] In socio-cultural terms, "quitting production" or escaping "the idiocy of rural life" and becoming an activist, a party functionary, and a propagandist frequently meant a life dedicated to previously unknown or limited intellectual activities— reading, writing, discussion, a life enriched by people and events.[63] Students were invited to CPSU congresses, plenary sessions of the ECCI, and congresses of the Comintern. Special literary gatherings were held to acquaint students with Russian and foreign classics, including works from eastern cultures. They came into contact with political elites—Stalin himself addressed the students in 1925—and cultural icons like Gorky and Mayakovsky made regular appearances.⁶⁴ Under what other circumstances could students hear Clara Zetkin speak at the third anniversary of the KUTV? "You will return to your countries and open their eyes, still blinded and spiritually backward, having never known equality. You will summon them and lead them in a social revolutionary struggle against all forms of theft and oppression of the working masses."⁶⁵

"Group A": Going to "The Country"

The Soviet Greek contingent (Group A) of the Greek sectors generally came from very poor peasant families, where one or both parents were quite often ill and unable to work or were deceased, leaving the children to fend for themselves. Like their "mainland" counterparts, Soviet-Greek students expressed an ardent desire to better themselves, but, as the majority had completed some years of Greek elementary school, they also expressed the desire to cultivate their Greek identity and establish links with their Greek peers at the KUTV and with the "mother country," Greece. It was a desire not easily satisfied in the context of the increasingly hostile political environment in Greece that saw many Greeks and Soviet Greeks returning to the Soviet Union to escape persecution or to treat illness. Some who wished to work in "the country," as Greece was frequently called, were held back by illness or refused permission on the grounds of inadequate performance and conduct. Only high competence and trust candidates were considered for work in Greece given that the KKE was outlawed and operated under increasingly strained conditions. Those who did not go to the country fulfilled their mission as Party organizers, teachers, and propagandists in the Greek settlements of the Soviet Union, essential cogs in the wheel of the Soviet project, at least until the tide turned against the nationalities.

Olga Kaloidou was among those who were assigned to the country to work as an undercover agent for the KKE in 1932. She was born in 1908 to Greek parents, poor peasants from Maykop, in the northern Caucasus, whose farm "couldn't feed the family of seven so the father had to work on tobacco fields."⁶⁶ Kaloidou joined him at the age of nine as an unskilled laborer. Following her father's desertion of the family in 1925 and her mother's death the following year, Kaloidou found refuge and purpose in the communist movement. She joined the Komsomol and quickly began to ascend through the ranks in the characteristic manner, working as women's leader in Khadyzhensk, Maykop, occupying various elected positions in the local Komsomol administration and the City Soviet. Her subsequent election as secretary of the local MOPR branch, and her work for the Society for the Assistance of Defense, Aviation, and Chemical Construction (OSOAVIAKHIM) all helped pave the path to the cadre universities and the "elimination of her illiteracy."[67]

She was summoned to the Regional Committee of the CPSU in the North Caucasus in 1928 to receive a recommendation for study at the newly opened Greek sector of the KUNMZ, in the same cohort as Hatzivasiliou. Kaloidou spent two years organizing local Greek communities in Ukraine and teaching at the Greek Teacher's College of Mariupol before she was assigned to work in Greece. One can see she had evolved from a person who considered herself to be illiterate, to teaching "History of the Class Struggle" to other "illiterates," and in fact showed great promise as an instructor.[68] Kaloidou spent two years (1933–1935) on assignment in Greece, the details of which were not disclosed, before being officially "withdrawn" in the summer of 1935 for "underperforming" following her husband's arrest and a compromised operation. On her return to the USSR, like many of her peers, Kaloidou worked as a propagandist and organizer in the Greek settlement of Krymsk in the Azov-Black Sea Region.[69]

Stella Kerasidou completed Greek elementary school "with honors," but her Russian secondary education was interrupted by her father's death in 1916 and the family's ensuing economic hardship. After the end of the tumult of the Civil War, which had caused the family to relocate on a regular basis, Kerasidou completed her secondary education, which had been made free when Georgia became a Soviet republic in 1921. In the same year she commenced work as an office clerk at the port authority of Batumi and joined the Union of Water Transport Workers, a decision that would alter the course of her life. Kerasidou became active in what she refers to as "social work," organizing Greek female garment factory workers, being elected to the union board on women's behalf, and laying down the foundations for what she called her "new life."

Sent to Moscow by the Union in 1922 to pursue her studies, she experienced a chance encounter with a group of Greek political immigrants from Turkey that proved fateful. Among them was future KKE leader

Nikos Zachariadis, then a freshly minted member of the Komsomol who encouraged Kerasidou's interest in the Greek trade union movement and "influenced her to study at the KUTV." She was accepted as a "minorities" student by National Minorities Central Committee in 1923, which noted her "appropriate social background," her involvement in the Water Transport Union, a "willingness to study," and surely, the support of an already well-connected Zachariadis; she transferred to the Greek (International) sector of KUTV the following year.[70] Kerasidou joined the Komsomol in 1924, and in 1925 was directed by the Balkan Section of the Comintern to depart for Greece to help out the Greek Communist Party and the OKNE, a turn of events that would seal her friendship and loyalty to Zachariadis, and by extension, her own security in the tumult that was to follow.

Kerasidou spent five years in Greece (1925–1930) working in the KKE as an underground operative. Upon her arrival in Athens in 1925, she became a member of the KKE and was elected to the Regional Committee of OKNE, and then to the underground Central Committee of the organization in 1927. Charged with the mission of "rebuilding a failed organization," she also worked as an OMS liaison—facilitating communication between the Central Committee of the KKE and the ECCI.[71] The OMS (Otdel mezhdunarodnykh svyazey) was the highly secretive International Liaison Department of the Comintern. Established in the early 1920s, it was a network of couriers, radio operators, and other specialists whose responsibilities ranged from clandestine communications and forgery of identification and travel documents to overseeing the leadership of national communist organizations and distributing Soviet funds to them. Indeed, Stavridis makes frequent references to "Stella from the KUTV" in his account of their shared experiences of underground life along with Chrysa Hatzivasiliou and Central Committee member Leandros Kritikos in the *yiafkas* (safe houses) of Athens. He also provided a rare reference to her involvement in the international communist women's movement, specifically her collaboration with Hatzivasiliou and Magda Kresinski, a representative of the Communist Women's International who visited Greece on behalf of Ruth Fischer to help grow the women's movement in Greece.[72] Kerasidou was "recalled" to the Soviet Union in 1930 as a "failed mission," after multiple imprisonments and remote island exiles. A subsequent attempt to re-enter Greece in late 1930 was thwarted by heightened police surveillance at Greek ports that saw her arrested and returned to the Soviet Union with the assistance of the Soviet Embassy in Greece, leaving behind her second husband, Kimov, a KKE cadre and KUTV alumnus, to languish indefinitely inside the Greek prison system.[73]

Kerasidou did not become the leader she was earmarked to be, in the Greek Communist Party, the ECCI, or the CPSU, but did fulfill some of her own personal ambitions. Upon her return to the Soviet Union and on the recommendation of the Politburo of the KKE Central Committee, she enrolled into the short (nine-month) courses of the MLS and commenced *aspirantura* (postgraduate study). She became an instructor at the MLS, teaching Party history and construction, in 1933, and indeed was recognized as an outstanding teacher and colleague in the Greek sector, the academic equivalent of a Stakhanovite.[74] The Great Terror caught up with Kerasidou, however, in January 1938, when she was dismissed for being associated with relatives who were in trouble with the law. The MLS itself and the entire Comintern education system was shut down later that year, but Kerasidou was transferred to the adult education system of the Soviet Union as a teacher and inspector after her dismissal, eventually working in the Greek section of a foreign publishing house. In 1944, when her file ends, Kerasidou was an employee of the Greek editorial board of the all-Russia radio committee -vrk- in Tiflis/Tbilisi.[75]

Olga Papadopoulou was literate, "read and wrote well" in Greek, though her Russian was poor. Her "dream was to go to secondary school" but poverty and displacement allowed only three years of elementary Greek school, which she completed with honors. She worked in a tobacco factory and in 1920, aged fourteen, found employment as a factory hand/janitor at the Podolsk mechanical works of Gossheveimachina (state sewing machines), formerly known as Zinger, which set her on a new course.[76] Papadopoulou's circumstances were not uncommon. Child labor was outlawed by the Revolution but resurfaced after the destruction of the Civil War when labor laws were revised to make possible the speediest possible reconstruction. In this revision the age at which minors could begin work was dropped to fourteen, but from the ages of fourteen to sixteen the labor day was to be only four daytime hours. Other limitations on older children remained the same.[77]

In 1924, at age eighteen, Papadopoulou joined the Komsomol despite negligible political training, but she quickly acquired organizational responsibilities within an agricultural workers' cell in Pioneria, Sevastopol, and a women's council. In quick succession she became a member of the

Komsomol cell bureau, and secretary of the editorial board of the Komsomol at Zinger. These competencies led to a recommendation for study at the KUTV by the Soviet Minorities Commission in 1925, thereby clearing the path for further learning and a regular monthly sum of thirty rubles, allocated by the Minorities Commission to the families of all KUTV students. This also enabled Papadopoulou to contribute to the care of her "dependents," her parents and grandparents (her mother died in 1926, and her father was disabled), along with her three older brothers, all of whom also worked for or were aligned with the RCP.[78]

Papadopoulou worked very hard to demonstrate her eligibility for transfer from the "general" sector of KUTV to the Greek sector (International), as she desired to be with her "Greek comrades who were being prepared to be sent to Greece" and to work in her "native country Greece after graduating from the University," even though she had never been there.[79] After undertaking an eight-month evening course in political literacy, the Minorities Commission noted that she was indeed a strong candidate for transfer and for international assignment. Papadopoulou's knowledge, level of interest, diligence, engagement, and overall preparedness were well above average.[80] She was promptly transferred to the Greek sector, "on the recommendation of Comrade Dimitrov," and assessed as "useful for working in Greece."[81] Papadopoulou spent seven years (1927–1934) alternating between work as an underground operative and an organizer, in her words, undertaking "serious work" for the Central Committee of the KKE "that required a lot of confidence and trust, and that other people were afraid to do." She was given orders by the CC to work at a printing shop of a major German manufacturer in Gouva, near Athens, where she organized a strike action, later moving to a textile factory near Athens and in the Piraeus, and then to the working-class refugee neighborhood of Kaisariani and Veria in the north, where she worked mostly among national minorities, especially Pontic Greek peasants who came from Russia.

In Thessaloniki, Papadopoulou facilitated secret communications in the manner of an OMS liaison and wrote for the communist newspaper *Rizospastis*, sending her news coverage from Greece to the Greek newspaper she had worked for in the Soviet Union, *Kommunistis*, published in Rostov on the Don. The relationship between state and Party was evident in the Greek press, which was monitored completely and strictly. The pre-Revolutionary Greek newspapers were closed, replaced by others that served the Party and the construction of socialism. The first was *Haravgi* (1918) published in Batumi (Anastasiadis was the editor). Two years later

Spartakos was established in Novorossiysk, under Sakarelos, a well-known Greek communist with an international career. In June 1921, upon the decision of the Regional Committee of the Communist Party of Georgia, the weekly *Kommunistis* was established in Batumi, regarded as the successor to *Spartakos*. It was based at Rostov on the Don and evolved into the most important Greek publishing center in Russia, with the biggest circulation of all the Greek papers. It maintained close relations with *Rizospastis* too. It was the official publishing arm of the Party in the area of Azov and the Black Sea. The publisher had exclusive rights to the publication of Greek school textbooks; it also published political philosophical and literary books, CPSU decisions, and speeches and writings of Stalin and other prominent officials[82]

Papadopoulou returned to the Soviet Union through MOPR channels in 1934 due to illness, specifically inherited syphilis and tuberculosis that she claimed to have acquired in Greece.[83] She found work as a librarian at the State Academic Library of Narcomtyazhprom (the Ministry of Heavy Industry), where she was employed till at least 1963 when her file record ends, thus outlasting the excesses of Stalinism and the mountainous challenges of chronic ill health that Papadopoulou instrumentalized deftly and consistently in numerous letters she wrote to university and other state authorities requesting assistance with employment, family income support, pension, medical care, and other matters.[84]

Agency in Conformity

Unlike many of their compatriots in the Soviet Union, Stella Kerasidou, Olga Papadopoulou, and Chrysanthi Kantzidou navigated the years of the Great Terror and the Stalinist turn against "enemy minorities" relatively unscathed, a feat attributable to a combination of their ability and willingness to conform to the ebbs and flows of Stalinism and to relationship networks within the party that protected them, and perhaps also to good fortune. In 1937, at the start of the Terror, Kerasidou came under state suspicion for her association with ex-husband Andronikos Haitas and her Party mentor, Valesky, both of whom were declared "enemies of the people."[85] Haitas had a leading role in the factional infighting between his Stalinist/Right faction and the Trotskyist/liquidarists represented by Pouliopoulos/Maximos, a dispute in which Kerasidou, in the customary manner of communists terrified of ostracism and "excommunication," emphasized her support of the Comintern line.⁸⁶ This was compounded in 1938 by the arrests of both her brother and brother-in-law by the NKVD for non-Party misdemeanors.⁸⁷ In her report to human resources of the Comintern, Kerasidou explained that her family never liked her brother-in-law, because he was from a bourgeois family and pulled her sister away from her education and from the Komsomol after they married.⁸⁸ In characteristic submission, Kerasidou lamented her "blindness" and poor political judgment regarding her ex-husband, Haitas (pseud., Sifnaios), and for not "helping to expose him in time especially since she knew of his involvement in the factional conflict in the Party."⁸⁹ When the police discovered letters during a house search in Athens in 1929, she blamed her brother during the interrogation, claiming that all materials found in the house they shared belonged to him. She was nevertheless exiled for communist activities for two months.⁹⁰

In a "closed door meeting" of Group B, MLS student Stella Kantzidou (pseud., Kaiti Vasiliou) repented for making a "serious political mistake" by omitting the political activities of her brother from her autobiography:

> I didn't think of this matter as an important one or related to my responsibilities as a Party member, and I almost forgot about it. Now I realize that I wasn't sincere before my Party, I lied to Personnel Department, but at that time I thought I was sincere before the Party. I didn't inform that my brother unconsciously joined the fascist organization EEE in the town of Drama. One day he was arrested as a suspected communist but later was released as an EEE member.... He was recruited by deception. He was told that it was a cultural and educational organization. When he came to know the real nature of the organization, he contacted the communists and worked on an assignment to destroy the organization from the inside.... I fully understand that not telling the truth was anti-Party and I condemn my act.⁹¹

According to the record, Kantzidou received nothing more than a reprimand for "breach of secrecy" despite the rapidly changing political climate of 1937. Kerasidou and Kantzidou both fell into line with a language and a culture that encouraged denunciation and ritualized acts of confession, criticism and self-criticism, and self-discipline designed to foster political loyalty and cohesion. They promptly distanced themselves from individuals, comrade or kin, who roused state suspicion and threatened their position in the Party, their livelihood, liberty, and indeed their lives.⁹² Addressing the doggedness of communist loyalty characteristic across the board, which often came at great personal cost to one's liberty, safety, and familial bonds, Murphy refers to a process of liminality that was involved in the communist life. Once having crossed the threshold and declared Party allegiance, communists found it all the harder to step back. Membership of a group with pariah status had a certain irrevocability about it.[93] Crossing the threshold may have been more an issue for middle-class activists who had breached the bounds of respectability than for activists in working-class cultures, but it was an even bigger issue for women than for men given the prevailing gender norms.

Like Kerasidou and Kantzidou, Papadopoulou both conformed to the system and worked the system for her own ends. Like many Soviet citizens, Papadopoulou wrote numerous letters to the Soviet authorities, including to Khrushchev, Stalin, and Manuilsky, mostly inquiries and requests regarding pensions, employment, and applications for and replacement of passports and essential identification documents.[94] She was a gifted writer. Her autobiographical narrative and the various letters she wrote in Russian, her second language, to the KUTV and other state authorities were fully utilized opportunities to solve problems and advance her circumstances by casting herself as a life-long victim of circumstance and the ill will of others, of general misfortune, a tragedy of unfulfilled potential. As the historian Golfo Alexopoulos states, after the Revolution people presented themselves as worthy subjects before Soviet authorities, making a point of their proletarian origins and working-class achievements, and often making claims of hardship. Implicit in this style of self-presentation was the belief that a hard life entitled someone to political membership in the new proletarian state, a form of redemption for all those who had suffered under the Old Regime.[95] In a dramatic concoction of truth, strategy, and embellishment, Papadopoulou does not flinch from narrating a childhood steeped in abject poverty, family discrimination and neglect, ill health, loneliness, and often destitution, surviving only by her wits. Her narrative also betrays a shrewd and resilient operator, a person of high intelligence with an irrepressible determination to survive.

The most notable of her letters was addressed to Khrushchev, written in 1962, and displayed what Hellbeck, Fitzpatrick, and other scholars have described as the "confessional" qualities in the widespread practice of letter writing to Soviet authorities.[96] Public letter writing, that is, sending a letter to prominent Party members, governmental institutions, or newspaper editors, ranked among the most widespread and important practices of Soviet democratic participation. The roots of this practice extended back to imperial Russia, when peasants and nobles alike composed petitions to the tsar on any number of matters ranging from violent landlords to harsh sentences for crimes. The Soviet government sought to set itself apart from its imperial predecessor by democratizing the practice of letter writing; no longer would those writing to the authorities approach them as subjects making demands on the state, but rather as citizens or civic-minded activists whose missives constituted acts of participation in the life of society at large. Basic literacy campaigns in the 1920s and 1930s also helped more and more people to gain the literacy skills necessary to compose letters. In this sense, letter writing was a profound validation of the Soviet regime's success and legitimacy.[97]

Papadopoulou offered "an account of her life to the Party of Lenin," that was finally being "steered" by the "reliable hands" of Khrushchev. It is a compelling example of the style and rhetorical tactics used in what Kozlov refers to as an "interested denunciation."[98] Papadopoulou insisted that she wanted nothing but to "to die with a clean conscience," to account for her life to the Party of Lenin and to make peace with herself, after having "lived as a corpse for the last thirty years," and for not being "given a chance to take part fully in the building of Communism," by virtue of her bouts of illness but primarily because of the exclusionary tactics of the Greek Communist Party under Zachariadis. Papadopoulou attributed her fractured reputation in the Party to the Party itself and the slander of Zachariadis, in particular.

Papadopoulou's denunciation of Zachariadis, a devoted Stalinist, was very purposeful in the climate of de-Stalinization ushered in by Khrushchev some years earlier, for it maximized her chances of being heard and her requests fulfilled: "I think that the steering wheel of the ship that was steered by Lenin has come into reliable hands only now. I have confidence in you and that means that I have confidence in the Party that you are leading."[99]

The confession served several unstated purposes, primarily those of preparing the ground for an imminent pension application and attempting to correct a tainted reputation that would shame and possibly disadvantage her son after her death.[100] While Papadopoulou's narrative as presented in letters and autobiography exemplify what Fitzpatrick calls a "useable self," a dramatic, bold, and candid self also leaps off the page, demonstrating once again that Bolshevik subjectivities were not as totalizing and censoring as authorities hoped and intended, and the Soviet state efforts to instill a single subjectivity were not as successful as scholars have mostly argued.

Papadopoulou was strident about what may be construed today as a "glass ceiling" in the Greek Communist Party, which she did not attribute explicitly to gender, but contextualized in terms of the lapsing values and misjudgments of the Greek Communist Party itself, in thrall to Zachariadis, and whose higher circles mistreated and exploited her "for a bowl of soup." The corrupted culture was most evident in the personality cult that had grown around Zachariadis, who was always surrounded by "comrades virtually licking his boots, but I was not able to do it."[101] Contrary to Lenin's principles and the principle of internal party democracy,

> [Zachariadis] would discard comrades without any regard for the consequences. My error was that I was a fanatical adherent of the true ideas of Lenin. In the archives of the Institute of Marxism-Leninism there might be all sorts of lies and nonsense from Mr. Zachariadis. But I consider myself clean and I have adhered to the principles of Lenin, and I have been giving all my energy to society even though I was expelled from the party.[102]

Papadopoulou's strident tone notwithstanding, dependence on the Party and fear of losing favor or being ousted from it constituted both an existential and material threat for cadres and devout functionaries, even in the less perilous period under Khrushchev.[103] As Nancy Adler's work has shown, even prisoners of the Soviet gulag—many of them falsely convicted—emerged from the camps maintaining their loyalty to the Party that was responsible for their internment. Reflecting on what appears to be boundless and irrational loyalty, it is useful to recall that the party had replaced everything—bad and good—or as the Greek writer and communist Elli Pappa had said, "the Party was God" (*to komma itan o Theos*).[104] On the other hand, as Papadopoulou wrote in her letter to Khrushchev, God gave her family nothing.[105] For her, and many communists of her generation, the demands, excesses, and absurdities of Party life remained a price worth paying to "wipe the slate clean."

5

Chrysa Hatzivasiliou
An Icon without a History

The life of the singular and elusive figure of Chrysa Hatzivasiliou/ Hadjivassiliou (pseud., Alexandra Nikolai Armand, Mary), the original inspiration for this book, merits much greater attention than the sources permit. The minutes of Party meetings and publications, her own correspondence and writings, and scattered references in the memoirs of those who knew her offer personal glimpses of the personality: learned, measured, conscientious, modest, dignified, a person of intellect, of presence and authority, commanding respect, a "beautiful person" (*oraios anthropos*), and dedicated to the Party.[1]

The first biographical entry for Hatzivasiliou appeared in Branko M. Lazitch's *Biographical Dictionary of the Comintern* (1973), which effectively summarized the data in her Comintern file.[2] The historiographical void is the sum of many factors: her premature death in 1950 canceled the possibility of memoir and interview, and as Ivo Banac states in reference to the anomaly of the Dimitrov diary, it was highly atypical for professional revolutionaries at this level to leave any trace of their activities in the moment. The continuing inaccessibility of the KKE archives and the workings of hegemonic masculinity also have a share in the glaring void that persists even after the explosion in Civil War historiography that began in the 1980s.[3]

Her Comintern file adds very little to the picture, consisting only of the *anketa* and brief student reports; the conspicuous absence of an autobiography perhaps connotes her sensitive political status. Hatzivasiliou was a committed communist-feminist, intellectual, comrade, and wife; her privileged background, rank, and authority in the Party also distinguished her from many of the female communists of her generation. But she surely shared with her contemporaries the sense of belonging and purpose that the world of communist activism provided, so eloquently expressed in the quote by Wolfgang Leonhard that opens this book.[4]

Background

Like many of her generation, she came to politics early. Hatzivasiliou was born in 1903 to a family of prosperous peasants in the city of Aidinio (Aydin), a fig-growing district of western Asia Minor, sixty miles southeast of Smyrna. The Battle of Aydin (1919) was one of the first and most infamous battles of the Greco-Turkish War, described by the *New York Times* as "a vast sepulchre," an appalling spectacle of desolation and destruction where hundreds of Greek and Armenian women, children, and priests lie in nameless graves—victims of massacres by Turks after Greek forces retreated under fierce attack by Turkish irregulars in the summer of 1919.[5]

The city had lain in ruins since 1919 but Hatzivasiliou managed to complete her secondary education before fleeing to Greece with her father in 1922. Her proficiency in French, as noted in her *anketa*, corroborates fellow communist Eleftherios Stavridis's recollection that she had attended a French Catholic high school run by nuns in Odemisio (Odemis), in Smyrna (Izmir) province, where most of the schools attended by the Levantine community were located.[6] Stavridis is referring to one of the foreign schools, many of them French and German missionary schools that proliferated in the Empire from the nineteenth century. There is little doubt that the Hatzivasiliou household enjoyed a considerable degree of prosperity, also noted in her Comintern file, as foreign schools were the exclusive preserve of wealthy Ottomans, who preferred them for their superior reputation. Aidinio is eighty-six kilometers from Odemisio, serviced by the Smyrna–Aidinio railway that required at least two hours of travel at that time. It is very likely that Hatzivasiliou was one of many students from the hinterland and neighboring towns of Smyrna who attended these schools in the city as boarders, a factor that resulted in a growing number of people who saw themselves as Smyrniots.[7]

Hatzivasiliou was barely eighteen when the exchange of populations agreement between Turkey and Greece hurled her family into the drama of expulsion, displacement, and economic turmoil in the new homeland of Greece. She joined the communist movement not long after her arrival. Upon arriving in Athens, having completed secondary school, she found office employment immediately, first as a secretary/typist, and then as an accountant in various private commercial offices in the cities of Salonika and Athens. Within two years she had joined the Union of Office Workers and the OKNE, and in 1925, at the age of twenty, she joined the KKE. Hatzivasiliou steadily built her profile in the Party as a member of the Athens and the Salonika OKNE committees, and as a member of the Greek Communist Party District Committee in Athens. Within three years, her talents and potential, more readily recognized, one assumes, in the heady context of Bolshevization, placed her on a leadership path. In 1928 she made the clandestine voyage to Moscow to commence her revolutionary training at the KUNMZ, she remained there for a period of three years.

"A Fearless and Experienced Revolutionary"

At the KUNMZ, Hatzivasiliou was known as Alexandra Nikolai Armand, an amalgam of Alexandra Kollontai and Inessa Armand, the names of prominent figures in Communist Women's International. It is not known if the patronym "Nikolai" was her actual father's name. The French-born Russian politician Inessa Fyodorovna Armand (born Elisabeth-Inès Stéphane d' Herbenville, 1874–1920) was an "old Bolshevik" and a feminist, a leading figure at the 1915 and 1920 International Women's Conferences of the Second and Third Internationals. An important figure in the pre-Revolution communist movement, Armand was virtually forgotten, another casualty of Stalinist censorship, in part due to her relationship with Lenin. The opening of Soviet archives in the 1990s has stimulated new research, although many valuable sources remain inaccessible. The much better known and historicized Alexandra Mikhailovna Domontovich (Kollontai) (1872–1952) was a significant figure in the Bolshevik Party during the Russian Revolution and became arguably the most influential woman in the new Soviet society. She was appointed commissar of Social Welfare by Lenin after the Revolution and remained committed to the connection between socialist revolution and the emancipation of women throughout her life. In 1919, Kollontai and Armand formed Zhenotdel, a Soviet government department dedicated to the rights and needs of women. Kollontai took over the leadership of Zhenotdel after Armand's death in 1920. Like Armand, Kollontai also fell out of

FIGURE 15. Chrysa Hatzivasiliou, 1928 (pseud., Alexandra Nikolai Armand) Photo courtesy of RGASPI.

favor with the Party as she became increasingly critical of its growing bureaucracy and its heavy-handed management of factories and workers. She was sidelined from Party politics by being given diplomatic posts abroad, and eventually retired to Moscow where she died in 1952.[8]

Hatzivasiliou's term at KUNMZ consolidated her growing reputation as a hardworking, committed communist and her loyalty to the Party. Her performance defied a chronic health condition, probably leukemia, that constrained her practical work and would eventually claim her life. The first practical that involved physical work at a factory in the first year gave way to less physical work in the following years in which Hatzivasiliou excelled—two months of the summer as a political educator and factory organizer in Greek villages, serving in the women's council, and writing for the factory newspaper.[9] In the winter of 1930 she worked in collectivization for two months in the Greek village of Merzhanovo (Rostov), and as a factory organizer before being relieved of her duties due to ill health.

In 1931, her final year of study, the University Rector signed off on Hatzivasiliou's readiness to be "used for organizational and propaganda work," in familiar language:

> Academic abilities and the ability to work on her own are above the average. Her grades are good. A significant growth has been noted. During all this time, she has been hardworking and persistent in her work, disciplined in her studies, and kept good relations with the fellow students. Party allegiance is

FIGURE 16. Inessa Fyodorovna Armand (1916; photo courtesy of RGASPI) and Alexandra Kollontai (circa 1900; photo by Universal History Archive/Universal Images Group via Getty Images)

good. During all the period of study did not show any deviation. Received no party sanctions. Was active in the socialist competition.[10]

Her return to Greece in 1931 coincided with the return of Zachariadis who was subsequently appointed General Secretary of the KKE by the Comintern.[11] The growing dominance of the Stalinist faction under Zachariadis did not impede Hatzivasiliou's rise through the ranks of the Party—she was a figure Zachariadis respected—but it was the exception that proved the rule. At the 6th Congress in December 1935, she became the first woman to be elected to the Central Committee of the KKE.[12] At the 2nd Panhellenic Conference of the KKE in 1942 during the War, she was elected to the closely guarded male preserve of the Politburo. The Politburo, or Political Bureau of the Central Committee of the Communist Party, was the highest policy-making body in the Party. To be elected to the Politburo, a member had to serve on the Central Committee. The Central Committee formally elected the Politburo in the aftermath of a Party Congress. Members of the Central Committee were given a predetermined list of candidates for the Politburo (with only one candidate for each seat); for this reason the election of the Politburo was usually passed unanimously. The more power the General Secretary had, the stronger the chance was that the Politburo membership were passed without serious dissent.[13]

Post-War Consolidation

Hatzivasiliou reached the peak of her trajectory in the glow of victory after the War and before the outbreak of civil conflict, chairing the proceedings of the 7th Party Congress in October 1945, at which she was re-elected to the Politburo and to the newly formed Secretariat of the Politburo, and appointed leader of the women's movement.[14] She belonged to a small group of elite communist women of the era who broke through the glass ceilings of their respective Central Committees, but who received far more scholarly attention than Hatzivasiliou, assisted by multi-archival access and a considerable volume of their own writings. Her contemporaries include Romanian Communist Party leader Ana Pauker (1893–1960), to whom Hatzivasiliou was likened by *Time* magazine; the Spanish Republican leader Dolores Ibárruri (1895–1989), known as "La Pasionaria"; Bulgarian communist leader Tsola Dragoicheva (1898–1993); German Communist Party leaders Clara Zetkin (1857–1933) and Ruth Fischer (1895–1961); and Elena Stasova (1873–1966).[15] Pauker served as communist Romania's foreign minister in the late 1940s and early 1950s and became the world's first female foreign minister when she took office in December 1947. She was also the unofficial leader of the Romanian Communist Party right after the Second World War. Dolores Ibárruri was appointed General Secretary of the Central Committee of the Spanish Communist Party in exile following the popular front defeat in the Spanish Civil War, a position she held from 1942 to 1960. Tsola Dragoicheva was a member of the Central Committee of the Bulgarian Communist Party (BKP) from 1936 and of the Politburo (1940–1948, 1957–1982), a representative of the BKP in the Fatherland Front (OF) from 1942, secretary of the OF after the communist seizure of power (1944), president of the Women's National Union, and finally, the minister of communications (1947–1957). She had also been to the International Lenin School.

Clara Zetkin had been an important influence in Hatzivasiliou's writings on the "woman question." She joined the new Communist Party of Germany in 1919, becoming a member of its Central Committee and serving in the Reichstag (federal Lower House) from 1920. She was elected to the presidium of the Third International (1921) but lost much of her influence after Lenin's death in 1924. Ruth Fischer (1895–1961) was the co-founder of the Communist Party of Austria (1918) and became famous as the chair of the Communist Party of Germany (KPD) in the Weimar Republic (1924–1926); then she fell afoul of Stalin for her Trotskyist views and was expelled in August of 1926. After 1945 she became a staunch anti-Stalinist activist and became associated with the anti-communist crusade in the US, where she authored the best-selling volume *Stalin and German Communism*. Stasova, an "Old Bolshevik" who survived the spy mania and state terror of the Soviet Union in the 1930s, became secretary of the Central Committee, the most important promotion she received and the highest office any woman ever held in the Russia's Communist Party. But her tenure was very brief, attributed by Clements to persistent patriarchy but, in contrast to Hatzivasiliou, also to Stasova's own lack of intellectual confidence and unwillingness to become involved in the politics of the Politburo and the Central Committee.[16]

Clements notes that the Old Bolshevik women (*Bolshevichki*) lost considerable rank after the Revolution. Conditions of emergency and the ideological commitment to women's equality had long been the two great facilitators of women's participation in the Party. The emergency had never been greater than during the civil war, and commitment to women's emancipation no less determined, but the war seemed to have strengthened the masculinist cast of Bolshevik political culture.[17] It has been argued that Hatzivasiliou and her European counterparts were regarded as honorary males in the Party establishment, with the exception of Spain's Dolores Ibárruri, who was regarded and self-presented as a "sort of Earth Mother of War," in an adaptation of the tradition of Republican motherhood.[18] It took courageous and tenacious women to challenge the biases of male communists. Such was the courage and tenacity of Hatzivasiliou, or "Alexandra Armand."

Hatzivasiliou was married to fellow OKNE member, Comintern graduate, and future Party executive Petros Roussos. Roussos also rose rapidly in the Party upon the instatement of Zachariadis as General Secretary in 1931. He was elected to the Central Committee of the KKE in 1935, the same year as Hatzivasiliou's election, a position which he held till 1973.[19] However, his career never cast a shadow over Hatzivasiliou's status, achievements, and legacy, in the way that the political lives of most Greek male communists overshadowed the often considerable activism of their communist wives and partners.[20] This is as much a testament to her character as to her talents and dogged commitment to the Party. Roussos and Hatzivasiliou did not have children, unusual even for communists of this era who lived much of their lives in perilous circumstances, including regular police violence and stretches of imprisonment, but continued to create families. Hatzivasiliou's chronic ill health may also have precluded the possibility of children and cleared the path to total dedication to the Party and her rapid rise in the leadership.[21] It is reasonable to argue that Hatzivasiliou's family and first loyalty was to the Party. The same was true of many communists including her husband who promptly estranged himself from Hatzivasiliou after she lost favor with Zachariadis at the 5th Plenum in 1949. Roussos remained in the CC until 1973, making him one of the few members of the inner circle of the Party to survive the purges.

Hatzivasiliou's *komatikotita* (party-mindedness) is beyond question, and she has been judged harshly for it, no doubt on account of her gender. In the context of a diatribe on the leftist monopoly of the historiography of the Axis occupation of Greece, Petros M. Staikos takes particular issue with Mark Mazower's description of Hatzivasiliou as a KKE activist (*agonistria tou KKE*) in his book *Inside Hitler's Greece*, remarking, "Of course, Hatzivasiliou was a great *agonistria* [fighter], but she fought only for the domination of the KKE in Greece, and this is as true before her 'education' at the Soviet KUTV, as after."[22] This evaluation is exemplary of an entrenched skepticism about communist agency, especially in relation to female communists who choose the party. In any case, her devotion did not shield her from the retributive chaos that gripped the Greek Communist Party in exile following the communist defeat in the Civil War in 1949.

Crime and Punishment after the Civil War

Judged by Zachariadis to be among those responsible for the communist defeat in the charged atmosphere of the aftermath, Hatzivasiliou was "retired" from her Politburo duties due to ill health at the Party's 5th Plenum in January 1949, but not before being interrogated and accused of "anti-Party opportunism" (*antikommatikos opportounismos*), and thereafter being ostracized from the Party. She had been a cautious voice on matters of strategy and direction as civil conflict beckoned; her opposition to armed insurrection at the key junctures of 1945 and at the 3rd Plenum of 1947 were now evidence of her "defeatism"; Hatzivasiliou was a "waverer," too keen to reach compromise with the "bourgeois establishment." She was thus implicated in the process that led to the decimation of the Greek

Democratic Army during the subsequent Civil War.²³ She had also been among the members of the executive who spoke out against authoritarianism in the Party, that the members "have no voice, criticism is repelled, self-criticism is absent, and the resulting status quo is one in which only shrewd, pragmatic, but incapable elements can thrive."²⁴ For these transgressions, Hatzivasiliou died alone in a Budapest hospital a year after the close of the Civil War, on November 14, 1950, at the age of forty-six, ostracized by the Party to which she had dedicated her life and best work.²⁵ According to the Party obituary, her funeral was attended by Hungarian party representatives, members of the political refugee community in Hungary, and comrade Petros Roussos.²⁶

Her illness and premature death spared her the humiliation of formal expulsion and certain exile, or worse, which befell other members of the leadership at this time. Her obituary appeared one month after her death, published in the newspaper *Foni tis Gynaikas* (Woman's voice) of the Greek branch of the communist Women's International Democratic Federation (in exile), of which Hatzivasiliou had been the president. The obituary was symptomatic of the times: a brief and impersonal account of her achievements.

> In 1925 she joined KKE and advanced into the highest leadership positions of the party. She was exiled to the islands of Ag. Stratis and Kimolos during the fascist dictatorship of Metaxas. With the invasion of German fascists, she threw herself heart and soul into the organization of the national liberation struggle. In the post-Varkiza period, she represented the EAM women's movement at the founding conference of the Women's International Democratic Federation and was a member of the Executive Committee up until its second conference.²⁷

The main aim of the obituary was to convey Hatzivasiliou's regret for her "serious errors of judgement," and her denunciation of the comrades who had leveled similar criticisms at Zachariadis' decisions. "In a letter addressed to the 11th KKE Conference, comrade Chrysa condemned the sewage [*ocheto*] of Vapheiadis, the views of Partsalidis, and the treachery of Karagiorgis; she acknowledged her own errors and reasserted her commitment in the fight to preserve the unity and monolithic status of the Party."²⁸ In a final act of redemption, she spent her final days translating Stalin's *Marxism and the National Question* and *The National Question and Leninism*.

Hatzivasiliou thus determined to make her peace with the Party to which she had dedicated a lifetime of unwavering service and loyalty.

As the late Elli Pappa poignantly remarks in her memoir:

> It wasn't easy to be a member of the KKE in the Stalinist years unless your mission was to climb the ranks. If this was your ambition, the second precondition was an ability to turn a blind eye to every crooked, unacceptable, suspicious act you might witness. To respond as a corpse might respond if you were not naturally biologically blind.... *Kommatikotita* [party-mindedness] meant total submission to the Party leadership line.... The Party lived in its own reality and believed that everybody had to do the same.[29]

The truest tribute to Hatzivasiliou at that time appeared in a short statement added to her file after her unceremonious discharge from the Party leadership, in which CPSU official V. A. Vedyushkin described her as "a prominent member of the KKE, and a strong organizer of the female workers in Greek cities, who enjoyed authority among communists and workers as a fearless and experienced revolutionary."[30]

The rehabilitation of Hatzivasiliou and the other leaders who had fallen from the graces of the KKE would occur some years later. The process of de-Stalinization spearheaded by Khrushchev in February 1956 and the split in the KKE (and international communism) after the Hungarian uprising in November the same year would bring the Zachariadis era to an end. Zachariadis was expelled from the KKE the following year.

A second commemoration for Hatzivasiliou took place in 1960 on the tenth anniversary of her death, to the day. It featured a segment in a radio broadcast by Foni tis Alitheias (Voice of Truth), the Bucharest-based radio station of the Party in exile. This tribute was far more generous in spirit and detail, befitting the shift in the political environment after 1956:

> Chrysa belonged to a generation of fighters whose self-sacrifice, intellectual and spiritual gifts, and indomitable activism built the solid foundations of the Communist Party of Greece before and during the War. Her entire life was dedicated to the lot of the working class. From the day she entered the ranks of the Communist Youth as a young woman in 1925 until her last breath, she had no other concern but to help spread the word of the Party to the places where working people lived and

worked. A loyal soldier of communism, herald of the immortal teachings of Marxism-Leninism, student/researcher of Greek problems, she developed her gifts in tireless daily dedication to the organization and enlightenment, for, with, and among the people. Inside the daily struggle and her own effort at self-sufficiency, she developed into one of the professional revolutionaries, without whom the working class could not have established its party, the KKE, admired by friends and feared by its enemies. Her self-abnegation, her sharpness, energy, courage, and candour, her ability to speak to the soul of ordinary people in combination with the proper modesty and dignity that befits a communist soldier, she advanced into the leadership of KKE from as early as 1935.[31]

Consistent with Party doctrine, and as historian Angelika Psarra points out, the achievements and legacy of Hatzivasiliou were framed strictly in terms of the Party's contribution to the Greek people and to the women's movement, rather than as the achievements of Hatzivasiliou or the women's movement itself.[32] Hatzivasiliou herself had attributed the mass politicization of women and their legendary participation in the Resistance to the efforts of the KKE over the long durée. "The serious and united response by women against the fascist dictatorship both before and after its establishment, their courage in the face of persecution and pursuit, imprisonment, and torture by the Metaxas-Glucksburg axis is not unrelated to the work undertaken by KKE to engage the female population of Greece. Indeed, it's a direct outcome of this commitment."[33] By 1960 Hatzivasiliou had shifted from pariah to martyr, and now belonged to "the pantheon of fighters from the people who, with their work and sacrifice, raised the Greek Communist Party, the National Resistance movement, the movement for Democratic Change, to its present eminence."[34]

The "Woman Question" in 1946

Hatzivasiliou's essay "The KKE and the Woman Question in Greece" was probably published in the early part of 1946, conceived and written during the small window of lingering optimism between the Dekemvriana (December Events) and the descent into full-scale civil war, the first "hot" conflict of the Cold War.[35] The Dekemvriana refers to a series of clashes fought during World War II in Athens from December 3, 1944, to January 11, 1945. The conflict was the culmination of months of tension between Left and

Right resistance factions, and ultimately between the popular communist resistance coalition and the British army.

By the end of the Second World War, Winston Churchill considered the influence of the Greek Communist Party within the Resistance coalition to have grown stronger than he had calculated. He proceeded to intervene in a highhanded attempt to restore the unwanted monarchy and suppress the entire republican Left. Britain thus switched allegiance to back the supporters of Hitler against its own erstwhile allies. During a victory day celebration in the center of Athens, RAF Spitfires and Beaufighters were strafing leftist strongholds as the Dekemvriana, also known as the Battle of Athens, began between the Greeks and the British alongside supporters of the Nazis against the partisans. This upheaval and its suppression set the stage for the civil war of 1946 to 1949.[36]

Hatzivasiliou's projections for the fate of Greek women and the communist movement remained cautiously optimistic at the time of writing in 1946, buoyed by the magnitude of the women's movement spawned by the unprecedented mobilization of Greek women during the occupation, the spirit of collaboration that held sway in the politically diverse women's movement in the early post-war period, the outcomes of the Party Congress in October 1945, and the creation of a strong left-feminist international organization embodied in the Women's International Democratic Federation (WIDF), whose Greek branch Hatzivasiliou would lead.[37] Hatzivasiliou was a Marxist feminist in the German tradition. Her essay is a standard Marxist historical analysis of women's predicament grafted onto Greek conditions, and both respectful and dismissive of the feminist project, especially in Greece. Greatly influenced by Friedrich Engels, August Bebel, and Clara Zetkin, who she quotes extensively, Hatzivasiliou considered the notion of private property as the basis of all social problems—including, and especially, women's degraded social, cultural, political, and economic status—and its destruction as the only resolution.

In the essay, Hatzivasiliou launches the classic Marxist critique that underscores the tension between feminism and the liberal capitalist order—which dogged the woman question in the most developed capitalist nations—as inherent and irreconcilable, but nevertheless superior to the "swamp waters" of pseudo-capitalism that rendered feminism entirely futile in Greece. But even a cursory reading leaves little doubt as to her implicit recognition of gender as highly politicized terrain and an important if secondary analytical category in considerations of women's predicament and its resolution.

The KKE held its 7th Congress in Athens from October 1 through 6, 1945, at which it founded a new Central Committee (Kendriki Epitropi) and Politburo (Politiko Grafeio) of the Central Committee. Hatzivasiliou was appointed to both. At this Congress, the Party declared the need to boost their number of women members to 50 percent. The establishment of a Women's Section at the highest level of the Party structure thus aimed to resolve this question; Hatzivasiliou would direct the Women's Section at the top level of the Central Committee Secretariat.

In November 1945, two months after the Congress, Hatzivasiliou and the journalist Dido Sotiriou flew to Paris to attend the World (International) Congress of Women, which founded the WIDF. They attended as members of the EAM and were joined by Elli Danos and Fani Simiti of the Panhellenic Union of Women, one of the most leftist women's organizations to emerge from the Resistance period, with numerous branches established across Greece. Paris-based Tatiana Gritsi-Milliex, a famed Greek novelist and journalist, delivered the address for the Greek delegation due to a delay in Hatzivasiliou's arrival. Gritsi-Milliex made several presentations to the Congress, emphasizing the contributions of Greek women to the antifascist movement in Greece, the tragedy of the violent government backlash, and the persecution of those who had fought in the Resistance following the German withdrawal at the end of 1944. Gritsi-Milliex pleaded that "the women of France send women in Greece a message of protest, of solidarity and encouragement that will comfort them in their isolation and bring them a breath of hope for the freedom and justice that their sacrifice so abundantly deserved."[38]

Two months later, in February 1946, the Panhellenic Federation of Women (POG; Panellinia Omospondia Gynaikon) was established under the directorship of Hatzivasiliou and promptly set about the task of harnessing the energies of the women's movement that had grown out of the period of occupation and resistance. In the same year, Hatzivasiliou penned her essay on the "Woman Question." The first POG conference, held in May of 1946, enshrined interorganizational cooperation; indeed, it became the umbrella organization for all groups concerned with suffrage. This secured the support of bourgeois feminist groups for whom the campaign for the political rights of Greek women had been a longstanding goal. The election of Avra Theodoropoulou, the president of the feminist Syndesmos gia ta Dikaiomata ton Gynaikon (League for the Rights of Greek Women), as the general secretary reinforced the spirit of communist-feminist collaboration.

Chaired by Theodoropoulou, the conference sessions were concerned with the status of women in public and private law, workplace reforms, children's welfare, and education. Maria Svolou, also a POG member, explained that "a resolution for full franchise rights was submitted to the Chamber of Deputies, but it has not yet found any place on the orders of the day." Svolou's subsequent article was later published in the leftist press, bemoaning the fact that "only Greek women in all of Europe do not have the right to be elected in the representative bodies of the nation; the powers that be show no signs of recognizing this right." This was a unique, albeit short-lived, moment in time when communists and feminists like Hatzivasiliou and Theodoropoulou reconciled pre-war feminist goals with a belief in the power of mass politics to effect change. POG was formed during a phase in which the KKE and the EAM resistance coalition envisaged sharing power with the established pre-war political parties, and communists and liberals accepted or accommodated feminist ideas as a part of a new approach to and analysis of the vastly changed post-war world in which they believed women were destined to play a central part. Hatzivasiliou transferred these values in her contribution to the Party's policy in 1945/1946 that also emphasized reconstruction, reconciliation, compromise, cooperation, insistence, and peaceful democratic development as the only viable prospect in Greece after the War.[39]

The essay, however, ends on a sober note, as Hatzivasiliou, the clear-sighted pragmatist, gives in to the reality of escalating civil conflict. Hatzivasiliou concludes with an appeal to Greek women to join in the coming battle against the "Asiatic forces of conservatism" in Greece, in which nothing less than their hard-won gains were at stake.[40] This orientalizing rhetoric, deployed by Hatzivasiliou to discredit the forces of conservative nationalism, would be turned on the communists as the tide turned against them during the Greek Civil War.[41] This language would become a tragic refrain in the communist campaign to recruit more women to the front line in the desperate end stages of the communist effort during the Greek Civil War.[42]

CONCLUSION

The Transnational Social History of Greek Interwar Communism

In December 1924 the Greek Communist Party made a commitment to bring internal party culture and operations into alignment with Comintern principles. I've argued that this facilitated a greater and more systematic engagement with women, essential for a marginal party that aspired to become a "revolutionary party of the proletariat." At the same time interest in gender-based understandings of the "woman question" and the women's movement, at least as conceived in the *Theses of the Communist Women's Movement*, lost traction at the Comintern. The Comintern's focus on the emancipation of women came to be understood entirely in terms of the workplace by the end of the 1920s, and any notion of the "special subordination" of women in communist propaganda or campaigning came to be regarded as a capitulation to bourgeois feminism. This book is an effort to break open and contextualize this apparent paradox of Bolshevization by focusing on the perspective "from below."

The KKE's alignment with the Comintern line was crucial to its renewed engagement with and organization of women from 1925. The "work among women," though consistently evaluated as "inadequate" at Party meetings, would surely have met with greater lethargy and resistance outside the tutelage of the Comintern, in the organic conditions of entrenched male dominance and general inertia. Moreover, the mobilization of "women as workers" had a particular resonance in the Greek context as Bolshevization coincided with the refugee crisis, the consequences of the ethnic cleansing of 1.3 million Orthodox Christians refugees, mostly Anatolian Greek women and youth, from their homelands in Asia Minor and their relocation to a "motherland" that was ill-prepared to absorb them. The integration of the refugees into the Greek economy both revolutionized Greek industry and expanded the ranks of the working poor, subjecting a vulnerable and unprotected female industrial labor force, in particular, to unprecedented levels of workplace exploitation. The KKE opened itself rhetorically and organizationally to women at this time, and found its female constituency among these vast numbers of toiling women, for whom class was of greater vital interest and anxiety than the Comintern's turn away from gender-based understandings of the "woman question" and commitment to the women's movement.

Those among them who embarked on the path of the professional revolutionary are perhaps Greek interwar communism's most obscured protagonists. Placing them at the center of this study is an act of historical recovery: an effort to document the historical agency, and indeed the very existence, of a group whose anonymity as underground operatives and outlaws was axiomatic. Reading across the *ankety* and the individual autobiographical narratives, one can discern a shared belief in the progressive direction the lives of the authors had taken as members of the communist movement along with the sacrifice, risk, compromise, hypocrisy, disappointment, fear, mistreatment, and loss endured at different times by all the subjects examined in this study. Membership in the elite cadre system offered food, shelter, healthcare, and a basic income. Ideology, further learning, political engagement, and professional training endowed cadres with a sense of purpose and belonging, a measure of social respectability, and fostered confidence and self-respect. Formal instruction in mass mobilization, organization, party structures, and conducting mass meetings could only be provided by Comintern universities at that time.

In his conversations with Apollo Davidson, Moses Kotane spoke of how the Lenin School and KUTV had enormously broadened his horizons and how he valued the fact that they had helped him to believe in himself and taught him "to think politically."[1] Perhaps the most important influence on such students who occupied the lowest social rung was being looked upon, treated, and taught as future political leaders. Where else would Stella Vamniatzidou, an illiterate refugee originally from Raedestos, Anatolia, working in tobacco in Kavala, who had never been to school and could barely sign her name, become an activist for the unemployed, an organizer of strikes and rallies, and a valued political leader, respected as a devoted comrade?[2] Most of the students/cadres examined here had received enough formal schooling for basic literacy but not enough to break the cycle of toil and poverty into which many were born. These "parvenus" became low- to mid-ranking functionaries, making up the ranks of the specially trained and highly mobile undercover agents, organizers, propagandists / political provocateurs, and liaisons, moving between Greece and the Soviet Union, and beyond as circumstances demanded and permitted.

The Greek case study reaffirms the importance of approaching the relationship of the Comintern and its affiliated parties, of the "center and the periphery," as a reciprocal albeit frequently fraught exchange between conscious actors, between university and student, between the party and its membership, between the party and its mass organizations. Even a cursory examination of the file data suggests that the cadres were far less the "products" they are understood by many scholars to have been, or the "raw material" (*yliko*) that the Comintern and the KKE wished to mold and "utilize" as they saw fit, than rational actors and determined beneficiaries of an education system *they* in fact utilized to recast their subjectivities and redirect their life's fortunes. For the subjects in this study, the risks and personal sacrifices demanded by communism's alternative universe were risks surely worth taking for those whom "even god had failed." This is expressed in characteristically dramatic terms by Papadopoulou who recalled her mother's last words in her epic letter to Khrushchev: "'I am dying, and I see no shame in my children being communists. I believed in God, but God would not give me anything. For me Lenin is higher than God.' And she asked me to revenge her sufferings."[3] Papadopoulou was in good company. As the scholar John Murphy has said, the story of socialism and communism is a saga of idealism and cynicism, revolution and repression, power and powerlessness. The world is still grappling with age-old questions regarding governance, equality, justice, and freedom—socialism and communism attempted to answer these questions definitively. In that they failed, but in doing so, they highlighted the importance of the questions themselves and of the ordinary people whose lives hang in the balance, waiting for answers.[4]

The period explored in this social history of Greek interwar communism was framed by great global events—Ottoman imperial collapse on the one hand, and Soviet empire-building on the other—that shaped the rest of the twentieth century and whose legacies resonate into the present. The conclusion of the Greek-Turkish War in Asia Minor and the subsequent Lausanne Peace Treaty (1923) reshaped the landscape of southeastern Europe and the Middle East and became a landmark event in the modern history of the refugee experience. The population exchange had an eventful afterlife. It became a template for demographic politics and partitions across the globe—from Central Europe (Nazi Germany) to South Asia (India/Pakistan) and the Middle East (Israel/Palestine). Likewise, *derzhavnost* (great power-ness) is the thread that links the Russification of the Comintern and its institutions to its ultimate demise, and the persecution of national minorities during the Great Terror with the fight Ukrainians are waging today for their very existence.

The world of the Greek Cominternians confirms that the history of Greek communism cannot be approached as a merely national one. The existence of a significant ethnic Greek minority in the Soviet Union and the eventual admission of its youth into the (international) Greek foreign sectors of the Comintern universities had historic consequences. For Soviet Greeks, basic Greek literacy acquired in the Greek schools established in the Greek settlement before and throughout the Soviet period, had been the critical factor in their trajectory, determining their access and ability to integrate into the Greek sectors for foreign students, which then became the launching pad for establishing links with "the country" and working for the KKE. The universities presented a unique and unprecedented opportunity for cultural interaction and collaboration between Greek nationals and Soviet Greek students, revealing the latter's often fervently expressed desire to improve their command of their mother tongue and to galvanize an existing ethnic Greek identity through formal instruction and social interaction with their Greek compatriots that admission to the international or Greek sector provided. The bond with Greekness was further consolidated when a selection of Soviet Greek graduates traveled to Greece "on assignment" to work with the KKE as undercover agents, party organizers, advisers, liaisons, and activists in the women's movement alongside their "native" comrades, consolidating their links with the Greek Communist Party and with Greece. Soviet Greeks were critical to the development and running of the Greek sectors of the universities in the context of ongoing resources deficits—the dearth of qualified Greek teachers and administrators, typists and translators, a void that was increasingly filled by bilingual Soviet Greeks after the opening of the Greek sector of KUNMZ in 1928 and the MLS in 1932. Both Greek and Soviet Greek students worked as propagandists in the Greek settlements of the Soviet Union whose more prosperous *kulak* populations remained famously resistant and indeed hostile to the ideals and policies of the Revolution. In short, the Greek Cominternians were vital to the advancement of both the Greek communist and Soviet projects, forcing one to rethink the actors, the boundaries, and the geographies that shaped Greek and Soviet communism. A mere snapshot of the lives of these Greek Cominternians highlights the importance of shifting national boundaries, refugee flows, transnational connections, displacement, and identity in the development of the Greek communist movement. The history of Greek communism is nothing if not a transnational one.

The movement of refugees, casualties of protracted territorial conflict that defined the late Ottoman period, and the excesses of Greek and Turkish nationalism that turned Anatolian Greeks and Turkish Muslims into objects of exchange in 1922 revealed itself as inseparable from the history of Greek communism. The dominance of (male) refugees in the leadership of the Greek Communist Party from 1924 is well known if not well understood, as is the fact that many of these figures had attended the Comintern universities. But the female cohorts were also predominantly of refugee backgrounds—refugees from Asia Minor who had fled to Greece in the course of the Greco-Turkish War, or Soviet Greeks from the poorer ethnic Greek (Pontic) peasant communities of the Soviet Union, who had made Russia their homeland in the course of the conflict-ridden nineteenth and twentieth centuries. For the poorest among them, the Russian Revolution presented a new channel, an alternative pathway to survival, with new opportunities for education, work, and advancement that were especially inconceivable to female members caught in the vortex of poverty, hunger, displacement, and patriarchal culture. Examining the trajectories of these two groups brought together by communist ideology highlights the gender-inflected history of refugee radicalization in the history of transnational Greek communism between the wars, in terms of both push and pull factors. To be sure, communism's persistent patriarchal core remains in full view as class-based taxonomies of oppression and emancipation coexisted with hegemonic male dominated leadership, the pretense of gender "neutrality," and pervasive anti-feminism. On the other hand, war, displacement, and poverty had particular impacts on the (refugee) girls and women in both Greece and the Soviet Union that found synergies in the broader field of agency and social mobility offered to female activists and revolutionaries that was unique to communist membership.

The predominance of Anatolian Greek refugees in the history of Greek and Soviet communism invokes Philip Mansel's studies on the Greeks of

Smyrna, whose Greek identities were not shaped by nation-states, which, quoting Haddad, Mansel referred to as "prisons of the mind," even though Smyrna had become a hive of Greek nationalism.[5] Mansel's idea tempts one to speculate on a possible link between Levantine cosmopolitanism and the appeal of communism, that is, that ethnic Greek identity in hybrid or non-national contexts is naturally drawn or open to the internationalist dimensions of communism. But the subjects of this research, with the exception perhaps of Hatzivasiliou, who may have considered herself to be a Smyrniot, led lives that differed markedly to Mansel's wealthy cosmopolitans from Smyrna, Alexandria, Beirut, or Odessa, even though they too were Ottomans and Russian imperial subjects whose Greek identities were not boxed in by nationalist logic.

More pertinent to the relationship between refugees and interwar communism than the cosmopolitan character of their ancestral homelands were the radicalizing effects of poverty, displacement, and "identity vulnerability"; the combined experience of violent expulsion and displacement and the declining importance of religious identity in the post-Ottoman adoptive lands called into question many of the social and political givens of refugee culture and identity. Among the refugees transplanted into Greece after 1922 who also faced the brutal conditions of resettlement, youth were particularly vulnerable, caught between old and new, between childhood and adulthood, and treated ambivalently by both their own and native societies. The vast numbers of girls and young women in particular, who constituted the majority of the refugee industrial workforce, were among its most valuable yet most exploited members, with little or no representation as workers or citizens. The passage of refugee youth into the OKNE and the KKE suggests that the shocks of the post-1922 interwar environment presented a juncture for generating novel forms of thought and behavior, one capable of transforming identities.[6] The preponderance of refugees in the Greek sectors of the Comintern universities after 1924 corroborates the argument that (refugee) women and youth, whose political behavior as nonvoting citizens has long been overlooked in the scholarship, were an important and growing constituency for the Greek communist movement, a movement that, in turn, and unlike any other, energetically sought to mobilize and absorb them.

Menelaos Haralambidis has argued that the refugees of Asia Minor constituted the "steam engine" (*atmomichani*) of the Resistance against the Axis occupation of Greece, explaining that in Athens and Piraeus the majority of Resistance participants in the various organizations of the communist-led

EAM coalition were of refugee background. This was reflected in the number of casualties in the refugee communities, with the heaviest tolls exacted in the "red neighborhoods" of Kokkinia, Kaisariani, and Nea Ionia, as it was in the fact that the largest Nazi raids or roundups (*bloka*) took place in refugee suburbs that were EAM strongholds.[7] Likewise, Thessaloniki, one of the most industrialized cities of the Ottoman Empire, became a communist stronghold by virtue of the large labor force (industry, trade, and transportation) dominated by refugees after 1922 in conjunction with the long tradition of working-class and socialist politics.[8]

Haralambidis makes no mention, however, of one of the most defining features of the EAM Resistance movement—the unprecedented mass mobilization of women, many of them refugees, into all facets of the movement. In this book, I have hoped to convey that the mobilizational success of the EAM Resistance among women cannot be understood without taking into account the earlier interwar period. In a 1942 report, Theodoros Skaloubakas, an officer of the state security service stationed in Sochos, a regional unit of Thessaloniki, stated that his predecessor had left him a list of one thousand names of communist women operating in the region. After some further investigation, he discovered that many of the women had been placed on the list as children, some as young as twelve, all of them tobacco workers from the region who had entered the communist movement in the 1920s, all of them paying members of Ergatiki Boitheia.[9]

Between the wars, Greek and Soviet Greek communist women, many of them refugees, graduates of the Comintern's cadre universities assigned to or returning to Greece, invested more than a decade working as propagandists, provocateurs, and organizers of female industrial workers and students, effectively preparing the ground for the conflict to come. All female professional revolutionaries did their part for the women's movement (*gynaikeio kinima*), or "the work among women," on both Greek and Soviet soil, a contribution that varied in degree only. As the appointed leader of the Greek communist women's movement from 1943, Chrysa Hatzivasiliou stands virtually alone in the acknowledgment of her activism in this domain. But as she herself states in the 1946 essay:

> Today's armies of organized women have been formed in great part due to the considerable effort and sacrifice of communist men and women as individuals and as an organized collective. Party members endured long prison sentences and exiles, beatings, and assault in the effort to guide the female worker and the employee down the path that led to the committee,

to the struggle, and to her rights. . . . The daily systematic effort made to enlighten working women and girls about economic and political issues has freed them from the lethargy of social slavery and superstition. It awakened their political perception and judgement and played a part in shaping the new contemporary Greek woman, released from both suffragettism and from the traditional patriarchal custom of the medieval harem. The national liberation war further consolidated this new contemporary Greek woman.[10]

The extent of cadres' participation in the Resistance effort requires considerable research. The historical record acknowledges very little about Chrysa Hatzivasiliou despite her singular status and contributions to the Resistance, the communist movement, and the Party; Olga Bakola and Stella Kantzidou are referenced briefly in the odd communist memoir. This first examination into the long-obscured history of this earlier generation of communists does make clear that, far from a being a ragtag group affiliated loosely with the Party through friends and husbands, women were among the Party's first Moscow-trained professional revolutionaries, a group who helped define and indeed embodied the Party's revolutionary aspirations, shaped its transformation, and in the process, as I have shown in this book, transformed themselves. This vanguard, which had spent years working and organizing women in Greece (and in the Greek settlements of the Soviet Union) before the War, was nothing if not instrumental in preparing the ground for the KKE/EAM's staggering mobilizational success among women and men during the German occupation, a phenomenon that had dramatic and far-reaching consequences for the European twentieth century.

APPENDIX 1

KUTV Curriculum for Academic Year 1925/26

Given the focus of this book on education I have included a sample of the Comintern curriculum. This example, including a list of subjects offered and samples of content within some of those subjects, is from the first-Year KUTV curriculum, which outlines the subject areas and examples of subject content and knowledge requirements.[1]

Subjects Offered

1. Russian
2. Mathematics
3. Natural Sciences
4. Economic Geography
5. Political Economy
6. History of Social Forms
7. Russian and World History
8. History of RSDLP, Leninism, and Party-Building
9. Historical Materialism
10. Soviet System
11. Economic Policy
12. Party Work

I. Subject: Economic Geography

1. Physical and political map of the world (isotherms, active weather, minerals, main countries, changes after WWI, map of colonies before and after WWI).
2. Physical and administrative maps of USSR (rivers, seas, lakes, mountains, islands, and peninsulas; Soviet Republics, autonomous republics and regions, state borders of USSR and neighboring countries).

II. Subject: World Economy

1. Geographic and international division of labor: general factors.
2. Regions of production and consumption of coal, oil, iron ore, cotton, wheat, machinery, and textile. Methods of distribution of goods.
3. The principal countries producing of the above-mentioned goods.
4. The main types of countries. List the most important countries.
5. Most significant countries in world trade and capital exports.
6. The global market. How do world prices influence local production? How do world markets influence the global distribution of labor?
7. Which countries export capital and why do they do it? What is the essence of the export of capital? What are the implications for countries exporting capital and for countries importing capital?
8. The changes in world trade and export of capital after World War I.
9. Main railways in Europe, Asia, Africa, and America and their economic significance.
10. Main sea routes, ports, and canals.
11. The impact of colonial politics on the international division of labor.
12. The essence and general characteristics of the world economy.
13. Signs of growth in the world's economy.
14. The changes in the world's economy after WWI: total damages, losses, and gains, moving centers.
15. Business and political groups in the world's economy.

III. Subject: USSR

1. The role of the USSR on the world's economy.
2. Natural historical conditions of distribution of labor in USSR.

3. The type of national economy in the USSR.
4. In which direction—industrial or agricultural—did the national economy of the USSR develop?
5. Natural and labor resources for the development of the national economy in the USSR.
6. Main characteristics of industry and agriculture.
7. How did agriculture develop in the USSR? How did it change after the Great October Revolution?
8. Distribution of labor in the agricultural sector in the USSR.
9. Main regions in production of wheat, rye, barley, cotton, and flax.
10. Main herding areas and regions of livestock production.
11. Intensive and extensive economy.
12. The regions of intensive farming in USSR.
13. Main signs of class stratification in rural areas.
14. Comparison of the situation before and after the revolution.
15. What is the correct approach to the study of class stratification in the Soviet countryside?
16. Communication and interaction between agriculture and industry. The role of agriculture in the industrial development of this country.
17. Prewar and postwar industrial world: geographical and political factors. Industrial growth after the Revolution.
18. Geographical distribution and value of small industry.
19. Geographical distribution and value of iron ore industry and textile industry.
20. Main issues in the industry of USSR: geographic factors in industrial recovery.
21. Transport in USSR. Most common types of transport in USSR.
22. Main features of Soviet domestic and foreign trade. Major distribution centers.

REQUIRED SKILLS

1. Read complex tables.
2. Use statistics.
3. Read charts.
4. Figure out functional dependence on charts and statistical tables.
5. Search multiple sources.
6. Select relevant literature on simple economic issues
7. Plan and write theses, reports, etc.

IV. Subject: Russian Language

1. Relatively fluent reading, correct emphasis, and pronunciation.
2. Ability to read a text (up to two pages) and define the main idea. Create a precis. Ability to locate and express information relevant to the discussion themes.
3. Ability to read the text and to present an oral summary.
4. Written tasks: basic rules of spelling, word-building, and use of prepositions.
5. Basic rules of punctuation.

V. Subject: History of the Revolutionary Movement

A. BASIC FACTS OF THE HISTORY OF THE REVOLUTIONARY MOVEMENT AND VKP(B):

1. Liberation of the peasants.
2. Development of revolution after the Liberation.
3. Origins of the Russian Social Democratic Labor Party (RSDLP)
4. The Split in the Party (Bolsheviks versus Mensheviks)
5. The 9th of January.
6. General Strike.
7. December Uprising.
8. Slogans "Revolutionary-Democratic Dictatorship" and "8-Hour Working Day."
9. Liquidators (a faction of the Mensheviks in the RSDLP).
10. The Lena Execution.
11. Newspapers *Zvezda* and *Pravda*.
12. Imperialist War.
13. Turn from Imperialist War to Civil War.
14. February Revolution.
15. Duality of power: all power to the Soviets.
16. July Events.
17. October Revolution.
18. Decree of Peace and Land.

B. ABILITY TO CONNECT THE ABOVE NAMES AND FACTS WITH THE WAY THE PROLETARIAT AND ITS PARTY CAME TO POWER.

VI. Subject: History of Social Forms

Each student must be able to recognize main social forms of human development:

1. Prehistoric/primitive people.
2. Clan system.
3. Feudal system.
4. Trade capitalism.

Ability to answer the following about the listed societies:

1. Methods of economy management.
2. Economic structure.
3. Social structure.

VII. Subject: Natural Sciences

A. BIOLOGY

1. Clear understanding of metabolism.
2. Cell structure of the body.
3. Nutrition and physiological value of food. Nervous system.
4. Plant nutrition.
5. The role of solar energy.
6. Sexual reproduction and breeding.
7. Evidence of natural origins of life. Darwinism.
8. Who is the closest relative of humans?

B. PHYSICS AND CHEMISTRY

1. Physical concept of labor and methods of measurement of labor.
2. Understanding various kinds of energy, energy transfer, and energy conservation.
3. Methods of heat measurement.
4. Efficiency measuring.
5. Understanding the issue of electrification and its historical significance.

APPENDIX 2

The Greek Communist Party and the Woman Question (1946)

Chrysa Hatzivasiliou

General Observations

Before we engage our main theme, which is the position and actions taken by the KKE in respect to the social problem referred to as the "woman question," it is essential to look back upon the origins and evolution of the problem throughout the history of humankind.

It is not a new issue. It is as old as the separation of society into those who have the means of social production, social wealth, and social goods in their individual possession, in this way securing their own economic and political power. On the other hand, there are those people who work but do not own property; they are subordinated by necessity to the first group both economically and politically.

The social essence of the woman question is the subordinate position occupied by women in society as persons and as citizens. It is a status quo based on subjugation and oppression that has been imposed upon woman, which has lowered her status to one laden with obligations but no rights.

This condition of women evolved alongside class divisions that emerged in human society during the primitive phases of its organization.

Historically, it is long beyond dispute that when the economic and productive role of men in primitive society was established, matriarchal right was abolished, and with it the rights of women. Ever since, the subjugation and oppression of women has undergone different stages according to economic development and the shifting nature of class society. In essence, however, it has not changed, as the original cause has not changed. That is, the organization of society on the basis of class exploitation and oppression, and the exploitation of the weak by the strong, continues.

Engels states:

> The subversion of matriarchal right signaled the world historical defeat of the female gender. Man took the wheel in his hands even within the home, woman was humiliated, subjugated, became a slave of his whim and a tool of reproduction. This humbled condition of women, which revealed itself primarily amongst Greeks of the heroic and moreso the classical period, was glorified and concealed bit by bit, assuming various forms but never abandoned. (Engels, *Origins of the Family*, 1945, p. 84)[1]

The subversion of women's power during the first steps of human history is justified (by advocates of women's enslavement) on the basis of noneconomic and ahistorical causes, and theories of women's "bodily and biological inferiority," of "intellectual inferiority and disability."

In this way [they] separate this social problem from society and sociology and place it in the realm of biology. They take this problem as a permanent and unchangeable given, and regard it as natural that women retain the status of second-class human beings forever, regardless of economic and social conditions. These perceptions, however, are losing ground daily when confronted with the findings presented by scientific research and the study of social phenomena.

The subjugation of women was a direct consequence of the change in the economic organization of the human race and coincides with the appearance of class stratification. In the same book Engels states: "The first class antagonism that appeared in history coincided with the growth of competition between men and women ... and the first instance of class oppression was the oppression of the feminine by the masculine."

With the passage of time and social progress, the subjugation of women has changed form. From femicide and the medieval harem, from her blatant position as subservient beast of burden in the villages, she passes to a covert and refined subjugation within the bourgeois home. Here her humble position is gilded with the eternal appearance of equality in the family, but it is entirely dependent on the good will and character of the husband and head of household. But if, for whatever reason, family relations are strained, the position of women in law and society is brought into clear focus. It is then that woman finds herself totally unprotected, vulnerable to the whims of her husband who has every right to humiliate her as a person and even as a mother. The law was made to serve the interests of men who possess economic might and power. The law rests on the belief that woman is a natural slave and servant of man, cast aside by social production and by life itself.

But just as economic factors determined the subjugation of women, so too have economic factors eased manifestations of this slavery and servitude. Economic factors have substantially changed the position of women in production and in the home, despite the fact that the laws of this class society continue to uphold a partial view of woman, even in instances where her political equality is recognized.

We can thus conclude that since the commune constituted the basic unit of early human social production, woman, who oversaw the process, was a crucial cog in the wheel of social production and a key economic entity with analogous rights and access to power. With the development of technologies came the separation of the workplace from the home; people became involved in agriculture and stockbreeding and the home lost its social character to become an auxiliary sphere dependent on the means of social production. Women who were involved only in the home thereafter stopped playing a crucial role in social production and thus became subservient to the person who possessed productive power, that is, man. However, with the continuing tide of technological innovation and economic development, women's work became essential once again to the means of social production. The new era in textiles and handicrafts—which emerged with industrialization—was in dire need of women's contributions. The productive potential of women was pushed into the marketplace; the entry of women into the economic zone paved their way to freedom and independence. Economic independence leads to political and social freedom and emancipation. This is precisely why the systematic organized movement for the rights of women emerged after women entered the workforce and became decisive actors in the economic life of society.

This movement formed a part of a general uprising staged by the new bourgeoisie against the feudal order; it began with the French Revolution of 1789 and continued intensely and diffusely into the nineteenth century. By the middle of the nineteenth century, in various countries of Europe and North America a movement for the rights of women had fully emerged that called itself feminism.

The aims and ambitions of this movement, despite its excesses and the diatribes against men in its early phase, and the capitulation implicit in its separation of the woman question from the totality of social problems as if it were a self-contained question, framed [the issue] within the context of the same democratic system that had defined equality and freedom in relation to only half of humanity in the first place. Because feminism did not place the women's question correctly within a broader social context or consider the problem in historical terms—genesis, evolution, and eradication—it is the product or outcome of an injustice it cannot even explain. In this way the woman question has been left flapping in the wind, ostracized from broader society. The movement could only see resolution as far as obtaining the right of women to vote, that is, in legislative reform. Feminism did not even try to approach the root of the problem, which lies in the way that the relations of social production have been constituted, that is, on the basis of class segregation. Feminism thus was and is a reformist movement operating within the constraints of the capitalist status quo. Its aims and content therefore accept the terms and serve the interests of capitalism. Without wishing to reduce its progressive role, its powerful articulation of the problem of women in the public arena, we cannot ignore the contradiction feminism embodies, its internal inconsistencies and tensions, and the reactionary class interests it serves. The liberation and emancipation of women is limited by the extent to which it complements or interferes with the interests of the capitalist oligarchy.

The socialist movement that emerged alongside feminism had a correct and clear perception of the woman question from the outset. It sees the woman question as a social phenomenon with historic significance. Socialism has considered this question from its genesis to its eradication and shaped an approach to the problem within a broad reformist social movement. Without ceasing to organize and mobilize working women around their direct economic and political interests, around the essential reforms that enable them to tear away from the capitalist status quo, the socialist movement dissolved all the delusions spread by feminism, enlightened by a scientific social analysis of the woman question. It was not detached from the general struggle of the exploited and the oppressed, envisaging a restructuring of society free of exploitation and oppression. The rationality of this approach is demonstrated clearly in the situation women in the urban centers of the Soviet Union found themselves during the interwar period.

There were countries in Europe in which the reformist aims of feminism held sway for a considerable period. In pre-war Germany, Austria, and democratic Spain, the political rights of women had been recognized. But when a more reactionary capitalist regime took power in fascist form, the fragility and instability of those reforms became apparent. "Back to the kitchen!" was the key fascist slogan directed at women. This was realized, although not substantially, because women's contribution to the war economy under fascism became essential. However, fascism did abolish all of women's formal economic, political, and legal rights.

At the same time in the Soviet Union, where socialism was being implemented, the woman question was resolved politically, legally, and economically without reservation and fractiousness, with all the radical open-handedness of the social revolution, from the very first day that the power of the workers was established. All the humiliating laws that shaped public and private life, even in the most progressive democratic countries, were dismantled, and the systematic effort of state and society began to raise the status of woman politically, professionally, and intellectually so that she can stand side by side with man as his equal, across all the realms and manifestations of social life.

In speech made by Lenin at a women's conference in Moscow in 1919, he stated:

> All the bourgeois liberation movements dating back tens and hundreds of years were defined by the demand to abolish archaic laws, and to institute legal equality between men and women. But not even one of these democratic countries, not even the most progressive democracies realized this demand. Because where capitalism dominates, where individual ownership of land, factories, and businesses remains paramount, where capital continues to dictate, men will always seek to preserve their privileges and rights.

The Soviet government, as a government of the workers, realized within the first months of its power the most radical transformation of the law as it pertained to women. Not a single law that kept women in a secondary position was left standing in the Soviet Union. I am speaking exclusively about those laws that used the social vulnerability of women to keep them in a convenient and often humiliating position, such as the laws around divorce, children out of wedlock, and the right of women to ask for support from the father of their children. Lenin continued in his speech: "The status of women from the perspective of legal and political rights in the Soviet Union must appear ideal to even the most progressive states. Yet we know very well that this is just the beginning" (Clara Zetkin, *Lenin on the Woman Question*, 55).

The current postwar situation of women in various countries only reinforces the Soviet perspective. At this time reforms in women's rights have become even more radical and profound in the countries where power has passed into the hands of workers, where democracy is not limited to political but also to social content, for example, in the People's Democratic Republics of southeastern Europe.

The only conclusion that can be drawn from this state of affairs is that the rights and accomplishments of women, the reforms that women achieve in their struggle within a capitalist paradigm, can only be fortified, stabilized, and deepened; the social problem of women's inferiority can only begin to be redressed radically and substantially if it is combined with the struggle for broader radical change in society.

The Woman Question in Greece

Following the general synopsis of this social problem, we can examine the specific case of Greece.

THE ECONOMIC SOCIAL AND POLITICAL STATUS OF GREEK WOMEN

In modern Greece women continue to occupy the position that the (Asiatic) eastern past bestowed upon her—Asiatic civilization in conjunction with Byzantine Roman law.

Economic development has, of course, disturbed many of the social preconceptions and many of the backward traditions and customs. In law, however, as regards the rights of women, the medieval Byzantine code of law still applies.

Even today, after so many legal reforms have been instituted across Europe, North America, and in Asia, in Greece, according to the current civil code—whether it is the modified version of the Sofoulis government or the interpretation of the 4th of August dictatorship before it (an interpretation embraced by the current government)—Greek women carry the status they occupied in Roman law. That is, [they carry] the status of minors or intellectually disabled persons.

But Greek women are a critical constituency in our national economy. From the time of the Balkan Wars to the present, Greek women as a group have stormed the realm of production in factories, offices, freelance professions, trade. Their role in the productive power of the nation is ever-expanding. The most important sectors of our industry, predominantly light industry (textiles, tobacco, chemical, and confectionary) all rely on female labor power. The 1928 census indicates the number of working women in urban and rural centers at 633,435, of whom 99,712 are involved in industry, 434,623 in agriculture, and the rest in public service jobs, paid domestic labor, etc.

The statistical service of IKA (the largest social security organization in Greece) in 1940 calculated the number of insured women working in industry and offices, excluding public servants, domestic servants, and villagers, to be 142,000.

Evelpides' book *Agriculture in Greece* states that the participation of women in the agricultural sector, in accordance with 1939 figures, amounts to approximately seventy-five million drachmae in women's *merokamata* [remuneration for a day's work] and ninety-four million in male *merokamata*.

In arboriculture [*dendrokomia*] 28,736,000 out of a total 59,181,000 *merokamata* is the product of female labor, that is, approximately 48.5 percent. In livestock breeding, out of 103,082,000 *merokamata*, 32,368,000 are female labor-based, that is, approximately 31.4 percent. In the agricultural cottage industry, we have 12.7 million drachmae worth of *merokamata* in female labor; only 2.7 million is the outcome of male labor.

In the professions, in freelance work, the public service, etc., women's participation is essential and significant. But the neo-Hellenic state that has developed on undemocratic foundations has impeded every progressive development. It has naturally made no exception in relation to the lot of women.

We cannot view the problems of women's status separately from the social totality that took root in our land as soon as the popular democratic movement of 1821 was snuffed out, and a Bavarian absolutist administration under Otto was imposed, assisted by foreign—mainly British—interests. This turn of events signaled the defeat of progressive forces in the new Greek nation and the reinstatement of conservative regressive elements. The social development of Greece was struck down by moral lapse. It was derailed from the course followed by the liberal bourgeois democracies of Europe before it. Instead, it took the road of feudal subservience to the rich landed classes [*kotsabasides*] who continued to rule Greece in the post-revolutionary period. These are the roots of Greek women's subordinate status today.

This economic and political compromise made by weak and foreign-worshipping Greek capital, its subservience to contemporary reactionary forces, both local and foreign, determined our evolution as a nation. A tortuous evolution full of back-and-forth movements. This weighed and continues to weigh disastrously on the elevation and emancipation of women in Greece.

The Bavarian administration, the plutocratic oligarchy, guardian of powerful interests, cultivated the Megale Idea chimera—the resuscitation of the Byzantine Empire. Part of this irredentist political program drew on ancestral glories, thus seducing the people and deflecting their attention from urgent domestic issues. In this way ancient customs and traditions in law and in every political realm, every anachronism and superstition, was cultivated and legitimated. On February 23, 1836, by Royal Decree, the Byzantine civil code (Roman law) regulated relations between individuals. This law, which regulated relations between citizens in the Byzantine Middle Ages, was to govern relations in the neo-Hellenic monarchy of the nineteenth century, the century that was defined elsewhere in Europe by national liberation and democratization. This Byzantine law, as is well known, classified women as inferior beings, accorded them a "diminished personal status" [*meiomeni prosopiki katastasi*]. The strangulation of the progressive forces of 1821 thus determined the status of Greek women whose legal expression was formulated on principles governing the medieval harem. Women did not enjoy a human status within the family or society. All the laws and many of the customs offended women's basic human dignity. Women's life and fate was determined and governed by their brothers and fathers in the paternal home, or by the husband, the master, within the marital home. Furthermore, as the political formation of the Greek state and foreign oppression impeded the growth of industry, of wealth-generating resources, and our economic progress, Greek women too were deprived of playing an independent role in economic development and production for the longest time. Their participation in cottage industry and the agricultural economy, which has been significant and serious, as we have seen, is still stifled by the structure of the small household, a structure that continues to dominate the agricultural economy. Statistics of 1929 indicate that 37 percent of agricultural households have between a quarter acre and 2.5 acres of land [1 and 10 *stremmata*] of land, and 35 percent of households/businesses have between 11 and 30 *stremmata*. This rigid economic scale (agricultural household) plays a restrictive role in social production. Small-scale cultivation of whichever type, and the dated technology, usury, et cetera., do not allow for significant trade potential; trade is restricted within the narrow boundaries of the closed economy, that is, of the household itself, which barely generates enough income to cover its own needs.

Women in these households, besides carrying out work in the fields and tending to the animals, also need to cover the basic domestic needs of the family members, such as clothing. If things were different, that is, if the harvest was greater for the market and industrial products were cheaper, they would get these goods from the market. But this could only happen if we had industry. Had industry been allowed to develop unimpeded, it would not have invited antisocial protective measures that impede consumption and cripple our national economy. There would be no vast gulf between the prices of agricultural and industrial products which make the latter inaccessible to farmers. In these conditions of small-scale agricultural production, the emergence of women as an independent productive force is stifled. This economic backwardness is the root cause of women remaining in the home as the slaves of regressive custom and superstition, the objects of legal humiliation.

The brilliant contribution of women to the national liberation movement of 1821, their unrivaled collective and individual heroism, was buried in the reactionary darkness that snuffed out the national democratic uprising of the nation. The military heroism of Tsavelaina, Bouboulina, Harikleia Daskalaki, Haido, Despo, and so many other women of Mani, Roumeli, Macedonia, Zaloggo, Kiougi, Arkadi, Naoussa—all these bright pages in our national struggle were written with the collective sacrifice of the women of Greece, alongside and equal to men. But they were not enough to break down the wall of medieval Byzantine superstition and perception that isolated Greek women from the public realm and made of them social outcasts, disinherited them in the newly formed Greek state.

Greek women lived in the darkness of illiteracy and ignorance. Only in 1837 did the Philo-educational Society [Philekpaideftiki Etaireia] found the first schools for girls in Athens; in 1885 girls were allowed into the University of Athens, recall the pioneering Panayiotatou sisters. The family home was constantly preoccupied with the problem of raising the dowry for the family's "undesirable" females. Lament and mourning would fill the home, dramas would ensue when the misfortune of a female child—*tsoupa* rather than *paidi*—was inflicted on the family. Common illiteracy, which continues to afflict our nation, impacts far worse on women. Before the recent war 57.45 percent of the female population was completely illiterate, 69 percent semiliterate.

In the nineteenth century this was the predicament of the majority of Greek women. In countries where the chains of feudalism had been broken and liberal bourgeois democracies were being established, a women's movement—feminism—emerged, which pursued reforms, especially equal political rights, that would improve the status of women. As we have seen, the French Revolution of 1789 had addressed the issue of women's parity, and the subsequent industrial development of Europe and America strengthened and spread this principle. In the nineteenth century the granting of political rights to women had already commenced. In 1848 the first feminist conference took place in America.

These economic and political conditions were not yet present in Greece. Several progressive and virtuous women who understood that women's situation was closely related to a general need for democratization played a significant role behind the political scene without forming a specific women's movement. For example, Kaliope Papalexopoulou, the widow of a senator of 1821, following the heroic contributions of women in 1821, played a great role in politics. She took a very active part in the organization of the anti-Otto uprising of 1862, for which she was recognized and honored by the people as an equal to her male counterparts upon visiting Athens.

However, as industrial development lagged behind in Greece, the terrain was not fertile for a serious women's movement, for European-style feminism. Trade-brokered capitalism in Greece, subservient to foreign capital, was satisfied with its parasitic profits and did not pursue greater industrial development. Every progressive initiative was snuffed out from its very beginnings. By extension, the preconditions for the development of a strong and broad feminist movement were hampered, if not impossible.

In 1836 Panayiotis Sofianopoulos supported the emancipation of women in his newspaper *Proodos* [Progress]. He was a lone voice in the desert. Much later, after the collapse of the Bavarian administration, a group of progressive women began to form a women's movement; the negative reaction was much greater than anything witnessed in more economically and politically developed countries. In conclusion we can say that addressing the woman question in Greece as a social problem was impeded in the same way that our general social development was, by the conditions created in Greece by antinational politics defined by foreign subservience and perpetrated by a reactionary plutocratic oligarchy.

GREEK FEMINISM

Kallirhoe Parren (née Siganou) from Rethymno, Crete, was the first woman who seriously and systematically undertook the task of organizing a feminist movement in Greece. In 1888 she established *Efimeris ton Kyrion* [The ladies newspaper] and founded several women's organizations, such as the Union of Greek Women in 1879 and the Greek Women's Lyceum in 1911. Regardless of the direction Parren's feminist movement took, its historical significance in Greece is beyond dispute. Kallirhoe Parren articulated the woman question in a systematic fashion before a hostile public comprising men and women who were blinded by tradition and superstition. With the passage of time and in the face of the unrelenting reaction that Greek feminism endured, feminism's progressive message assumed a quieter tone until it was silenced completely by compromise and capitulation to Byzantine anachronisms. In her final years, Parren was forced to abandon her calls for political equality completely and became preoccupied with philanthropic and cultural pursuits. She made feminism so unrecognizable that it was eventually applauded even by Achilleas Kyrou on the fiftieth anniversary of her political career, during the Metaxas dictatorship.[2] The Greek Women's Lyceum of today has been transformed into a center of social display for our royalist "aristocracy." Nevertheless, the efforts of Parren constituted a milestone and must be regarded as a significant turning point in the history of Greek women's struggle for their human rights.

The other feminist organizations, the National Council (est. 1918) and the League for the Rights of Women (est. 1920), were and remain more progressive. They emerged in an era marked by intense social and political turbulence, both within Greece and globally. They emerged alongside the victorious uprising of socialism following the First World War, which could not but have an impact on their programs and actions, no matter how foreign and distant from socialism these organizations were. These organizations pursued the rights of women with greater courage and decisiveness, but the outcome of their efforts was poor, precisely because they did not understand deeply enough the spirit of their times and relied instead on outmoded feminist dogmas that separated the women's movement from broader social issues. The conclusion to draw from studying the history of Greek feminism is that, in Greece, this bourgeois liberal movement had the same fate as other liberal agendas of the Greek bourgeois class. Feminism in Greece remained an inferior imitation of the European intellectual spirit;

a genuine, indigenous, progressive spirit could not emerge and flourish in Greece under the prevailing economic and political conditions.

THE WORKERS' MOVEMENT AND THE WOMAN QUESTION

During precisely the same period that Greek feminism struggled in the swamp waters of Greek underdevelopment [nineteenth century and the interwar period], attempting to remain autonomous but without a solid orientation, situated outside the social currents that shook the era, and faithful to the feminist dogma of separatism, a workers movement was emerging in our country. It was both professional and political, free of the utopian socialist and anarchist pretensions of its earlier phase in the second half of the nineteenth century. This movement aimed to lead the democratic reconstruction of modern Greek society and abolish every medieval reaction and anachronism. The workers movement of our country, from its inception, cultivated new progressive political and social customs and morals. Its view of the woman question as a social problem was clear and decisive. It was a view that came from a scientific engagement with the problem.

In November 1918 the political organization of the Greek working class was founded, the Socialist Workers Party of Greece [SEKE], which later became the Communist Party of Greece [KKE; 1925]. Its establishment signaled that the working class of our country had begun the process of their emancipation from the politics of the plutocratic parties. It signaled that the multifaceted struggle for a progressive democratic and socialist restructuring of society, for a genuine neo-Hellenic renaissance, shifted to the hands of the classes whose interests coincide with historic progress, with national improvement, a movement in the hands, that is, of working people.

All the economic, political, and ideological problems of our nation, which the vain plutocratic oligarchy and representatives of Byzantism and miserable irredentism wished to bury, flowed out of the time-machine and saw the light of science, and were offered to the lancet of sociological examination. Nor, of course, was the woman question left unexamined. The political party of the working people presented a clear position on this problem and its resolution, as well as on the direct economic and political reforms that needed to be instituted, based on scientific research and analysis.

The struggle for the rights of women is a part of the struggle for the abolition of every exploitation and oppression in society. It is a pillar of the struggle for the abolition of today's class status quo and mode of production, and for the establishment of people's power, of socialism. With their broad participation in production—industrial, textile, and agricultural—Greek women have proven to be the essential ally in the daily struggle of workers to better their existence. With their numerical strength, efficiency, and energy, their influence in the family and on their children, their ideological and spiritual formation, working women are the critical allies and guardians of every progressive struggle for reform.

Lenin told Clara Zetkin that if we did not have Russia's women, the proletarian women of Moscow and Saint Petersburg, it would be very difficult to win, it would have been impossible to win. The KKE, from its inception, stated its position clearly: the direct struggle for the economic and political rights of women, the recognition of parity of citizenship [*isotimias kai isopoliteias ton gynaikon*], were basic principles of its program. This position differentiated the Party from the other parties of the plutocracy, which to this day have not recognized these rights. This difference between the KKE and the other parties would not be substantial or serious if the decisions and declarations of the KKE were not accompanied by the practical measures necessary to realize the passions and aims of Greek women, so as to enable Greek women to organize and mobilize themselves politically. No representative body of the KKE in twenty-eight years of its history has ever neglected to state the importance of special organizational and enlightenment work that needs to be carried out among Greek women, the importance of monitoring and supporting local party organizations to support the forward march of Greek women.

During the elections of 1920, the still-young KKE put forward the political rights of women as a central plank of their platform; the call for "the hammer and sickle and the vote for the skirt," could be heard clearly alongside other matters during the independent pre-election uprising of the workers and the people. The KKE newspaper *Rizospastis*, in 1920 ran a series of articles on the woman question. The articles were written by Ioanna Komioti, a member of the Party. These articles do not just express her own view but the view of the Party on the woman question, which Komioti placed in its proper sociological context. The articles argue that "the vote is not the ideal for the working woman. It does not symbolize her liberation. The main issue that concerns her most of all is the social problem in its entirety."

The perseverance of the Party toward the specific goal of organizing and mobilizing women became greater and more systematic after 1927. From the 4th Congress onward, there would be no Party organization that did not address the matter, nor a Party decision that did not recognize that the organizational and political work that needed to be done to mobilize and politicize women, especially working women, lagged well behind. Let us refer to some of these agenda items despite the fact that they seem identical, because they show that the woman question is not only included in the Party agenda but is inseparable from it.

> The Party must systematize its work with women workers and with women in general, and must allocate sufficient resources to this purpose (4th Congress).
>
> a) Combating the indifference toward organizing the women's movement.
> b) Founding female committees from the center and local organizations.
> c) Encouraging the participation of women in factions [*fraxies*] and particularly within the trade unions that have a lot of women.
> d) Establishing a central publication for the women's movement (organizational decision of 1928).

The Communist International emphasized the following:

> Our neglect of women and the recruitment of women to the Party must be considered a typical expression of opportunism [*opportounismos*]. The fact that women dominate in an entire realm of production and that conditions in those areas are far below those of any other spheres of the working class points to the responsibility and duty of the Party and the trade unions to address this opportunistic devaluing of their work, and to pay attention to their organization. (5 March 1932, decision of the 4th plenary session of the Party)
>
> One of our weakest points is the recruitment of women workers into the Party, and our work among them. Tobacco workers, textiles workers, farm laborers, etc., compose vast and dynamic sectors of the Greek proletariat that we need to turn our attention to. (Organizational decision March 1932)
>
> We dictate a radical shift in our work among women and against the undervaluing of this work. (6th Plenary Session, 1934)

> We must heighten awareness in the Party, among cadres, about women workers and working youth who compose a massive majority of the exploited workforce in this country; without their loyalty and support we cannot claim to represent and support the working class. Today's pre-war and tomorrow's wartime situation beg the question more sharply than ever. No more delay, no more undervaluing and neglect can be allowed or accepted. (5th Conference, March 1934, organizational decision)

We observe thus that from 1934 onward, the Party adopted a crystal-clear perspective on the critical role to be played by women in the new war. In the election programs of the United Front and the Popular Front, where the KKE played a decisive role, the question of the political equality of women was clearly articulated, a principle absent from any other political program of the day. Furthermore, in September 1935, when the fascist intentions of the plutocratic oligarchy became apparent and the KKE prepared the Greek people to resist these plans, the participation of women in the antifascist struggle was emphasized. The decision of the 4th Plenary Session of the Party in September 1935 stated:

> For the successful struggle against fascism, the attack of capital, and the danger of war, the United People's Front demands the force of the nation's women. A serious obligation of the KKE is to achieve the formation of a united front of all antifascist elements across women's organizations, and to utilize all manner of organizational strategy to bring the thousands of women workers to the forefront of the antifascist struggle.

The specific political claims of women—parity and full citizenship—were and are synonymous with the democratization of social and political life. Women had to become an active militant force in the struggle for democracy, to become daring and fearless warriors against fascism, which brought back the Middle Ages with its raw primitiveness. For women this was encapsulated in the fascist slogan—"Women, back to the home!" Thus, the participation of women in the antifascist struggle was an issue that concerned the KKE, and as a result the cause of antifascist struggle and democracy has made considerable inroads into the world of women. The serious and united response by women against the fascist dictatorship both before and after its establishment, their courage in the face of persecution and pursuit, imprisonment, and torture by the Metaxas-Glucksburg axis is not unrelated to the work undertaken by KKE to engage the female population of Greece. Indeed, it is a direct outcome of this commitment.

From all we have discussed here, it becomes clear that the leadership of the Party, as well as its local branches, did not limit themselves to tokenistic calls for the recognition of Greek women's rights. They did not sit back and relax after measures and decisions were merely announced, but instead tirelessly went to work to organize, mobilize, and politicize the female population of our country.

The continuous monitoring of this work shows, as indicated in the quotations above, that our efforts are not as urgent and systematic as they ought to be. And these observations are not merely sterile, nagging criticism. They are an expression of the constant uneasiness of the communist in the face of what (he) knows he has to do. They are an expression of his "never rest" principle (as a communist's work is never done). Every such observation marks a new alert for the awakening of Greek women from the sociopolitical lethargy to which she was condemned by centuries-long slavery and exclusion. It signaled to communists a new urge for a new assault on the wall of segregation and exclusion long justified by an outdated, backward perception that sought to keep women out of public life. The effort toward the political and social awakening of Greek women was harder than the equivalent campaign in other countries, by virtue of our general economic and political backwardness relative to those countries, which I have discussed above.

Thanks to the systematic and tireless daily organizational and enlightenment work undertaken by the KKE, working women have begun to sense their place, to become politically conscious, and to fill the ranks of trade unions and other workers' organizations. Wages, working hours, social welfare for mothers and children, and employer's threats are all issues of concern for women, which nurture their new political conscience and their appetite for struggle.

Women workers and employees, members of KKE, found themselves in the front lines of the struggle to help raise the consciousness of other working women, to help them defy employers' threats and blackmail, and to cease being easy prey for exploitation and becoming, without wishing to, the cause of a general fall in wages.

Today's armies of organized women have been formed in great part due to the considerable effort and sacrifice of communist men and women as individuals and as an organized collective. The least of what they endured was being fired and condemned to hunger. But this was not all. They were also confronted by the standover men of employers, and by paid parastate militants who unleashed the entire spectrum of evil against them. Party members endured long prison sentences and exiles, beatings, and assaults in the effort to guide the female worker and the employee down the path that led to the committee, to the struggle, and to her rights.

In parallel with this tireless attempt to mobilize the working women of Greece around their economic interests, was the effort to help them get their political bearings. The daily systematic effort made to enlighten working women and girls about economic and political issues has freed them from the lethargy of social slavery and superstition. It awakened their political perception and judgement and played a part in shaping the new contemporary Greek woman, released from both suffragettism and from the traditional patriarchal custom of the medieval harem. The national liberation war further consolidated this new contemporary Greek woman.

It is without doubt that the inclusive multidimensional national resistance movement of our people places it among the frontline antifascist movements of the world. The occupiers and abolishers of national freedom and independence were not fought with arms alone by the Greek people. They were also fought with other forms of collective and individual action, which proved to be singularly effective in the global antifascist war. In our country, whenever the occupiers were found outside their quisling circles and the small number of their paid collaborators, they found themselves in a very hostile environment; they were obliged to be perpetually on guard.

They confronted scowling, scornful, and categorical hatred everywhere. Greek women were first and foremost in this arena of national resistance. They occupied the brightest pages of our national history but also the history of antifascism in the world. They were equal to men in all the facets of the national liberation war, and through their participation earned public recognition and appreciation. With their militancy, self-sacrifice, and self-denial, they smashed and dismantled the last vestiges of superstition; they caused a general progressive upheaval in the mentality of our people. The dynamism and value of women's intervention in public life has become so entrenched that the opposing perceptions of neofascist politicians seem positively foreign before public opinion. The KKE is proud for having played a significant role in women's political awakening and maturity.

As is well known, the KKE took the initiative in the organization of the national liberation front, placing all of its political influence and organizational might at its disposal. The organizational nucleus also comprised female cadres with considerable political and organizational experience in both legal and clandestine political activism and a belief in the struggle of the good and the just, an indomitable will and perseverance.

From the moment of its inception, EAM voiced its respect for the rights of women and invited them to join the struggle for our national liberation. EAM recognized this equality in rights and obligations and helped to draw women into all the facets of the national liberation war, from the simplest of relief work to the most dangerous of missions. The power of the people, which EAM established, finally recognized and incorporated officially the human rights of women, declaring women equal citizens of the Greek state. Greek women held administrative positions in local self-government. They organized whole sectors of the national liberation struggle, and in some sectors, female action and initiative dominated. In this limitless and equal field of activism, the Greek women of 1941 to 1945 smashed their own sense of inferiority, inherited from age-old servitude. In the course of daily struggle and sacrifice, their hesitancy retreated, as did a lack of trust in themselves and in their strength. The demands of the struggle were inexorable. Whoever decided to fight had to fight with their all, beyond their all. There were moments in which unpredictable factors arose and demanded daring initiatives without hesitation. Women who found themselves in positions of responsibility often had to confront these issues alone or the mission would be compromised, or the opportunity to hit the enemy would be lost. This forced women to rely on their own strengths, and with each such confrontation, confidence and faith in their capabilities and value grew.

The KKE did not cease to encourage and protect this trajectory of Greek women toward their own social and political liberation. This destination remained a Party-political goal. At the Panhellenic Conference of the Party (December 1942), as well as at the 10th Plenary Session (January 1944), the shift in the political trajectory of Greek women brought on by the national struggle was articulated. The decision of the 10th Plenary stated:

> For the first time in Greek history, the working women of Greece and all women participated in a national and popular struggle on a mass scale. The tens of thousands of members of KKE and the hundreds of thousands of members in the national liberation organizations make quite clear the readiness of Greek women to fight for a free and new Greece in which they will be equals. Our duty is to push women boldly to leadership positions, to guide their consciousness in an organized way into the great struggle.

Due to the tireless efforts of the KKE, the most committed militants of the towns and villages joined its ranks. The proportion of women in those villages is 20 percent of the total membership. Even though this figure does not meet the goals set by the Party, it is still very significant, an indicator of the extent of social and political change, and the shakeup that occurred these last years among the female population. Women themselves have recognized that the KKE has helped and continues to help them fulfill their potential. It is no accident that the most formidable of women fighters struggling for progress and justice emerged from conservative families with archaic traditions and perceptions about women; they are among the strongest and most valued members of the KKE. It is no longer rare for a man to be conservative, and worse still, a reactionary, an X agent or a monarchist, and as a consequence, for the women to be independent and democratic, for a brother and father to be X agents, and for the girl of the house to be in EPON.[3] These are all signs of the times, symptomatic of the deep changes that have occurred in the political and social mentality of women. This change did not occur spontaneously or by the mere passage of time. Rather, it is in the first instance, the outcome of conscious, persistent, daily, systematic, organizational political and enlightenment work carried out by our Party since the moment of its founding twenty-eight years ago.

The majority of female victims of this struggle for freedom and independence were communists. This shows that the role KKE played in Greek women's assumption of their heroic place in the pantheon of antifascist heroes is formidable.

Recall Electra and her contempt for her fascist torturers—with her fearlessness in the face of death she became a symbol of fighting valor [*agonistki levendia*], of sacrifice for higher human ideals that transcends Greek borders. Electra was a true child of KKE; KKE nurtured her and cultivated those ideals in her. Behind Electra stands Maro Mastraka, Kaiti Douka, Diamando Stathopoulou, Koula Soulioti, Kaiti Vitilia, and so many other famous and nameless heroines of our people, in the towns and the villages, who were all members and cadres of KKE.

As KKE was able to produce such heroic personalities and such women, it stands to reason that it was also instrumental in helping bring about change in the backward mentality of the male population of this country toward women, and in cultivating the ideological environment that made the recognition of women's equality as citizens possible. The radiance of women's sacrifice and the heroic virtues of communist women who fell for freedom and independence enthuses our female population and disarms every trace of stubborn backward skepticism.

Following the dark turn in the political situation of our country with the foreign invasion of December 1944, and predicting the neofascist currents of the post-December status quo, our Party emphasized to all its representative bodies a renewed focus on the female population of the country. The decision taken at the 11th Plenary Session of the Party (April 1945) states:

> The long national liberation struggle welcomes a new progressive force to the political stage, the mass political activism of women. The mass participation of women in all facets of the national liberation struggle—strikes, demonstrations, sabotage, and guerrilla warfare—has raised the militancy and activism of the nation to a new level. Women constitute a very serious force in the victory of the democratic struggle and the renaissance of Greece. The fascist reaction will do all it can to retract all the democratic rights women have gained during this period of national liberation struggle and to condemn them anew to illiteracy and obscurity from every political and progressive activity. The Party must intensify its efforts to develop and fortify the participation of women in all facets of the sociopolitical life of the country, equal to men.

The 12th Plenary Session of the Party stated as follows:

> Greek women will gain the same political and economic rights as men. There can be no popular democracy without the emancipation of women. The Greek mother will be protected so as she can give birth and raise her children without care or worry. Our working women will receive equal pay for equal work. Alongside male youth, female youth will also be released from heavy and unhygienic work that harms their health.

The foreign invasion of our country has temporarily interrupted our smooth democratic evolution. If this had not occurred and things evolved naturally as in all the other liberated countries, the women of Greece would be enjoying the rights and status they had gained and that were recognized by the people's government during the occupation. Women would be an active group in the economic reconstruction and in the political and moral regrouping of our country, as they are elsewhere in Europe. The woman question would have been integrated along with all the other democratic problems of our country into a program for its final and decisive resolution. Popular democracy would have taken all the economic, political, social, and intellectual measures necessary to free women not just at the level of discourse but also in practice, from slavery in employment, in the home, in law and society. Recognition would not be limited to formal parity and equal citizenship but would entail creating the conditions necessary for the successful realization of these legal rights.

Above all, the economic and social program of popular democracy would secure women's economic emancipation from the male head of household. Economic emancipation from men forms the foundation of women's social liberation. Equal pay for equal work. Social welfare measures that secure women and children from hunger, unemployment, and sickness create the conditions for a civilized and carefree life for subsequent generations. Educational institutions that offer women the capacity to cultivate their abilities, to build careers in all the realms of economic and social life as workers, technicians, skilled professionals, intellectuals, et cetera, would slowly and steadily close the gap between the achievement of men and women caused by historic political and social factors.

Since popular democracy in our country is a stepping-stone for further social economic and political development, a path to establishing new ways and new modes of production—that is, to socialism—the measures popular democracy will adopt in relation to women will prepare the ground for the radical solution to this social problem—a socialist solution.

However, the force and violence of the reaction in our country and the armed assistance of foreign powers are attempting to snuff out domestic democracy, and this needs to be urgently addressed and resolved. The reaction [*andithrasi*] is attempting to spread the darkness of an August Fourth with all of its catastrophic consequences for the nation. If the August Fourth regime of Glucksburg and Metaxas brought isolation and national catastrophe, the Hitler-fascist occupation will bring national treason, hunger, and destruction, the enslavement [*exandrapodismo*] of our people, and civil war; the new misadventure that is being prepared by the monstrosity of a government after the electoral comedy of March 31 will sow the seeds of national ruin in Greece.

This situation calls for a united popular response. The united columns of democracy formed by our people are coming head-to-head with the foreign-held [*xenodoulo*] front of the plutocratic monarcho-fascist oligarchy. The struggle for democratic development is a vital national necessity. The women of Greece have common interests. Their specific economic and political claims will not be satisfied except within the context of a democratic government. The oligarchy already showed what it is prepared to give Greek women, with its attitude to the globally recognized post-war political rights of women. Instead, it imprisoned, raped, murdered, and assaulted thousands of women. Greek women must unite their strengths with all the nation's forces. They must become creative forces of progress, a militant force against the monarcho-fascist oligarchy. The democratic unity of all the people cannot be realized without this half of the population.

THE KKE AND THE WOMEN'S MOVEMENT TODAY

The KKE, in its deep appreciation of the role played by women at this juncture of national history, during the 7th Congress declared the goal of building female Party membership up to 50 percent, including 50 percent of the leadership. This decision is very significant. Its importance transcends the Party itself and feeds into the general effort toward national progress, the mobilization of all the forces of the country toward the goal of shifting Greece away from its position as a backward, underdeveloped country, an international symbol of illiteracy and backwardness, the neofascist cancer.

This Party decision aims to create the necessary numerically significant vanguard which will patiently, persistently, systematically, and methodically lift the political and ideological level of working women. It will enlighten them as it did during the period of fascist occupation, it will light their path with a living example of activism, self-sacrifice, and active faith in the ideal. The implementation and realization of this goal of the 7th Congress means that the beneficial effects that the uprising of the nation has had on the mentality of the broad strata of women, will not fade. Women will not be engulfed by the darkness of superstition once again, as neofascist policy would like. On the contrary, women will cultivate themselves all the more. Day by day, more and more women across the entire country will become aware of the need to free themselves from slavery and servitude and strengthen their appetite for struggle.

The effect of this organized and systematic effort will not be embraced by women alone, but also by the male population of the country. The road to the realization of this decision will unleash many backward perceptions about women that continue to prevail in different ways, even among communist men, perceptions that have their origins in general backwardness.

In this sense the decision made by the 7th Congress of our Party will play a massive acculturating role.

Communists uproot and smash the effects and remnants of backward bourgeois perception in their very own ranks; through the broad political influence of KKE, simultaneously the mentality and the perceptions of broad sections of our people will be remade. When communists understand their basic duty to draw women into the ranks of popular movements and elevate them to equal status as freedom fighters, this perception will spread and dominate among the hundreds of thousands of supporters of our Party and by extension, the masses at large.

It is no secret that the bourgeois inheritance is very heavy. It takes a monumental effort to uproot these habits, a mentality that we have absorbed through education in the school, at home, and in society generally. A great effort needs to be made by communists to escape the conditioning by which women and their abilities are undervalued. In her memoirs of Lenin, Clara Zetkin recalled their discussions about women and the duties of the communist movement:

> Many regard the propaganda and activism, the awakening and revolutionary guidance, in relation to the female masses, as a completely secondary task, as a detail that is relevant only to communist women. This is a critical mistake. This is a divisive tendency, an inverse emancipation of women [*heirafetisi ton gynaikon ap tin anapodi*]. The mistake can be traced back to a historic fundamental devaluing of women and their abilities. Unfortunately, a certain adage is still relevant to many of our comrades: if you scratch the surface of a communist you will find a philistine. Naturally you have to scratch his weak point and that weak point will be his attitude toward women. (C. Zetkin, *Lenin on Women*, 40).

This backward mentality in Greece, whose causes we discussed earlier, is still heavy and demoralizing, and weighs heavily also on communists who have not liberated themselves far enough. The struggle of the Party against this mentality will not be restricted to within its own ranks but will rip open the darkness of superstition across society as a whole, by virtue of the Party's political influence. With the decision made in the 7th Plenary Session, the KKE showed itself once again to be the Party that fights with conviction for the specific rights of women and for the cultivation of the people; it is the Party that has taken on the woman question today as nothing less than a crucial part of the national problem, whose resolution is of historically unprecedented national necessity.

The way the KKE is handling the woman question distinguishes it completely from the parties of capitalism that are either openly hostile or mutter familiar and well-worn excuses about the political and intellectual disabilities of women, such as the People's Party [Laiko Komma] and all the fascist factions, or those that feign interest, like the Liberal Party [Komma Fileleftheron] and the old democratic parties. As for the People's Party and its fascist relatives, there is no need to examine their opposition as the fascist position on women is well known. It must be said that one manifestation of the counterfeit democracy of the so-called democratic parties is in the gap between the constant appeals to and recognition of human rights on the one hand, and their long-standing negative stance toward the rights of women on the other.

Besides KKE's program for the rights of women, besides the daily struggles for the realization of its economic and political aims, for the internal organization of its own forces, for the enforcement of an internal status quo of absolute equality between men and women, and the effort to elevate communist women politically and intellectually to be equals with their male counterparts, it also works to smash archaic backward perceptions about the social value of women. It has become an agent of acculturation of contemporary customs and morals, of civilized conduct and co-operation between people, irrespective of gender. Creating tens of thousands of communists among working women, clerks, intellectuals, and housewives, creates the necessary morality and critical mass which will mobilize Greek women into the struggle for democracy, to fight alongside the rest of our people and to achieve freedom, independence, peace, and normality for our country, and for their own humanity and recognition.

The decision of the 7th Congress burdens women in the KKE, in particular, because it is on their actions, their persistent effort to educate themselves and to liberate themselves from their inheritance, from the habits and psychology left by eons of social slavery, that the fortunes of the new policy chiefly depends. Communist women must dominate and prevail, invested with the virtue of their membership in the Party, their irreproachable character and morals, their serious appearance and measured gestures, their civilized conduct in both private and social life, their tireless actions and indomitable will, their undaunted and courageous contribution to the struggle for the liberation of Greek women from slavery. Communist women must feel deeply that there is no higher calling than to be a member of the KKE, the Party that is a pioneer, the indomitable soldier of freedom and civilization in our country, and decisive warrior of female liberation. Locating the woman question in science, history, and sociology, the KKE has always operated persistently and systematically toward its goal, never losing direction in the quest to improve the economic and political status of women, never neglecting to declare that the radical liberation of women was closely identified with the radical transformation of the entire social system. Popular democracy as a form of popular power whose final goal is to open the road for the socialist transformation of society creates very solid preconditions for the radical solution to the woman question.

In our country the road to popular democracy must pass through the struggle to subvert the establishment of a neofascist status quo imposed by Glucksburg. The struggle for democracy against monarcho-fascism, the implacable enemy of women's liberation, is the struggle for the rights of Greek women. The KKE as a unified whole, and its female members, in particular, are giving all they have without Party-political self-interest, to attract the progressive sectors of the Greek female population to the struggle for justice and civilization, the struggle for the human rights of Greek women. In this struggle, the KKE is showing itself to be in the service of the national interest, a warrior of consequence for Greek democracy.

CONCLUSION

Through this broad examination of the trajectory of the women's movement, we can conclude that the contribution of the KKE, as a mass movement with crystal clear aims, was foundational. We do not wish to argue that the KKE has done all it can for its part. It can do more and yield greater results if it was not also burdened by the suffocating atmosphere of backwardness, of backward eastern Asiatic morals from which it is very difficult to be liberated. KKE has issued its own confession on this matter through certain decisions it has made throughout its history. In spite of this legacy, however, whatever has been accomplished regarding the mobilization of women, their liberation from the mentality of the slave, while less than adequate, was primarily the achievement of the organized workers' movement (professional and political). It is above all the achievement of KKE, the tireless and persistent driver of the political campaign for the liberation of Greek women, a critical condition for the successful rebirth of our country. Historical factors invested the working class and its party with this duty. If this goal has not yet been fulfilled, or if it remains unfulfilled in the future, this would be to the detriment and loss of the working class and the Party.

If foreign intervention and Greek feudalism and its capitulation to foreign interests did not delay our country's progress, if in other words, the bourgeoisie had played its historic progressive role in Greece as it did in other countries, this progress would also be reflected in the predicament of women; there would have emerged a European-style feminism in Greece. This did not happen. Our feminist movement, anemic and weak from its birth, was unable to fulfill its progressive mission and influence and benefit Greek women through the creation and spread of an emancipated gender consciousness across broad cross-sections of the female population. On the contrary, in our country, feminism was hostile to those classes; it ignored their issues, passions, and claims, and for this reason it paid the price of isolation from the majority of women and persistent ignorance. Feminism had no impact on the people [*platia stromata*]. It was restricted to a very small class of progressive women of the middle and upper middle classes. The workers' movement led by KKE needed to prepare the ground accordingly, to draw Greek women out on a mass scale from the swamp of political and social ignorance and indifference, to cultivate and nurture them in them the consciousness of the free human being, to release them from the psychology of the slave, a condition that produced the defects the opponents of women's emancipation consider to be synonymous with the female gender and thus unchangeable. Today, it's not just a handful of enlightened men and women fighting against this backward perception. A whole army of women from the towns and villages is fighting—the Panhellenic Women's Conference was proof of this. The columns of pioneer women are growing daily, comprised of free women with a strong sense of their mission and their (moral) debt.

We are not saying, of course, that this progressive movement of women is a (philo) communist movement. On the contrary. It is a clearly progressive united effort, the product of objective historic need. But the contribution of the workers' movement and their Party—to the women's movement and to creating the social conditions so that the movement may bear fruit—is a fact. History will show this beyond a doubt.

Glossary of Terms

AUCP All Union Communist Party (Bolshevik Party)
Comintern Communist International (a.k.a. Third International)
CC Central Committee
CPGB Communist Party of Great Britain
CPC Communist Party of Cyprus
CPSU Communist Party of the Soviet Union, also referred to as the Russian Communist Party (RCP)
VKP(b) Vsesoiuznaya Kommunisticheskaya Partiia (bol'shevikov) (All-Union Communist Party (Bolshevik) and Kommunisticheskaya Partiya Sovetskogo Soyuza (Communist Party of the Soviet Union)
DKP Deutsche Kommunistische Partei (Communist Party of Germany)
DSE Dimokratikos Stratos Elladas (Democratic Army of Greece/GDA)
EAM Ethniko Apeleftherotiko Metopo (National Liberation Front)
EBE Ergatiki Boitheia Elladas (Labor Assistance of Greece)
ECCI Executive Committee of the Communist International
EGSEE Enotiki Geniki Synomospondia Ellinon Ergaton (Unitary Greek General Confederation of Labor)
EPON Ethniki Panellinia Organosi Neon (National Panhellenic Youth Organization)
GSEE Geniki Synomospondia Ergaton Elladas (Greek General Confederation of Labor)
KKE Kommounistiko Komma Elladas (Communist Party of Greece)
KOA Kendriki Organosi Athinas (Central Athens Organization)
KOMEP Komunistiki Epitheorisi (Communist review)

KUNMZ Kommunistichesky Universitet Natsionalnykh Menshinstv Zapada (Communist University for National Minorities of the West)
KUTV Kommunistichesky Universitet Trudiashchikhsia Vostoka (Communist University for the Toilers of the East)
MLS Mezhdunarodnaia Leninskaia Shkola (International Lenin School)
MOPR Mezhdunarodnoye Obshchestvo Pomoshtchi Revolutzioneram (International Red Aid)
NKVD Naródnyy Komissariát Vnútrennikh Del (People's Commissariat for Internal Affairs)
OKNE Omospondia Kommounistikon Neolaion Elladas (Federation of Communist Youth of Greece)
OMS Otdel Mezhdunarodnykh Svyazey (International Liaison Department)
OSOAVIAKHIM Obshchestvo Sodeyctviya Oboronye, Aviatsionnomu i Khimocheskomu Stroitelstvu (Society for the Assistance of Defense, Aircraft, and Chemical Construction)
PCF Parti Communiste Français (Communist Party of France)
PDEG Panellinia Dimokratiki Enosi Gynaikon (Panhellenic Democratic Union of Women)
PEEA Politiki Epitropi Ethnikis Apeleftherosis (Political Committee of National Liberation)
RSC Epitropi Apokatastasis Prosfygon (Refugee Resettlement Commission of Greece)
RGASPI Rossiiskii Gosudarstvennyi Arkhiv Sotsial'no-Politicheskoi Istorii (Russian State Archive of Socio-Political History)
RKSM Vsesoyuzny Leninsky Kommunistichesky Soyuz Molodyozhi (All-Union Leninist Young Communist League); usually known as Komsomol
RSDLP Russian Social Democratic Labor Party
SDG Syndesmos gia ta Dikaiomata ton Gynaikon (League for the Rights of Women)
SEKE Sosialistiko Ergatiko Komma Elladas (Socialist Workers' Party of Greece)
SSR Soviet Socialist Republic
VUZy Vysshie Uchebnye Zavedenii (Higher Education Institution)
WIDF Women's International Democratic Federation
USSR Union of Soviet Socialist Republics
UWCL Universal World Confederation of Labour

Notes

ACKNOWLEDGMENTS

1. International Committee for the Computerization of the Comintern Archive, "Communist International (Comintern) Archives at the Library of Congress: The INCOMKA Project," Library of Congress Research Guides, accessed June 18, 2024, https://guides.loc.gov/comintern-archives/incomka-project.

INTRODUCTION

Epigraphs. Wolfgang Leonhard, *Child of the Revolution*, trans. C. M. Woodhouse (Collins, 1957), 215; Ella Winter, *Red Virtue: Human Relationships in the New Russia* (Victor Gollancz, 1933), 91; "Letter to Khrushchev," File of Olga Papadopoulou (Vlasova/Spiridovna) f. 495, op. 207, d. 159, 16, Rossiiskii Gosudarstvennyi Arkhiv Sotsialno-Politicheskoi Istorii (hereafter, RGASPI).

1. The Greek word for female Bolshevik, *Bolsevika/Bolshevika*, is an adaptation of the Russian *Bolshevik* (masc) and *Bolshevichka* (fem).
2. The Treaty of Lausanne, or the Treaty of Peace with Turkey, was signed on July 24, 1923, by the British Empire, France, Italy, Japan, Greece, Romania, and the Serb-Croat-Slovene state, on the one part, and Turkey, on the other part. The Lausanne Project, 2017, https://thelausanneproject.com.
3. Exceptions were made for Greeks residing in Constantinople and on the islands of Imvros (Gökçeada) and Tenedos (Bozcaada), on the one hand, and Muslims residing in Western Thrace, on the other. According to figures for 1928, the refugee population numbered 1,221,849: 1,104,216 from Turkey (Asia Minor, Pontos, Thrace, Constantinople/Istanbul); 48,027 from Bulgaria (Treaty of Neuilly-sur-Seine, 1919); 58,526 from Russia (Caucasus and other regions); and 10,080 from Albania, Serbia, Dodecanese, and elsewhere). "Collection of the Main Statistical Data Concerning the Exchange of Populations and the Rehabilitation of the Refugees," compiled by A. A. Pallis, member of the Council of the Committee for the Rehabilitation of the

Refugees (CRR), Athens, 1929. ELVEN_GR_58171, Eleftherios Venizelos Archive, Benaki Museum (hereafter Venizelos Archive).

4. See Margarite Poulos, "Beyond the Ballot Box: Rethinking Greek Communism between the Wars," *European History Quarterly* 52, no. 1 (2022): 43–64. An exception is a very recent paper by Grigoriadis and Moschos who attempt to demonstrate the link by analyzing the electoral results of the interwar period (1932 and 1936) using OLS modelling. Theocharis N. Grigoriadis and Dimitrios Moschos, "Farewell Anatolia: Refugees and the Rise of the Greek Left," *European Journal of Political Economy*, no. 77 (2023): article 102281, https://doi.org/10.1016/j.ejpoleco.2022.102281.

5. According to a memorandum from Brainerd P. Salmon, special commissioner of the Minister of Public Assistance in Greece, 40 percent of the refugee population was composed of males—14 percent under the age of twelve, 8 percent between twelve and twenty-one, 19 percent over twenty-one (mostly elderly). The female majority was composed of children under twelve (14 percent), young adults between fourteen and twenty-one (13 percent), and adults over twenty-one (19 percent). The refugees were thus not infrequently referred to as *pathitikon* (costly but nonproductive) in expenditure reports. See "Report on the Condition of the Refugees," October 1923. File 131, EL_VEN_GR_27533, Venizelos Archive; Speros Vryonis Jr., "The Labour Battalions in the Ottoman Empire," in *Cultural and Ethical Legacies: The Armenian Genocide*, ed. Richard Hovannisian, 275–91 (Routledge, 2006).

6. Memorandum of B. J. Salmon, "Report on the Condition of the Refugees," October 1923, File 131, ELVEN_GR_27533, Venizelos Archive.

7. Poulos, "Beyond the Ballot Box," 50.

8. Jacob Zumoff, *The Communist International and US Communism, 1919–1929*, Historical Materialism Book Series, vol. 82 (Brill, 2014), ch. 7.

9. Minutes of the General Meeting of the Party Circle, 24/3/1929, KUTV International Greek Sector, f. 532, op. 2, d. 83, 24–25, RGASPI.

10. This includes key figures Chrysa Hatzivasiliou, Petros Roussos, and Avra Vlassi Partsalidou, among others.

11. For a concise survey of the debate according to John McIlroy and Alan Campbell see "Bolshevism, Stalinism and the Comintern: A Historical Controversy Revisited," *Labor History* 60, no. 3 (2019).

12. KKE, "On Bolshevisation: The Educational Program of the Party. Instructions of the Executive Committee on Educational Work." *KKE: Episima Keimena 1925–1928* (Document 212) (Syghroni Epochi, 1974), 16. Communist Party publications are sold at the communist bookshop Sygroni Epochi and are available through ASKI archive (both in Athens).

13. See, for example, the very influential work of Angelos Elefandis, *H Epaggelia tis Adynatis Epanastasis: KKE kai Astismos ston Mesopolemo* [The promise of the impossible revolution: The Greek Communist Party and the bourgeoisie between the wars] (Themelio, 1976); Andonis Liakos, *Ergasia kai politiki stin Ellada tou mesopolemou* [Labor and politics in interwar Greece] (Nefeli, 1993).

14. Notable examples include Kevin McDermott and J. Agnew, "Bolshevising the Comintern, 1924–8," in *The Comintern: A History of International Communism from Lenin to*

Stalin (Palgrave, 1996); McIlroy and Campbell, "Bolshevism, Stalinism"; Tim Rees, "Deviation and Discipline: Anti-Trotskyism, Bolshevization and the Spanish Communist Party, 1924–34," *Historical Research* 82, no. 215 (2009): 131–56; Zumoff, *The Communist International*.

15. The scholarship focused on women and gender in the Resistance includes Janet Hart, *New Voices in the Nation: Women and the Greek Resistance 1941–1964* (Cornell University Press, 1996); Tasoula Vervenioti, *H gynaika tis adistasis: H eisodos ton gynaikon sti politiki* [The reluctant woman: The entry of women into politics] (Odysseus, 1994); Margaret Poulos, *Arms and the Woman: Just Warriors and Greek Feminist Identity* (Columbia University Press, 2010); Eleni Fortouni, *Greek Women in Resistance: Journals, Oral Histories* (Delphini Press, 1986); Deborah R. Altamirano, "Up in Arms: The Lives and Times of Women Activists in the World War II Greek Resistance" (PhD diss., UCLA-Santa Barbara, 1993), 449.

16. Lefteri Nea was subsumed by the youth wing of EAM, the Eniaia Panelladiki Enosi Neon (EPON; United Panhellenic Union of Youth) in 1943. See Vervenioti, *H gynaika tis adistasis*; "Electra, a Heroine of the People," *Rizospastis*, July 29, 2001; Avra Partsalidou, "Electra," *Bulletin of the Greek Democratic Army*, vol. 80 (1949).

17. *Ethniko Symvoulio: Periliptika praktika ergasion tis Protis Synodou tou—Koryschades 14–27 May 1944* [National Council: Summary of the Minutes of the First Synod—Koryschades 14–27 May 1944] (Euritania, 1988); T. Tsouparopoulos, *The Democratic Institutions of the Greek Resistance* (Politeia, 1989).

18. Donna Harsch notes that only one woman was ever a voting member of the Soviet Politburo. Galina Semyonova became a voting member of the CPSU under Gorbachev. Donna Harsch, "Communism and Women," in *The Oxford Handbook of the History of Communism*. ed. Stephen A. Smith (Oxford University Press, 2014), 492.

19. The Women's International Democratic Federation (WIDF) was the largest and most influential international women's organization of the post-1945 era. Founded in Paris in late November 1945, it has been characterized as a progressive, "left-feminist" international umbrella organization, with an emphasis on peace, women's rights, anticolonialism, and antiracism. The WIDF had a strong association with the communist world, and many, though not all, of its leading women were communists. See Francisca de Haan, "The Women's International Democratic Federation (WIDF): History, Main Agenda, and Contributions, 1945–1991," Women and Social Movements (WASI) Online Archive, October 2012, http://alexanderstreet.com/products/women-and-social-movements-international. For the Greek branch (PDEG) see Margarite Poulos, "'So That Life May Triumph': Communist Feminism and Realpolitik in Civil-War Greece," *Journal of Women's History* 29, no. 1 (2017): 63–86; Margarite Poulos, "Transnational Militancy in Cold-War Europe: Gender, Human Rights, and the WIDF during the Greek Civil War," *European Review of History: Revue Europenne d'histoire* 24, no.1 (2018): 17–35.

20. From the autobiographical essay of Allegra Felous (1953), f. 495, op. 207, d. 1060, 12, RGASPI.

21. Avra Partsalidou (née Vlassi), *Anamniseis apo tin zoi stin OKNE* [Memories of life in OKNE], 4th ed. (Syghroni Epochi, 1983).

22. *Achtides* refer to mid-ranking sections within the KKE hierarchy.
23. "Biographical report of Comrade Allegra Felous" (also appears as "Fegous"), f. 495, op. 207, d. 1060, RGASPI.
24. The best example of this scholarship remains Angelos Elefandis, *H Epaggelia*.
25. Victor Strazzeri makes a point of this in his recent article, "Beyond the Double-Blind Spot: Relocating Communist Women as Transgressive Subjects in Contemporary Historiography," *Gender and History* 36, no. 2 (2024): 755–74. https://doi.org/10.1111/1468-0424.12675.
26. I refer to philosopher Nanette Funk's essay in the *European Journal of Women's Studies*, in which she accuses non-anticommunist feminist scholars, or "revisionist feminist scholars," including Kristen Ghodsee, Francisca de Haan, and others, of uncritically touting the achievements of communist-era women's organizations, and by extension communist women's agency, ignoring the oppressive nature of authoritarian regimes in Eastern Europe. See Nanette Funk, "Knot So: A response to Kristen Ghodsee," *European Journal of Women's Studies* 22, no. 3 (2015): 350–55.
27. Sheila Fitzpatrick, *Tear Off the Masks: Identity and Imposture in Twentieth-Century Russia* (Princeton University Press, 2005), 13.
28. Jochen Hellbeck, *Revolution on My Mind: Writing a Diary under Stalinism* (Harvard University Press, 2006); Jochen Hellbeck, "Working, Struggling, Becoming: Stalin-Era Autobiographical Texts," *Russian Review* 60, no. 3 (2001): 340–59.
29. From Ville Laamanen, "From Communist to Cadre Outsider: Ideals, Opportunism, and Coping with Change in Moscow and Stockholm 1929–1948," *Scandinavian Journal of History* 45, no. 3 (2020): 334–59. Also see Nicolas Weill interview with Carlo Ginzburg, originally published in *Le Monde des livres*, October 3, 2022. Now available as "Carlo Ginzburg: 'In History as in Cinema, Every Close-Up Implies an Off-Screen Scene,'" *Verso Books* (blog), June 6, 2023, https://www.versobooks.com/blogs/5536-carlo-ginzburg-in-history-as-in-cinema-every-close-up-implies-an-off-screen-scene.

CHAPTER 1

A version of this chapter was published in the *European History Quarterly*. Poulos, "Beyond the Ballot Box."

1. Christian Gonsa, "Autobiografika keimena Ellinon kommouniston kai i istoria tou Ellinikou Kommounistikou Kommatos" [Autobiographical writings of Greek communists and the history of the Greek Communist Party] *Mnimon*, vol. 17 (1995): 121.
2. Elli Alexiou, *Apo Poli Konda* [Up close] (Kastaniotis, 1990); Partsalidou, *Anamniseis apo*; Kaiti Zevgou, *Me ton Yiani Zevgo sto epanastatiko kinima* [With Yiannis Zevgos in the revolutionary movement] (Athens, 1980). Partsalidou's memoir was written in the 1930s but only published after the collapse of the military dictatorship (*metapolitefsi*).
3. The Comintern's 5th Congress in June 1924 articulated the principles by which all national communist parties would transform into Marxist-Leninist "new" parties. For the "Twenty-one Conditions of Admission," see "Seventh Session: July 30," Minutes of Second Congress of the Communist International, Marxists Internet

Archive, accessed July 22, 2024, https://www.marxists.org/history/international/comintern/2nd-congress/ch07.htm

4. Once again, see Elefandis, *H Epaggelia*; Liakos, *Ergasia kai politiki*; Nikos Marantzidis, *Under Stalin's Shadow: A Global History of Greek Communism* (Ithaca, New York: Cornell University Press, 2023). See also the Greek Communist Party's own *Dokimio Istorias tou KKE* [Essays on the history of the KKE], vols. 1–2 (Syghroni Epochi, 2018); Anastasis Ghikas, *Rixi kai ensomatosi: Symvoli stin istoria tou ergatikou-kommounistikou kinimatos tou mesopolemou 1918–1936* [Rupture and integration: A contribution to the history of the labor-communist movement of the interwar period, 1918–1936] (Syghroni Epochi, 2010).

5. Mavrogordatos' work on class perception and consciousness in Greece has been very influential. G. T. Mavrogordatos, *Stillborn Republic: Social Coalitions and Party Strategies In Greece, 1922–1936* (University of California Press, 1992). See also Mark Mazower, "The Messiah and the Bourgeoisie: Venizelos and Politics in Greece," *Historical Journal* 35, no. 4 (1992): 888.

6. Nikos Potamianos, "Internationalism and the Emergence of Communist Politics in Greece, 1912–1924," *Journal of Balkan and Near Eastern Studies* 21, no. 5 (2018): 515–31. https://doi.org/10.1080/19448953.2018.1506288.

7. Angelika Psarra, "Feminism and Communism: Notes on the Greek Case," *Aspasia*, vol. 1 (2007): 213.

8. Figures cited in Menelaos Haralambidis, "Aspects of the Political Behaviour of the Refugees in Interwar Greece," *O dromos tis Aristeras*, July 27, 2011.

9. John V. Kofas, *Authoritarianism in Greece: The Metaxas Regime* (East European Monographs, 1983), 12.

10. Anna Karamanou, "The Changing Role of Women in Greece," in *Greece in the Twentieth Century*, ed. Theodore A. Couloumbis, Theodore C. Kariotis, and Fotini Bellou (Frank Cass, 2003), 284.

11. Chris Jecchinis, *Trade Unionism in Greece: A Study in Political Paternalism* (Labor Education Division, Roosevelt University, 1967), 50.

12. Figures cited in Karamanou, "The Changing Role," 284.

13. Letter from former prime minister Stylianos Gonatas to the Ministry of Education, on the spread of communist ideas in Macedonia, Thessaloniki, 30 March 1931, ELVEN_GR_25798, Venizelos archive.

14. These figures come from Elefandis, *H Epaggelia*, 424. See also Kostas Kostis, *History's Spoiled Children: The Story of Modern Greece* (Hurst, 2018); Giorgos Mavrogordatos, *Stillborn Republic: Social Coalitions and Party Strategies in Greece, 1922–1936* (University of California Press, 1983).

15. Avdela, *Public Servants of the Female Sex: The Division of Labor by Gender in the Public Service 1905–1953* [in Greek] (Research and Education Foundation of the Commercial Bank of Greece, 1990), 35.

16. Avdela, 35.

17. Zizi Saliba, *Gynaikes Ergatries stin Elliniki Biomichania kai Biotechnia 1870–1922* [Women workers in the manufacturing and craft industry] (Ethniko Idrima Erevnon (EIE), 2002), 23; Avdela, *Public Servants*, 37.

18. 1928 census statistics (Ministry of the National Economy of Greece) reproduced in Avdela, *Public Servants*, 36.
19. Avdela, *Public Servants*, 39.
20. The Greek Refugee Resettlement Commission (RSC; Epitropi Apokatastasis Prosfygon), established in 1923 under the auspices of the League of Nations, was an autonomous organization subject to international monitoring and tasked with monitoring and administering the resettlement of the refugees, but also with the financial reconstruction of the Greek national state at a time when Greece was in a dire state of emergency. See Elizabeth Kontogiorgi, *Population Exchange in Macedonia* (Oxford University Press, 2006).
21. C. A. Macartney, *Refugees: The Work of the League* (League of Nations Union, 1930), 110.
22. Macartney, *Refugees*, 110.
23. Dimitri Pentzopoulos, *The Balkan Exchange of Minorities and its Impact on Greece* (1962; repr., De Gruyter Mouton, 2021), 114.
24. Michael B. O'Sullivan, "The Greek Interwar Refugee Crisis as a Cause of the Greek Civil War, 1922–1949," *Historical Perspectives*, series II: vol. 15, article 8 (2010): 49.
25. Vilma Hastaoglou-Martinidis, "A Mediterranean City in Transition: Thessaloniki between the Two World Wars," *Facta Universitatis: Architecture and Civil Engineering* 1, no. 4 (1997): 502.
26. League of Nations, "The Settlement of Greek Refugees, Scheme for an International Loan, Protocol." Geneva, September 29, 1923.

    27. J. H. Simpson, "The Work of the Greek Refugee Settlement Commission," *Journal of the Royal Institute of International Affairs* 8, no. 6 (Nov. 1929): 599.
28. Leda Papastefanaki, *Ergasia, technologia kai fylo stin Elliniki viomichania: I klostoyfantourgia tou Pirea 1870–1940* [Labor, technology and gender in Greek industry: The textile industry of Piraeus 1870–1940] (Heraklion: Crete University Press, 2009), 378.
29. Papastefanaki, *Ergasia, technologia*, 95.
30. For an extended report on the crisis of unemployment, low wages, and rising inflation for working women between the wars, see "Presentation on Female Employment in Greece 1927–1935," Archive of Maria Desypri Svolou, GR-ASKI-0153b, *Contemporary Social History Archive* (ASKI), Athens.
31. Anastasia Kondaxi, "A Bourgeois Refugee Settlement: Nea Ionia Volou," Master's thesis, Aristotle University, Thessaloniki, 1993, 35.
32. Quote from "Presentation on Female Employment."
33. "Presentation on Female Employment."
34. See respectively, Maria Svolou, "Women Carpet Workers," *O agonas tis gynaikas* [Woman's struggle], vol. 41 (1927); and N. Pagratis et al., "Medical, Demographical and Social Aspects of Syphilis: The Case of Infected Sex Workers in Greece during the Interwar," *Giornale Italiano di Dermatologia e Venerealogia* 149, no. 4 (2014): 464.
35. "Presentation on Female Employment."
36. M. Riginos, *Structures of Production and Wages in Greece 1900–1936* (Historical Archives of the Commercial Bank of Greece, 1987), 195.
37. See Efi Avdela, "To the Most Weak and Needy: Women's Protective Labor Legislation in Greece," in *Protecting Women: Labor Legislation in Europe, the United States and*

Australia (1880-1920), edited by Ulla Wikander and Alice Kessler-Harris (University of Illinois Press, 1995).
38. Efi Avdela, "The Contradictory Content of Social Protection: Legislation on Women's Industrial Work, 19th–20th Century," *Istorika*, no. 11 (1989).
39. See Avdela, "To the Most Weak and Needy," 300.
40. Avdela, "To the Most Weak and Needy," 310.
41. A young woman's column: "Refugee Women," signed by "Elvira," in *Prosfygikos Kosmos*, December 11, 1927.
42. The articles from *O Agonas tis Gynaikas* include the following: M. Svolou, "Female Refugee Unemployment," nos. 1-2, 1923; M. Svolou, "The Greek Woman Worker," no. 12, 1924; Anna Papadimitriou, "From the Work of Refugees," no. 12, 1924; "Speech by Maria Svolou," no. 25, 1925; M. Svolou, "Women Carpet Workers," no. 41, 1927; M. Svolou, "Women at Work," no. 42. 1927; Anon., "Current Affairs," no. 56, 1927; Anon., "Current Affairs," no. 72, 1928; Anon., "Current Affairs," nos. 74/75, 1928; M. Svolou, "Persecution of Working Women," no. 95, 1929; Anon., "Current Affairs," no. 103, 1929; Anna Makropoulou, "On the Work of Women and Children," no. 114, 1930; Anna Makropoulou, "Women at Work: How Greek Women Work in Five Large Industries," no. 115, 1930; M. Svolou, "The Persecution Continues," no. 116, 1930; M. Svolou, "The Persecution of the Woman Clerk and the Union Organizations," no. 117, 1930; M. Svolou, "Two Measures, Two Standards," no. 119, 1930.
43. Svolou, "Women Carpet Workers."
44. Avdela, "To the Weak and Needy," 310. For a focused examination of the office clerk campaign see Avdela, *Public Servants*.
45. Svolou was exiled from Greece twice, with her husband, socialist Alexandros Svolos. The first occurred under the Metaxas dictatorship for her feminist activism (1936 to 1940), and the second in 1948, during the Greek Civil War, for her communist sympathies and active participation in the EAM Resistance. Following her return from exile in 1953 she ran for the Greek Parliament as a member of the United Democratic Left. She was elected twice and was a member of the Party's Central Committee. Sasa Moschou-Sakorrafou, *I istoria tou Ellinikou feministikou kinimatos* [History of the Greek feminist movement] (self published, 1990), 188; Dimitra Samiou, "Maria Svolou (born Desypri) 1892–1976," in *Biographical Dictionary of Women's Movements and Feminisms in Central, Eastern, and Southeastern Europe: 19th and 20th Centuries*, ed. Francisca De Haan, Krassimira Daskalova, Anna Loutfi (Central European University Press, 2005), 552–57.
46. Yiorgos Kokkinos, Vlassis Agtsidis, and Elli Lemonidou, *Memory, Identity, and Ideology amongst Pontian Greeks* (Taxideftis, 2011); excerpt reproduced in "The Left and the Refugees of 1922," *A Blog by Vlassis Agtsidis* [in Greek], https://kars1918.wordpress.com.
47. Kokkinos, Agtsidis and Lemonidou, *Memory, Identity*.
48. "The Refugee Question," *KKE Episima Keimena, 1925–1928* (KKE—Official Documents) 233/e (Syghroni Epochi, 1974), 77.
49. "The Refugee Question," 77.
50. *Rizospastis*, September 7, 1929.

51. *Rizospastis*, September 7, 1929.
52. The Friendship, Neutrality, and Arbitration Agreement signed by Venizelos and Ataturk in Ankara on October 30, 1930, consisted of twenty-eight articles, the most important of which stipulated the obligation of both states to refrain from signing any other political or economic agreement that would burden either party. See Areti Tounda-Fergadi, *Themata Ellinikis diplomatikis istorias (1912-1934)* [Themes in the history of Greek diplomacy] (Paratiritis, 1986), 246–48.
53. The Second Republic followed from the period of "crowned republic" under the monarchs of the Glücksburg dynasty and lasted until its overthrow in a military coup d'état that restored the monarchy. The Second Republic marks the second period in modern Greek history where Greece was not headed by a king, with the assemblies and provisional governments of the Greek Revolution being regarded as the First Republic.
54. Lily Macrakis, *Eleftherios Venizelos 1864-1910: The Making of a National Leader* [in Greek] (MIET, 1992).
55. Alexander Kitroeff, "The Greek State and the Diaspora: Venizelism Abroad, 1910–1932," *Classics Journal* 10, no. 1 (2020), https://classics-at.chs.harvard.edu/classics10-alexander-kitroeff-the-greek-state-and-the-diaspora-venizelism-abroad-1910-1932.
56. Constantinos Tsoucalas, *The Greek Tragedy* (Penguin, 1969).
57. For more on labor history and historiography in the late Ottoman period, see Donald Quataert, "Labor History and the Ottoman Empire, c. 1700–1922," *International Labor and Working-Class History*, no. 60 (2001): 93–109.
58. Andrew L. Zapantis, *Greek-Soviet Relations 1917-1941* (Columbia University Press, 1983); Andre Gerolymatos, *An International Civil War in Greece 1943–1949* (Yale University Press, 2016).
59. "Domestic cadres" is a term used by Milovan Djilas, *Rise and Fall* (Harcourt Brace Jovanovich, 1983), 128.
60. The high point of diaspora representation in the KKE leadership was 1934/35 when 50 percent of the new Central Committee was composed of diaspora Greeks, especially from Asia Minor (including Hatzivasiliou), as were all permanent members of the Politburo (Nikos Zachariadis, Mitsos Partsalidis, Vasilis Nefeloudis, Kostas Sklavainas, Yiannis Michailidis, and Yiannis Ioannidis). The dominance of diaspora Greeks in the leadership remained high but diminished in the 7th Conference of 1945 primarily due to the significant increase in the number of Central Committee members, while representation in the Politburo remained high, four out of seven members (56 percent) (Zachariadis, Hatzivasiliou, Partsalides, and Anastasiadis).
61. This is Angelos Elefandis's thesis in *H Epaggelia*.
62. See Vasilis Fouskas and C. Dimoulas, *Greece, Financialization and the EU: The Political Economy of Debt and Destruction* (Springer, 2013), 77.
63. "On the Doubling of Forces of the Party: Instructions of the Executive Committee," *Rizospastis*, April 24, 1925.
64. "On the Doubling of Forces."
65. Central Organizational Unit (Kendriko Organotiko Tmima), "On the Recruitment of New Members to the Party," *Rizospastis*, October 2, 1927.

66. Angelika Psarra, "The Different Faces of a Celebration: The Greek Course of International Women's Day 1924-2010," *Aspasia*, vol. 6 (2012): 46.
67. "The principles and program of the Socialist Workers Party (SEKE)," in KKE, *Episima Keimena 1918–1924* [KKE: Official Documents], vol. 1. (Syghroni Epochi, 1974). Angelika Psarra has argued that the Party's introduction of International Women's Day in Greece some months before the Congress (March 1924) was the first act within the framework of Bolshevization regarding women, an annual event that became "central in communist women's course along the path of politics." Psarra, "The Different Faces," 46.
68. Presented by "A," "The Movement of the Working Women of Greece," *International Press Correspondence* (English edition) 8, no. 90 (December 1928). Presentations also made by "Comrade Nicolaou," "Sifnaos" (pseud., Andronikos Haitas), and "Watis."
69. For example, B. T. "We Women," *Rizospastis*, Aug. 8, 1919; Marthe Bigot, "Le communism et la femme," translated in *Rizospastis*, Aug. 15, 1921. The Greek translations of Third International papers on the "woman question" were published in *Kommounistiki Epitheorisi* [Communist review] 2, no. 1 (1922): 29–41.
70. Komioti, like many communist women in Greece and elsewhere, was initiated into the Party through male patronage. She was the sister and wife respectively of SEKE co-founders and leaders Spiros Komiotis and Nikos Dimitratos. Ioanna Komioti, "Bourgeois and Socialist Feminism," *Rizospastis*, Feb. 5, 1920.
71. "Announcement of the Women's Office: To All the Working Women of the City and the Meadow," *Rizospastis*, January 25, 1925.
72. See "Organization Conference on the Work among Women," *International Press Correspondence* (English edition) 5, no. 56 (July 15, 1925). "A. Sgrudeos" may have been another pseudonym of Andronikos Haitas, also referred to "Sifnaios" in other Comintern reports. Born in Georgia, a former member of the Russian Bolshevik Party, and proficient in Russian, Andronikos Haitas was sent by the Party to Moscow in 1925 to represent Greece at the Communist International.
73. Eleftherios Stavridis, *Ta Paraskinia tou KKE* [Behind the scenes of KKE] (self-published, 1953).
74. "Greek Section," Communist University for the Toilers of the East, f. 532, op. 2, d. 82 and 83, *RGASPI*.
75. "Decision on the Youth Movement," *Rizospastis*, April 15, 1927.
76. "The Organization of the Socialist Workers Party (SEKE)" in *KKE Episima Keimena, 1918–1924*, vol. 1 (Syghroni Epochi, 1974), 21.
77. "Decision on the Youth Movement," *Rizospastis*, April 15, 1927.
78. Polymeris Voglis, *Becoming a Subject: Political Prisoners during the Greek Civil War* (Berghahn, 2002).
79. Students demonstrated against rising fees and a lack of resources, and for a general overhaul of education standards and conditions.
80. "Report by Commander in Chief P. Klados to Ministry of Military Affairs on communist activities," February 14, 1931. ELVEN_GR_20499, Venizelos Archive.
81. "Report by Police Commissioner G. Kalochristiannakis Regarding Communism in Thessaloniki in the Year 1930," August 2, 1930. EL_VEN_GR_24044, file 107,

Venizelos archive; "Report by Police Commissioner G. Kalochristiannakis Concerning Communist Propaganda in the Year 1932," November 29, 1932, ELVEN_GR_24955, file 114, Venizelos archive.

82. Achilleas Kalevras, "O kommounismos eis ta gymanasia," *Eleftheros Logos*, Dec. 11, 1925.
83. Avra Vlassi Partsalidou joined OKNE in 1926 and became a reserve member of the Central Committee of the KKE in 1945, and a full member in 1953. Very little is known of her background. She married fellow OKNE member, trade union leader, and one-time KKE Politburo member Dimitris Partsalidis, a Pontic Greek refugee from Trabzon (Trapezounda in Greek). See Partsalidou, *Anamniseis apo*, 20. Nothing is known of the background of Eleni Rousaki or Raika. Partsalidou refers to Rousaki as a student but elsewhere she is referred to as a tobacco worker.
84. "Report by I. Papagrigoriou on the arrest of member of the Greek Communist Party," March 12, 1931, Athens. ELVEN_GR_24181, file 108, Venizelos archive.
85. File of Agnia Apostolou and Electra Apostolou (Koula Drakou), f. 495, op. 207, d. 128, RGASPI.
86. *Rizospastis*, Mar. 12, 1925.
87. Raika, "The League of Women," *Rizospastis*, Mar. 12, 1925.
88. Raika, "Our Opinion," *Rizospastis*, April 4, 1925.
89. Her mentor Pouliopoulos led the Trotskyist faction within the Party; the Party purged them both at the end of 1927.
90. Her full name is a matter of contention. In the few references made to her, she appears as Raika Eirini Kondouri, Raika Komioti, or Eirini Koundouri Komioti.
91. Yianna Katsiamboura, "Protosocialist Feminism: Women Communists and Socialists of the Interwar Period" [in Greek], paper presented at Democratic or Socialist Revolution in Greece?: 80 Years after Pouliopoulos and His Era, at the Institute of Political and Social Research Pandelis Pouliopoulos, December 13, 2014, Athens. Available online at Institute of Political & Social Research, "Pantelis Pouliopoulos," http://ipsr-pouliopoulos.org/sites/ipsr-pouliopoulos.org/files/1412-katsiampoura-pouliopoulos.pdf, 5. There are a few exceptions, the most notable of which is the work of Greek journalist and historian Angelika Psarra.
92. See Katsiamboura, "Protosocialist Feminism." Psarra has argued that SEKE/KKE views on women's emancipation developed at the same time and in dialogue with feminist views on the subject. Angelika Psarra, "Women in Pursuit of Pleasure and the Vote," in *When Women Have Differences: Contradictions and Conflicts between Women in Contemporary Greece*, ed. Christina Vlachoutsikou and Laurie Kain Hart (Medusa, 2003), 187.
93. "Instructions from the Executive Committee: On the Doubling of the Forces of the Party May–June," *Rizospastis*, April 24, 1925. This is Psarra's characterization. See Psarra, "The Different Faces," 43–59.
94. A. Papadimitriou, "From the Work of Women," *Agonas tis Gynaikas*, vol. 12, 1924.
95. "The Movement of Refugee Widows and Orphans in Thessaloniki—the Terrific Success of Their Organization," *Prosfygikos Kosmos*, November 24, 1929.
96. File of Chrysa Hatzivasiliou, f. 495, op. 207, d. 13, RGASPI.
97. Karamanou, "The Changing Role," 284.

98. Nitsa Koliou, *Typo-photographic Panorama of Volos*, vol. 1 (self published, 1991).
99. Koliou, *Typo-photographic Panorama*, 54.
100. Anna Koumandaraki, "The Greek Trade Union Movement in Controversy: Against a State-Centred Approach to Labour Movement Theory," *Workers of the World: International Journal on Strikes and Social Conflicts* 1, no. 1 (2012): 130.
101. Anastasis Ghikas, "The Politics of Working-Class Communism in Greece 1918–1936" (PhD diss., University of York, 2004), 175.
102. "Presentation on Female Unemployment in Greece 1927–1935," GR-ASKI-0153b, Archive of Maria Desypri Svolou, Contemporary Social History Archive (ASKI), Athens.
103. Ilham Khuri-Makdisi, *The Eastern Mediterranean and the Making of Global Radicalism, 1860–1914*. (University of California Press, 2010), 155; Joel Beinin and Zachary Lockman, *Workers on the Nile: Nationalism, Communism, Islam, and the Egyptian Working Class, 1882–1954* (Princeton University Press, 1987), 50 -57; E. Tutku Vardagli, "Tobacco Labor Politics in the Province of Thessaloniki: Cross-Communal and Cross-Gender Relations" (PhD diss., Bogaziçi University, Turkey, 2011).
104. Gülhan Balsoy, "Gendering Ottoman Labor History: The Cibali Régie Factory in the Early Twentieth Century," *International Review of Social History*, vol. 54 (2009): 54. After the Second Balkan War, Thessaloniki and other Greek regions of Macedonia, like the tobacco center of Kavala, were officially annexed to Greece by the Treaty of Bucharest in 1913.
105. Mustafa Erdem Kabadayi, "Working in a Fez Factory in Istanbul in the Late Nineteenth Century: Division of Labour and Networks of Migration Formed along Ethno-Religious Lines," Supplement 17: "Ottoman and Republican Turkish Labor History," *International Review of Social History*, vol. 54 (2009): 77.
106. Balsoy, "Gendering Ottoman Labor History," 56.
107. Balsoy, "Gendering Ottoman Labor History," 64.
108. Thanasis Betas, "From the Tobacco Shop to the Cigarette Factory: Technological Changes, Gender and Surveillance in a Greek Cigarette Form in the Early 20th Century," *Advances in Historical Studies*, vol. 5 (2016): 61.
109. Note: the autobiography is handwritten, but probably not by Vamniatzidou. The writing is very sophisticated, but her signature shows that she is barely able to write. "Autobiography of Stella Vamniatzidou (Elena Agneva)," f. 495, op. 207, d. 109, 41, RGASPI.
110. "Autobiography of Elena Anemelou (Dimitrievna),", f. 495, op. 207, d. 199, 14-16, RGASPI.
111. Efi Avdela, "Class, Ethnicity, and Gender in Post-Ottoman Thessaloniki: The Great Tobacco Strike of 1914," in *Borderlines: Gender and Identities in War and Peace 1870-1930*, ed. Billie Melman (Psychology Press, 1997).
112. *Rizospastis*, February 24, 1928. According to official data there were 21,426 women employed in Greek tobacco, compared with 29,175 men in 1927; by 1932 the number of women and men had reached parity (19,500 : 20,000) although the number of employees dropped due to increasing mechanization of the industry. See "Presentation on Female Unemployment," archive of Maria (Desypri) Svolou.

113. *Kommounistiki Epitheorisi* [Communist review] 2, no. 1 (January 1929): 24–26.
114. Partsalidou, *Anamniseis apo*, 36.
115. Avra Partsalidou "On the Conquest and Organization of Women Workers," *Kommounistiki Epitheorisi* [Communist review], no. 7 (April 1933): 8.
116. Partsalidou "On the Conquest," 8.
117. Partsalidou, *Anamniseis apo*, 35.
118. *Rizospastis*, May 25, 1931.
119. Partsalidou, *Anamniseis apo*, 11.
120. Partsalidou, *Anamniseis apo*, 63.
121. Demetra Tzanaki, "Sex Work Is Work: Greek Capitalism and the Syndrome of Electra 1922–2018," in *Back to the '30s?: Recurring Crises of Capitalism, Liberalism, and Democracy*, ed. Jeremy Rayner et al. (Springer Nature, 2020), 376.
122. See Evangelos Kofos, "The Impact of the Macedonian Question on Civil Conflict In Greece (1943–1949)," in *Greece at the Crossroads: The Civil War and Its Legacy*, ed. John O. Iatrides (Pennsylvania State University Press, 2010), 278.
123. Partsalidou, "On the Conquest."
124. Profintern was a contraction of the Russian term Professionalye Soyuz Internationalny or, literally, Occupational Union International.
125. Barbara Foley, *Radical Representations: Politics and Form in U.S. Proletarian Fiction, 1929–1941* (Duke University Press, 1993), 218.
126. Partsalidou, *Anamniseis apo*, 53.
127. Partsalidou, *Anamniseis apo*, 9.
128. I refer, for example, to the Greek branch of the YMCA, Christianiki Adelfotis Neon (Brotherhood of Christian Youth) established in 1921, and Christianiki Enosis Neanidon (Union of Young Christian Women), the Greek branch of the World Young Women's Christian Association, established in Greece in 1923. For the ideological warfare exercised on the football pitch—the most popular sport in interwar Greece—see Giorgos Gasias, "The Case of the Football Associations in Greek Society between the Wars 1922-1936" (PhD diss., University of Crete, 2005). On international communism and sport, see Andre Gounod, "Sport reformiste ou sport revolutionnaire?," in *Les Origines du sport ouvrier en Europe*, ed. Pierre Arnaud, 219–45 (Paris: L'Harmattan, 1994).
129. *Rizospastis*, Dec. 28, 1924.
130. Papastefanaki, *Labour, Technology, and Gender*, 408.
131. *EBE Deltio*.
132. From *Apo ti Zoi ton Organoseon* [The life of the organizations], *EBE Deltio*, December 1935, 12–16.
133. *EBE Deltio*, Jan 1928.
134. *EBE Deltio*, Feb. 1, 1935.
135. *Rizospastis*, Aug. 15, 1930.
136. *EBE Deltio*, Jan. 1928.
137. Elli Pappa archive, A.E.9/02 Box 34, Greek Literature and History Archive (ELIA), Athens, Greece.

138. Autobiography of Aliki Kantza (Olga Bakola), f. 495, op. 207, d. 99, RGASPI. Bakola refers here to the Panhellenic Antifascist Women's Congress of 1933.
139. From "the life of the organizations" and "organizational matters," *Apo ti Zoi ton Organoseon, EBE Deltio*, Dec. 1935, 12–16.
140. *EBE Deltio*, Feb. 1, 1935.
141. Kostas Efthimiou, *Ergatiki boitheia kai koinoniki allileggi: Dyo paradigmata taxikis allilegias drasis stin ellada tou Mesopolemou* [Labor assistance and social solidarity: Two examples of class solidarity in interwar Greece] (Ekdoseis ton Synadelfon, 2014), 20–29.
142. Efthimiou, *Ergatiki Boitheia*, 119. According to Efthimiou, until the 1930s, the EBE was a much more mass organization than the KKE itself, which had a couple of thousand members in 1927. EBE made efforts to establish a greater mass character, expressing the needs of a broader cross section of the democratic or progressive social forces who faced challenges, but it quickly became identified with political choices and strategies and followed the fortunes of the KKE.
143. *Rizospastis*, Jan. 23, 1933.
144. Papastefanaki, *Labor, Technology and Gender*, 430.
145. Papastefanaki, *Labor, Technology and Gender*, 423. This is a long-held view, established by influential scholars such as Angelos Elefandis and Yiorgos Mavrogordatos.
146. "Language field" is a term used by Lito Apostolakou in reference to the political vocabulary that advocated workers should adhere to their class, party, or trade union, not to their employer or political patrons. Lito Apostolakou, "Greek Workers or Communist 'Others': The Contending Identities of Organized Labor, c. 1914–1936," *Journal of Contemporary History* 32, no. 3 (1997): 417.
147. In Vlassis Agtsidis, "Pontian Refugees in the 'Motherland,'" *Istoria tou Ethnous*, vol. 17 (August 2010): 23.
148. See Apostolakou, "Greek Workers," 409–24.
149. Partsalidou, *Anamniseis apo*, 58.
150. The Idionymo (Law 4229) introduced by the Venizelos government was a law "concerning safety measures for the protection of the social system and of freedoms." It aimed to penalize "insurrectional" ideas and, in particular, lay the basis for the prosecution of communists and anarchists, and for the suppression of unionist mobilizations. It was the first legal measure instituted against the KKE and initiated a series of emergency legislations activated by the Greek state against the Left thereafter. See Mazower, "The Messiah and the Bourgeoisie," 885–904.
151. Agtsidis, "Pontian Refugees," 23.
152. Andreas Kazamias, *Education and Modernization in Greece* (ERIC Clearinghouse, 1975), 83.
153. Kazamias, *Education and Modernization*, 83.
154. *Gazette of the Debates*, 4th Session, Library of the Greek Parliament, Athens, Greece, July 9, 1929 (National Printing Office, 1929), 91. Cited in Giorgos Kritikos, "From Labour to National Ideals: Ending the War in Asia Minor—Controlling Communism in Greece," *Societies*, vol. 3 (2013): 368.

155. *Gazette of the Debates*, 2nd Session; July 2, 1924, 13 (cited in Kritikos, 373).
156. Fotis M. Karamesinis, "Poinikopoiisi ton ideologikon andilipseon kai staseon stin Elliniki ekpaidefsi: Poines kai metra mesa sta ekpaideftika archeia tis periodou 1925–1929" [The criminalization of ideological perceptions and positions in Greek education: Crimes and punishments from the education archives of the period 1925–1929] (Postgraduate thesis, Ionian University, Corfu, 2015); Poulos, "Beyond the Ballot Box," 43–64.
157. "Letter from the Commissioner of Urban Police, Athens, to Venizelos," April 5, 1932, ELVEN_GR_ 24376, Venizelos archive.
158. Ghikas, *Rixi kai ensomatosi*.
159. Greek women gained full political rights in 1952 and exercised them for the first time in the elections of 1956.
160. "How Did Athenians Vote Yesterday?" *Acropolis*, February 12, 1934; "The Threat of the 'Red' Mayors in Various Towns of Northern Greece," *Acropolis*, January 26, 1934.
161. The All-People Front (*Pallaiko Metopo*), founded in 1935, was an electoral coalition formed between the KKE; the Common Front of Workers, Farmers and Professionals; and the United Front of Workers and Peasants that took 5.76 percent of the vote and won fifteen seats in the 1936 legislative elections. It participated in the elections of 1935 as Communists and Allies and took 9.59 percent, without electing any MPs.
162. "The Bloody May of '36 in Thessaloniki," *Rizospastis*, April 30, 2006.
163. Ioannis Metaxas, *Logoi kai Skepseis, 1936–1938*, vol. 1 (Govostis, 1969), 9.
164. In Anastasia Mitsopoulou, *Greek Anti-Communism in the Short Twentieth Century* (Epikendro, 2014), 30.
165. Sheila Fitzpatrick, *Education and Social Mobility in the Soviet Union 1921–1934* (Cambridge University Press, 2010).

CHAPTER 2

1. "Report of the Greek Delegation of the Comintern," Meeting of the Executive Committee of the Comintern, 26/31930, f. 495, op. 3, d. 160, 162–63. Fonds Francais de l'Internationale Communiste, Maison des Sciences de l'Homme de Dijon. My thanks to Anastasia Koukouna for sharing this material with me.
2. Christina Gilmartin, "Gender in the Formation of a Communist Body Politic," *Modern China* 19, no. 3 (1993): 314. For the party under Mao Zedong, see Wang Zheng, *Finding Women in the State: A Socialist Feminist Revolution in the People's Republic of China, 1949–1964* (Berkeley: University California Press, 2016).
3. Elizabeth Waters, "In the Shadow of the Comintern," in *Promissory Notes: Women in the Transition to Socialism*, ed. Sonia Kruks, Rayna Rapp, and Marilyn B. Young, 29–56 (Monthly Review Press, 1989).
4. On the communist reinstitutionalization of gender-role traditionalism after the Revolution, see Elizabeth Wood, *The Baba and the Comrade: Gender and Politics in Revolutionary Russia* (Indiana University Press, 2001).
5. Anna Krylova, "Bolshevik Feminism and Gender Agendas of Communism," in *World Revolution and Socialism in One Country 1917–1941*, vol. 1 of *The Cambridge History of*

Communism, ed. Sylvio Pons and Stephen A. Smith (Cambridge University Press, 2017), 444.
6. Fitzpatrick, *Tear Off the Masks*, 142.
7. "Report of the Central Committee to the Eighth Convention of the Communist Party of the USA." Cleveland, Ohio, April 2–8, 1934 (Workers Library Publishers, 1934), 123.
8. "On Bolshevization: The Education Program of the Party. Instructions of the Executive Committee on education work," *Rizospastis*, January 11, 1925.
9. Annie Kriegel, *The French Communists: Profile of a People*, trans. Elaine Halperin (University of Chicago Press, 1972), 264. This was not a characteristic of the individual file narratives consulted here but it appears to have been the case for KKE chief Nikos Zachariadis. See Nikos Zachariadis, *Istorika dilimmata, istorikes apandiseis: Apanda ta dimosievmena 1940–1945* [Historical dilemmas, historical responses: Complete published works 1940–1945] (Kastaniotis, 2011)
10. Zachariadis, *Istorika dilimmata*. This would be Zachariadis's second stint in the universities of the Comintern, having attended KUTV as a Soviet citizen before moving to Greece.
11. Marja Kivisaari, "Communists Are Not Born, They Are Made: The Political Education System of the French Communist Party," "Red Lives," special issue of *Socialist History*, no. 21 (2002): 70.
12. See John Halstead and Barry McLoughlin, "British Students at the International Lenin School," Ireland and the Spanish Civil War, accessed July 23, 2024, http://irelandscw.com/ibvol-MLSchool.htm.
13. Markovitis was executed in 1938 in the closing stages of the Great Terror. The author of his biography is his son. Marios Markovitis, *Ochi, den eimai echthros tou laou* [No, I am not an enemy of the people] (Epikendro, 2017), 115.
14. Stavridis, *Ta Paraskinia tou KKE*, 363–64.
15. Reference for Comrade Dimitropoulou, signed by Nikolaev, Jan. 28, 1934, f. 495, op. 207, d. 225, 6-33, RGASPI; "Letter to Dimitrov regarding Elena Dimitropoulou," File of Elena Dimitropoulou, f. 495, op. 207, d. 263, 2-4, RGASPI.
16. See KKE, *Dokimio Istorias tou KKE: 1919–1949* [Essays on the history of the KKE], vol. 1 (Syghroni Epochi, 2008); the memoirs of communist leader Vasilis Nefeloudis, *Aktina Θ* (Estia, 2007); the memoirs of leftist and journalist Periklis Rodakis, *Nikos Zachariadis* (Epikairotita, 2007); and the memoir of former general secretary of the KKE Grigoris Farakos, *B Pangosmios Polemos: Scheseis tou KKE kai Diethnous Kommounistikou Kendrou* [Second World War: Relations between the Greek Communist Party and the International Communist Center] (Ellinika Grammata, 2004). Bakola is mentioned in the work of historian Menelaos Haralambidis, *Dekemvriana 1944, H Machi tis Athinas* [The December Events 1944: The Battle of Athens] (Alexandria Press, 2014).
17. *Anketa* of Feodora Ignatievna Batman, f. 495, op. 207, d. 210, RGASPI.
18. Stratis Someritis, *I megali kampi: Martyries—anamniseis 1924–1974* (The great turning point: Testimonies—recollections), vol. 1 (Olkos, 1975), 80–87.
19. Zevgou, *Me ton Yianni Zevgo*, 46.

20. Partsalidou, *Anamniseis apo*, 36.
21. Markovitis, *Ochi, den eimai echthros*, 54.
22. Lefteris Apostolou, *O Aris Velouchiotis opos ton gnorisa* [Aris Velouchiotis as I knew him] (Filistor, 2003), 23.
23. Christian Gonsa, "Autobiografika keimena Ellinon kommouniston" [Autobiographical texts of Greek communists], *Mnimon*, vol. 17 (1995): 127.
24. I refer to the title of her book: Brigitte Studer, *The Transnational World of the Cominternians* (Palgrave Macmillan, 2015).
25. Markovitis, *Ochi, den eimai echthros*, 115.
26. Nikos Kazantzakis, *Russia: A Chronicle of Three Journeys in the Aftermath of the Revolution* (Creative Arts Book Company, 1989), 221; "Bolshevism in Theory and Practice," *Eleftheros Logos*, November 22, 1925.
27. Heinz Richter, "The Greek Communist Party and the Communist International," *Jahrbuch fur Historische Kommunismusforschung*, 111–40 (Aufbau Verlag, 2002). See also Elefandis, *H Epaggelia*; Zapantis, *Greek-Soviet Relations*, 169ff; Someritis, *H megale kampi*, 85.
28. Someritis, *H megali kampi*, 83.
29. Greek sources state that Hatzivasiliou attended the KUTV, but this is contradicted by her Comintern file which states clearly that she was a KUNMZ graduate.
30. John McIlroy and Alan Campbell, "Bolshevism, Stalinism and the Comintern: A Historical Controversy Revisited," *Labor History* 60, no. 3 (2019): 176.
31. L. J. Macfarlane, *The British Communist Party: Its Origin and Development until 1929* (McGibbon and Kee, 1966), 77–89.
32. Kriegel, *The French Communists*, 196.
33. Barry McLoughlin, "Proletarian Academics or Party Functionaries?: Irish Communists at the International Lenin School, Moscow, 1927–1937," *Saothar*, no. 22 (1997): 63.
34. See Gidon Cohen and Kevin Morgan, "Stalin's Sausage Machine: British Students at the International Lenin School 1926-1937," *Twentieth Century British History* 13, no. 4 (2002): 327–55.
35. Cohen and Morgan, "Stalin's Sausage Machine," 330.
36. Kivisaari, "Communists Are Not Born," 73.
37. Kriegel, *The French Communists*, 259–62. The cadres were at times referred to in communications between parties and with the Comintern as "assets."
38. Brigitte Studer, *The Transnational World of the Cominternians* (Palgrave Macmillan, 2015), 90, 97.
39. Berthold Unfried, "Foreign Communists and the Mechanisms of Soviet Cadre Formation in the USSR," in *Stalin's Terror*, ed. Barry McLoughlin et al. (Palgrave Macmillan, 2003), 175.
40. The sociologist Erving Goffman defined the "total institution" as "a place of residence and/or work where a large number of like-situated individuals cut off from the wider society for an appreciable period of time, together lead an enclosed, formally administered round of life." He included asylums, prisons, concentration camps, and English public schools like Eton. Goffman also emphasized, however, that resistance and the intransigence of inmates or students figured as much as transformation in the

total institutions he studied. That is, they did not embody any flawless model of control. Cited in Alan Campbell et al., "The International Lenin School: A Response to Cohen and Morgan," *Twentieth-Century British History* 15, no. 1 (2004): 57. See also Cohen and Morgan, "Stalin's Sausage Machine," 340.
41. Campbell et al., "The International Lenin School," 51–76.
42. Campbell et al., "The International Lenin School," 58.
43. John McIlroy and Alan Campbell, "Forging the Faithful: The British at the International Lenin School," *Labour History Review* 68, no. 1 (2003): 99–128. Other works that fall within the Soviet center/periphery genre include McLoughlin, "Proletarian Academics," 63-79; Alexander V. Pantsov and Daria A. Spichak, "New Light from the Russian Archives: Chinese Stalinists and Trotskyists at the International Lenin School in Moscow 1926-1938," *Twentieth-Century China* 33, no. 2 (2008): 50; Kivisaari, "Communists Are Not Born," 67-82.
44. McLoughlin and Campbell, "Forging the Faithful," 117.
45. The idea of a "loss of the self" originates with Hannah Arendt's influential analysis of totalitarian regimes, in *The Origins of Totalitarianism* (Penguin Books, 2017).
46. Jochen Hellbeck, "Working, Struggling, Becoming: Stalin-Era Autobiographical Texts," *Russian Review* 60, no. 3 (2001): 341.
47. Fitzpatrick, *Education and Social Mobility*, 19.
48. Much of the English-language literature draws on the work of Natalya Timofeyeva, "Kommunistichyeskii Univyersitet Trudyaschikhsya—Tsetr idyeinoi podgotovki ryevolyutsionnykh kadrov" [The Communist University for Toilers of the East: Center for Ideological Preparation for Communist Revolutionary Cadres] (PhD diss., Institute of Oriental Studies of the Academy of Sciences, Moscow, 1989); Julia Kostenburger, "Die Geschichte der Kommunistischen Universitat der nationalen Minderheiten des Westens (KUNMZ) in Moskau 1921–1936," in *Jahrbuch fur historische Kommunismusforschung*, no. 8-9 (Mannheimer Zentrum fur Europaische Sozialforschung, Aufbau Verlag, 2000–2001), 248–303.
49. Lisa A. Kirschenbaum, *International Communism and the Spanish Civil War* (Cambridge University Press, 2015); Brigitte Studer, *The Transnational World of the Cominternians* (Springer Verlag, 2015); Irina Filatova, "Indoctrination or Scholarship?: Education of Africans at the Communist University of the Toilers of the East in the Soviet Union, 1923–1937," *Paedagogica Historica* 35, no. 1 (1999): 65; Lana Ravandi-Fadai, "'Red Mecca': The Communist University for Laborers of the East (KUTV): Iranian Scholars and Students in Moscow in the 1920s and 1930s," *Iranian Studies*, vol. 48, no. 5 (2015): 718.
50. Filatova, *Indoctrination or Scholarship*, 64.
51. Ravandi-Fadai, *Red Mecca*, 713.
52. Meredith L. Roman, "Race, Politics and US Students in 1930s Soviet Russia," *Race and Class* 53, no. 2 (2011): 71.
53. Kirschenbaum, *International Communism*, 19.
54. Kirschenbaum, *International Communism*, 19.
55. McIlroy and Campbell, *Bolshevism, Stalinism and the Comintern*, 174.
56. McIlroy and Campbell, *Bolshevism, Stalinism and the Comintern*, 174.

57. Pandelis Pouliopoulos (b. 1899, Larissa, Greece) was among the founders of the Trotskyist movement in Greece. In 1924, he was a Party delegate to the 5th Congress of the Comintern, and later that year became general secretary of the KKE.
58. Cited in Papastefanaki, *Labor, Technology and Gender*, 404.
59. From J. V. Stalin, "The Political Tasks of the University of the Peoples of the East." Speech delivered May 18, 1925, at a meeting of students of the Communist University of the Toilers of the East. First published in *Pravda* on May 22, 1925. Now available in the Stalin Reference Archive, Marxists Internet Archive, 2005, https://www.marxists.org/reference/archive/stalin/works/1925/05/18.htm.
60. Artiom Ulunian, "The Communist Party of Greece," in *International Communism and the Communist International*, ed. Tim Rees and Andrew Thorpe (Manchester University Press, 1998), 190. Ulunian has drawn all the Greek KUTV data from one source: Timofeyeva, "Kommunisticheskhih Universitet Trudiashchiksia Vostroka."
61. See Masha Kirasirova, "The 'East' as a Category of Bolshevik Ideology and Comintern Administration: The Arab Section of the Communist University of the Toilers of the East," *Kritika: Explorations in Russian and Eurasian History* 18, no. 1 (2017): 8. See also the speech by Stalin, "The Political Tasks."
62. See respectively, Richter, "The Greek Communist Party," 131; "The 4th Conference of the Greek Communist Party of Greece, 10–15 December 1928" (Document no. 399), in *To KKE—Episima Keimena, 1925-1928*, vol. 2 (KKE—Official Documents) (Syghroni Epochi, 1974), 558.
63. The first attempt was made in 1920. In accordance with the decision made at the 2nd Congress of the SEKE (later renamed Greek Communist Party), Demosthenes Ligdopoulos would represent the Party at the 2nd Congress of the Comintern to negotiate entry into the Comintern order. *Kommounistiki Epitheorisi*, vol. 2 (Feb. 1921).
64. For example, in 1925, three out of twenty-one students in the Iranian sector of KUTV were women. Ravandi-Fadai, "'Red Mecca,'" 718.
65. "Letter to Komintern Administration and Comrade Frumkina (KUNMZ) from CPG Representative," August 31, 1927, f. 529, op. 1, d. 71, RGASPI. The slight was in all likelihood less to do with the quality of the training offered at the KUTV and more to do with the "eastern" identification.
66. I refer once again to the KKE's obligation to accept the Balkan Communist Federation's controversial position on Macedonian national independence, in support of the interests of the more important Bulgarian Communist Party. The KKE's policy on Macedonian independence damaged the party's appeal irreparably and served to legitimize state repression of the communist movement for decades thereafter. See Potamianos, "Internationalism and the Emergence of Communist Politics."
67. Edward B. Richards, "Soviet Control of the Third International," *Social Science*. 36, no. 1 (1961): 27.
68. See G. V. Antonov, "Communist University for National Minorities of the West," in *Great Soviet Encyclopedia* (1979). The Great Soviet Encyclopedia, 3rd Edition (1970–1979). Available through the Free Dictionary, © 2010, http://encyclopedia2.thefreedictionary.com/Communist+University+for+National+Minorities+of+the+West.

69. Antonov, "Communist University."
70. *Anketa* of Chrysa Hatzivasiliou, f. 495, op. 207, d. 13, RGASPI; *Anketa* of Lena Anemelou, f. 495, op. 207, d. 199; *Anketa* of Clio Dimitrievna Stai, f. 495, op. 207, d. 636, RGASPI.
71. The first phase was during capitalism's rise prior to World War I, the second being the short period after the crushing of the post-war revolutions when it seemed to have stabilized. This meant that a decisive and final revolutionary upheaval was also afoot and the sections of the Comintern had to make ready for the immediate advent of socialist revolution. Instead, there was the Nazi rise to power, the brutal destruction of the mighty German labor movement, and the resultant imbroglio of communist theory and practice. See Kevin McDermott and Jeremy Agnew, *The Comintern: A History of International Communism from Lenin to Stalin* (Palgrave, 1996).
72. Nicholas N. Kozlov and Eric D. Weitz, "Reflections on the Origins of the 'Third Period': Bukharin, the Comintern, and the Political Economy of Weimar Germany," *Journal of Contemporary History*, vol. 24 (1989): 387.
73. See Zev Katz, "Party Political Education in Soviet Russia 1918-1935," *Soviet Studies* 7, no. 3 (1956): 243.
74. "Information on Admission of Students to KUNMZ in 1929/1930," f. 529, op. 1, d. 71, RGASPI; "Academic Progress Report, Greek Sector KUNMZ, 1st semester academic year, 1929/1930," f. 529, op. 1, d. 306, RGASPI.
75. "KUTV Rules of Admission 1928/29," f. 532, op. 1, d. 65, RGASPI.
76. J. T. Murphy, "The First Year of the Lenin School," *Communist International*, September 30, 1927, 267.
77. Harry Haywood, *Black Bolshevik: Autobiography of an Afro-American Communist* (University of Minnesota Press, 1978) 198.
78. Bronska-Pampuch published her insider account under the pseudonym Alfred Burmeister in 1955, just after Stalin's death. Alfred Burmeister, *Dissolution and Aftermath of the Comintern: Experiences and Observations 1937–1947* (Research Program on the USSR, 1955), 9–10. See also Mette Skak, "Female Comintern Insiders," NANOPDF, May 16, 2018, https://nanopdf.com/download/female-comintern-insiders_pdf.
79. See Joni Krekola and Ole Martin Running, "International Cadre Education of Nordic Communists," in *Red Star in the North: Communism in the Northern Countries*, ed. Sven Egge et al., 292–302 (Oslo: Orkana Forlag, 2015).
80. Markovitis' estimation of the size of the Greek sector is supported by the fact that the MLS also hosted a Party organization for the Greek students headed by Grigoris Skafidas, and a trade union organization headed by Yiannis Pandelias. Markovitis, *Ochi, den eimai echthros*, 142–43.
81. *Anketa* of Lidiia Ivanovna Petrova, f. 495, op. 207, d. 65, RGASPI. According to Markovitis there were still eleven Greek students enrolled in 1936, the volatile year of the university's closure, when many, including Lidiia Ivanovna, fell victim to Stalin's purges. Markovitis, *Ochi, den eimai echthros*, 140.
82. *Anketa* of Feodora Ignatievna Batman, f. 495, op. 207, d. 210, RGASPI.
83. See Robert Levy, *Ana Pauker: The Rise and Fall of a Jewish Communist* (University of California Press, 2001), 207.

84. Kivisaari, "Communists Are Not Born," 78.
85. "KUTV Minimum Subject Requirements," f. 532, op. 8, d. 104, 8, RGASPI.
86. "Teaching Department KUNMZ," f. 529, op. 1, d. 70, RGASPI.
87. "KUTV Rules of Admission," f. 532, op. 1, d. 131, RGASPI.
88. Krekola and Running, "International Cadre Education," 296.
89. Report to Sixth Plenum of Executive Committee of the Communist International (ECCI) 1925–6 f. 495, op. 164, d. 500, RGASPI.
90. See Katz, "Party Political Education."
240. For more on the Institute of Red Professors see Michael David-Fox, *Revolution of the Mind: Higher Learning among the Bolsheviks, 1918–1929* (Cornell University Press, 1997) 133–91.
91. "Minutes of Meeting of the Greek Party Circle of September 14, 1926," f. 532, op. 2, d. 82, 10, RGASPI.
92. "Minutes of General Meeting of Greek and Albanian Party Circle," Dec. 14, 1928, f. 532, op. 2, d. 83, 13, RGASPI.
93. "Teaching Department KUNMZ," f. 529, op.1, d. 70, 3, RGASPI. For a discussion of similar problems in the Irish sector of the MLS, see McLoughlin, "Proletarian Academics," 74.
94. Vasilis Nefeloudis, *Martyries 1906–1908* [Testimonies 1906–1938] (Okeanida, 1984), 194–97. Cited also in Markovitis, *"No, I Am Not an Enemy,"* 141–43.
95. *Anketa* of Kaiti Vasiliou, f. 495, op. 207, d. 98, RGASPI.
96. The nature of this voluntary status is not explained but may suggest that her position was self-funded, or not subsidized by the Comintern.
97. "Character reference, compiled by comrades M. M. Makroyani and Petrova," dated May 29, 1937, File of Clio Dimitrievna Stai, f. 495, op. 207, d. 636, 27, RGASPI.
98. Markovitis, *Ochi, den eimai echthros*, 140.
99. Nikos Zachariadis had undertaken postgraduate study at the MLS (circa 1929-1931).
100. M. Offerle, *Les partis politiques* (Paris: Presses Universitaires de France, 1987).
101. Filatova, "Indoctrination or Scholarship?," 65.
102. Katz, "Party Political Education," 242.
103. Serbo-Croat(ian) was the term used to refer to the South Slavic language spoken in Serbia, Croatia, and elsewhere in the former Yugoslavia, and the term used in the referenced source. Since the breakup of Yugoslavia, the names of the individual languages have generally been preferred.
104. Philippe Bourrinet's *An Ambiguous Journey: Ante Ciliga (1898–1992)* is based largely on Ciliga's own writings, especially *The Russian Enigma* (Ink Links, 1979). Ciliga argued that his students embodied a great paradox of the Soviet system. Coming from the working class, they were the parvenus of the system, and therefore "the worst enemies of any authentic workers' movement"; an authentic workers' movement would necessarily "seek the annihilation of the whole bureaucratic system." Philippe Bourrinet, *An Ambiguous Journey: Ante Ciliga (1898–1992)* [Dec. 12, 1992], trans. George Gordon, 1993, *Left-Disorder*, http://www.left-dis.nl/uk/ciliga.htm.
105. Wolfgang Leonhard, *Child of the Revolution*, trans. C. M. Woodhouse (Collins: 1957), 75.
106. Quoted in Kivisaari, "Communists Are Not Born," 66–82.

CHAPTER 3

1. Stavridis, *Ta Paraskinia tou KKE*, 231.
2. *Anketa* of Olga Papadopoulou (pseud. Olga Vlasova Spiridovna), f. 495, op. 207, d. 159, RGASPI.
3. McLoughlin, "Proletarian Academics," 74–75.
4. Loukas Karliaftis (pseud. Kostas Kastritis), "The Birth of Bolshevism in Greece," *Revolutionary History* 3, no. 3 (spring 1991), https://www.marxists.org/history/etol/revhist/supplem/karliaft.htm. Karliaftis, a leading figure of the Greek Trotskyist movement, uses the terms Bolshevization and Stalinization, in the context of the KKE, interchangeably. For an overview of the debate on similarities and distinguishing features of each, see John McIlroy and Alan Campbell, "Bolshevism, Stalinism and the Comintern: A Historical Controversy Revisited," *Labor History* 60, no. 3 (2019).
5. Loukas Karliaftis, "Stalinism and Trotskyism in Greece" *Revolutionary History* 3, no. 3 (spring 1991), https://www.marxists.org/history/etol/revhist/backiss/vol3/no3/staltrot.html. Extract from an article originally published in *Diethnistis* (Internationalist), 1979.
6. Nefeloudis refers here to the Stalinist leadership represented by the "troika" Zachariadis, Ioannidis, and Michaelidis. See Nefeloudis, *Martiries*, 52-61.
7. Richter, "The Greek Communist Party," 111–40.
8. Quote taken from Mario Kessler, "Resisting Moscow? Ruth Fischer and the KPD", in *Weimar Communism as Mass Movement 1918-1933* ed. Ralf Hoffrogge and Norman LaPorte (Lawrence and Wishart, 2017).
9. Stavridis, *Ta Paraskinia tou KKE*, 230. Stavridis served as general secretary of the KKE in 1925-1926. He was expelled from the Party in 1928 and became an ardent and outspoken anticommunist.
10. See Emmanouil Pratsinakis, "Contesting National Belonging: An Established–Outsider Figuration on the Margins of Thessaloniki, Greece" (PhD diss., Universiteit van Amsterdam, 2013), 54; Ioannis Hasiotis, *Oi Ellines tis Rossias kai tis Sovietikis Enosis: Metoikesies kai ektopismoi* [The Greeks of Russia and the Soviet Union: relocations and displacements] (Thessaloniki: University Studio Press, 1997); Markovitis, *Ochi, den eimai echthros tou laou*, 128.
11. The CPSU is also often referred to in Comintern documents as the Russian Communist Party (RCP).
12. Former KKE leader Eleftherios Stavridis, for example, makes this reference. See his *Ta Paraskinia tou KKE*.
13. "Paterouli" could have been a pseudonym; it was a commonly used nickname for Stalin by Greek communists; it translates to uncle, or sacrosanct/wise father. There is no specific reference to Pontic origins in the *ankety* of students.
14. Ravandi-Fadai, for example, notes that students in the Iranian sector of the KUTV were not necessarily Party members. See *Red Mecca*, 719. For more on communization, see David-Fox, *Revolution of the Mind*, 80.
15. See Krekola and Running, "International Cadre Education."

16. For the KKE numbers see Elefandis, *H Epaggelia*, 319. Elefandis draws partly on the work of Branko Lazitch in *Les Partis Communistes d'Europe* (Les Iles d'Or, 1956), 212. According to these Comintern data the KKE membership numbered 1,320 in 1920, 6,000 in 1934, and 17,500 in 1936.
17. *Anketa* of Chrysa Hatzivasiliou, f. 495, op. 207, d. 13, RGASPI; *Anketa* of Lena Anemelou, f. 495, op. 207, d. 199, RGASPI; *Anketa* of Clio Dimitrievna Stai, f. 495, op. 207, d. 636, RGASPI.
18. The dominance of Soviet Greeks in the Greek sector of KUNMZ pertains to female students only. University records for the period from 1928 to 1930 state that Soviet Greeks were a numerical minority in the Greek sector of the KUNMZ. Specifically, of forty-three student enrollments recorded in the Greek sector during this period, thirty-one were listed as Greek nationals, ten as Soviet Greeks, and two as "political immigrants" whose admittance was coordinated by the ECCI. These records make no reference to gender, but it is reasonable to assume that most of the Greek nationals were male. See "Information on Admission of students to KUNMZ," f. 529, op. 1, d. 71, 3, RGASPI; "Minutes of the General Meeting of the Greek and Albanian Party Circle," f. 532, op. 83, d. 3, 3, RGASPI.
19. See Paschalis Kitromilides, "Greek Irredentism in Asia Minor and Cyprus," *Middle East Studies* 26, no. 1 (1990): 3–17.
20. Reference to the Greek situation in the file of Feodora Ignatievna Batman, f. 495, op. 207, d. 210, 14, RGASPI.
21. "References and Work Record of Yevgenia Andreevna Dimitropoulou," f. 495, op. 207, d. 225, 1-6, RGASPI.
22. *Anketa* of Stella Vamniatzidou (pseud., Elena Agneva / Yiannoula Nikolaides / Elena Arnova / Stella Vudanya) f. 495, op. 207, d. 98, RGASPI; Kaiti Vasiliou / Chrysanthi Kantzidou f. 495, op. 207, d. 98, RGASPI; Olga Bakola (pseud., Aliki Kanda) f. 495, op. 207, d. 99, RGASPI.
23. See KKE, *To KKE sto Italo-Elliniko Polemo 1940–1941* [KKE during the Greek-Italian war] (Syghroni Epochi, 2015), 229.
24. "Questionnaire of Chrisoula Vagia," f. 495, op. 209, d. 183, 1–11, RGASPI.
25. File of Lidiia Petrova, f. 495, op. 207, d. 65, 20, RGASPI. An additional file belongs to Vera Georgievna Karayianni, who travelled to Moscow to work as a typist in the Greek sector of the MLS on the recommendation of the KKE. Karayani came from a family of tobacco workers in Athens, who had joined the Workers' Union and the Party in 1927 and began employment in the Greek sector of the MLS in 1932. "Information on Vera Kirianovna Karayianni" f. 495, op. 207, d. 222, 10, RGASPI.
26. File of Lidiia Ivanovna Cherman (Petrova), f. 495, op. 207, d. 65, 12, RGASPI.
27. Nefeloudis, *Martiries*, 52-61. Cited also in Markovitis, *Ochi, den eimai echthros*, 141–43.
28. See V. Maos. "Plythismiakes exelixeis ton Ellinon Pontion stin proin Sovietiki Enosi kai stin Ellada" [Demographic developments of the Greek Pontics in the former Soviet Union and in Greece], in *Pontic Immigrants from the Former Soviet Union: Social and Economic Integration*, ed. K. Kasimati (Secretary General for Greek Returnees and European Social Fund, 1992), 538.

29. *Kulak* in Russian means a "fist." When used by the communists to refer to rich peasants, it alludes to their alleged fist-like hold on their poorer brethren. Vladimir Lenin saw the *kulak* as a "village bourgeoisie" that would be crushed by a socialist revolution. This was achieved during Stalin's "revolution from the top" that mandated collectivization and "dekulakization." See Moshe Lewin, "Who Was the Soviet Kulak?" *Europe-Asia Studies* 18, no. 2 (1966): 189–212; Lynne Viola. "The Campaign to Eliminate the Kulak as a Class, Winter 1929–1930: A Re-evaluation of the Legislation," *Slavic Review* 45, no. 3 (1986): 503–24; Robert Conquest, *The Harvest of Sorrow: Soviet Collectivization and the Terror–Famine* (Oxford University Press, 1986).
30. See A. Popov, "From Pindos to Pontos: The Ethnicity and Diversity of Greek Communities in Southern Russia," *Bulletin: Anthropology, Minorities, Multiculturalism*, vol. 5 (2004): 84–90; Anton Popov, "Making Sense of Home and Homeland: Former Soviet-Greeks' Motivations and Strategies for a Transnational Migrant Circuit," *Journal of Ethnic and Migration Studies* 36, no. 1 (2010): 67–85; Pratsinakis, *Contesting National Belonging*; Eftichia Voutira, "Post-Soviet Diaspora Politics: The Case of the Soviet Greeks," *Journal of Modern Greek Studies* 24, no. 2 (2006): 379-414.
31. This background is drawn from Neal Ascherson's masterful *Black Sea: The Birthplace of Civilization and Barbarism* (Vintage, 1996), 17.
32. See Ioannis Hasiotis, *Oi Ellines tis kai tis Sovietikis Enosis* [The Greeks of Russia and the USSR] (University Studio Press, 1997); A. Xanthopoulou-Kyriakou, "The Diaspora of the Greeks of the Pontos: Historical Background," *Journal of Refugee Studies* 4, no. 4 (1991): 357–63; E. Sideri, *The Greeks of the Former Soviet Republic of Georgia: Memories and Practices of Diaspora* (University of London, 2006); Pratsinakis, *Contesting National Belonging*.
33. Hasiotis, *Oi Ellines tis Rossias*; Eftichia Voutira, *The "Right to Return" and the Meaning of "Home": A Post-Soviet Greek Diaspora Becoming European?* (Lit Verlag, 2012).
34. I. T. Stogiannis, *What I Saw in Soviet Russia: Phenomena and Other Things* [in Greek] (Vradini, 1934), 287.
35. A. Karpozilos, "Pontic Culture in the USSR between the Wars," *Journal of Refugee Studies* 4, no. 4 (1991): 366.
36. *Kosmos* newspaper (Odessa), no. 49, March 9, 1907, cited in Irena Bogdanović and Walter Puchner, *Elliniko theatro stin Odysso 1814–1914: Agnosta stoicheia gia Ellinikes parastaseis stin poli tis Filikis Etaireias kai stis Pareuxeinies Hores apo Rosikes kai Ellinikes Efimerides tis Odyssou* [Greek Theater in Odessa 1814–1914: Unknown aspects of Greek performance in the city of the Friendly Society and in the Black Sea areas, as presented in Russian and Greek newspapers of Odessa] (Paravasis, 2013), 207; Walter Puchner, "Greek Cultural Activities in the Black Sea around 1900," in *Ethno-Cultural Diversity in the Balkans and the Caucasus*, ed. Thede Kahl and Ioanna Nechiti, 242–56 (Austrian Academy of Science, 2019).
37. Bogdanović and Puchner, "Greek Theater in Odessa," 204.
38. Vlassis Agtsidis, *Parefxinios Diaspora* [Black Sea diaspora] (Adelfoi Kyriakidi, 1997); Vlassis Agtsidis, *Pontiakos Ellinismos: Apo tin Genoktonia kai to Stalinismo stin Perestroika* [Pontic Hellenism: From the genocide and Stalinism to perestroika] (Thessaloniki: Adelfoi Kyriakidi, 1997).

39. See Sofia Illiadou-Tachou and Alexia Orfanou, "From Tsarist Russia to the Soviet Union: The Effects of Civil War on Grecophone Education," in *Democratisation of Education: Historical Perspectives*, ed. Zanda Rubene, 131–40 (University of Latvia Press, 2015).
40. Terry Martin, "An Affirmative Action Empire: The Soviet Union as the Highest Form of Imperialism," in *A State of Nations: Empire and Nation Making in the Age of Lenin and Stalin*, ed. Ronald G. Suny and T. Martin (Oxford University Press, 2001), 73.
41. Roger Markwick, "Ukraine and Great Russian Power: Christian Rakovsky versus Josef Stalin 1922-1923," *Historical Materialism* (blog), January 27, 2023, https://www.historicalmaterialism.org/blog/ukraine-and-great-russian-power-christian-rakovsky-versus-joseph-stalin-1922-23.
42. Markovitis, *Ochi, den eimai echthros*, 65.
43. See Vlada Baranova, "Local Language Planners in the Context of Early Soviet Language Policy: The Case of Mariupol Greeks," in "1917 en Russie: La Philologie a l'epreuve de la Revolution," special issue, *Revue des Etudes Slaves* 88, no. 1–2 (2017): 97–112.
44. Apostolos Karpozilos, "The Greeks in Russia," in *The Greek Diaspora in the Twentieth Century*, ed. Richard Clogg (Macmillan, 1999).
45. R. M Dawkins, "The Pontic Dialect of Modern Greek in Asia Minor and Russia," *Transactions of the Philological Society* 36, no. 1 (1937): 18. See also Baranova, "Local Language Planners."
46. On literacy and language see Dawkins, "The Pontic Dialect"; Hasiotis, *Oi Ellines tis Rossias*; Karpozilos, "Pontic Culture." On the singular cultural integrity and "historic Pontic separatism," see Anthony Bryer, "Greeks and Turkmens: The Pontic Exception," *Dumbarton Oaks Papers*, no. 29 (1975): 113–48.
47. "Resolution Bearing on the Matter of Summer Internship, Greek Sector, KUNMZ," dated Nov. 8, 1929, f. 529, op. 1, d. 306, 3, RGASPI. On the subject of language and education in the Pontic Greek communities of prerevolutionary Russia and the Soviet Union, see Voutira, *The "Right to Return."*
48. Sokhum-born (Pontian) Andronikos Haitas (Sifnaios) had graduated from the "general" KUTV sector, before going to Greece in 1922 and joining the SEKE/KKE.
49. "Autobiography," File of Yefrosinia Diamantidou, f. 495, op. 207, d. 482, 14, RGASPI.
50. "Letter to Rector, Comrade Frumkina," June 3, 1935, File of Daria Mikhailovna Yarmosh, f. 495, op. 207, d. 467, 15, RGASPI.
51. "Letter to Comrade Kupriyanov," dated Oct. 8, 1925, File of Olga Papadopoulou (Vlasova), f. 495, op. 207, d. 159, 20, RGASPI.
52. M. Pratsinakis, "Contesting National Belonging," 48.
53. "KUTV Meeting of the Greek Circle: Resolution to Address the Linkage between General Course Students and International Students," f. 532, op. 2, d. 82, 8, RGASPI.
54. "Annual Report on the Work in the Greek Sector, KUNMZ 1932-1933," f. 529, op. 1, d. 312, 13, RGASPI.
55. As was the case for Kerasidou, who was asked to translate Stalin's "Questions of Leninism" into Greek. "Letter from Comrade Parishev, Publishing House of Literature in Foreign languages, to Comrade Gulyaev," ECCI Human Resources Department,

dated March 2, 1940, *Anketa* of Olga Ivanova (Kerasidou) f. 495, op. 207, d. 169, 10, RGASPI.
56. "KUNMZ Rector Frumkina to Kultprop" (Department of Cultural and Educational Propaganda). Central Committee, VKP(b), July 9, 1934, f. 529, op. 1, d. 71, 3-4, RGASPI.
57. "KUNMZ Rector Frumkina to Kultprop" (Department of Cultural and Educational Propaganda). Central Committee, VKP(b), July 9, 1934, f. 529, op. 1, d. 71, 3-4, RGASPI.
58. Kriegel, *The French Communists*, 253.
59. Nikos Zachariadis had undertaken postgraduate study at the MLS (circa 1929-1931).
60. Kostas Grizonas, *Kokkinoi drapetes 1920–1944* [Red fugitives 1920–1944] (Glaros, 1985), 21.
61. Halstead and McLoughlin, "British Students."
62. "Biographical Report of Comrade Allegra Felous" (also appears as "Fegous"), f. 495, op. 207, d. 1060, RGASPI.
63. "Report on Summer Internship Working Yalta District in Dec. 3–Jan. 20, 1929," f. 529, op. 1, d. 306, 1, RGASPI.
64. "Report on Summer Internship Working Yalta District in Dec. 3–Jan. 20, 1929," f. 529, op. 1, d. 306, 1, RGASPI.
65. "Annual Report on the Work of the Greek Sector, KUNMZ, 1933-34," f. 529, op. 1, d. 71, RGASPI.
66. See Hiroako Kuromiya, "Ukraine and Russia in the 1930s," *Harvard Ukrainian Studies* 18, no. 3 (1994): 331. See also Violetta Hionidou and David Saunders, "Exiles and Pioneers: Oral Histories of Greeks Deported from the Caucasus to Kazakhstan in 1949," *Europe-Asia Studies* 62, no. 9 (2010): 1,479–501.
67. The contribution of Vlassis Agtsidis to this history is especially noteworthy. See, for example, Agtsidis's "The Persecution of the Pontic Greeks in the Soviet Union," *Journal of Refugee Studies* 4, no. 4 (1991): 372–82. See also Terry Martin "The Origins of Soviet Ethnic Cleansing," *Journal of Modern History* 70, no. 4 (1998): 813–61. For the deportation of Soviet Greeks to Kazakhstan see Hionidou and Saunders, "Exiles and Pioneers"; I. Dzhukha, *Grecheskaya Operatsiya* (Aleteiya, 2006); N. L. Pobol and P. M. Polian, eds., *Stalinskie deportatsii 1928–1953* (Materik, 2005); Nikolay Bugay, *The Deportation of Peoples in the Soviet Union* (Nova Publishers, 1996).
68. This information appears, for example, in Markovitis's rare account of the fate of the Greek students at the KUNMZ and the MLS at this time based on his father's diaries. See Markovitis, *Ochi, den eimai echthros*.
69. File of Lidiia Petrova Ivanovna/Cherman, f. 495, op. 207, d. 65, 12, RGASPI. See also Golfo Alexopoulos, "Stalin and the Politics of Kinship: Practices of Collective Punishment, 1920s–1940s," *Comparative Studies in Society and History* 50, no. 1 (2008): 91–117.

CHAPTER 4

1. Jochen Hellbeck, "Working, Struggling, Becoming: Stalin-Era Autobiographical Texts," *Russian Review* 60, no. 3 (2001): 341.
2. Hellbeck, "Working, Struggling," 15.

3. *Kulak*, in Russian, means a "fist" and was used by communists to refer to rich peasants. Lenin saw the *kulak* as a "village bourgeoisie" that would be crushed by a socialist revolution. See Lewin, "Who Was the Soviet Kulak?"; Viola, "The Campaign to Eliminate"; and Conquest, *The Harvest of Sorrow*.
4. In the dominant interpretation of Bolshevik thought led by Igal Halfin, Leopold Haimson, Stephen Kotkin, and Sheila Fitzpatrick, "class consciousness" is understood as the ultimate goal in the Bolsheviks' interaction with the working class. Accordingly, working-class identity was a state of mind and thus accessible to non-proletarian classes as long as they "assume the proletarian point of view." Krylova has since introduced the concept of "class instinct" to explain the Bolshevik obsession with "social origins," as the guiding principle of social governance and organization after 1917. The Bolsheviks believed that workers were unique carriers of the proletarian class instinct that made a part of their personality essential and innate. For the Bolsheviks, class position was an environment out of which class instinct evolved and made workers who they were—revolutionaries by instinct. See Anna Krylova, "Beyond the Spontaneity-Consciousness Paradigm: 'Class Instinct' as a Promising Category of Historical Analysis," *Slavic Review* 62, no. 1 (2003): 1–23.
5. Kritikou was possibly the wife or relative of Leandros Kritikos, also a KUTV alumnus and one-time member of the Central Committee of the KKE. See the reference to Kritikos in Stavridis, *Ta Paraskinia tou KKE*, 93. Bolshevik shorthand here refers to the standardized language and categories characteristic of all *ankety*. Scholars such as Stephen Kotkin refer to this as "Bolshevik speak," where the speaker/writer does not necessarily mean or believe everything he/she says. Rather, the expression signals a willingness to participate *as if one believed,* and it signals that one recognizes the rules (and the discourse) of an agreed-upon reality. See for example Stephen Kotkin, *Magnetic Mountain: Stalinism as a Civilization* (University of California Press, 1995).
6. "KUTV Character References of Students in the Greek group," f. 532, op. 2, d. 83, RGASPI.
7. "Record of Party Work, Member and Candidates of the Party Circle of the Greek Sector," f. 532, op. 2, d. 82, 8, RGASPI.
8. *Rizospastis*, Sept., 22, 1930; March 22, 1931; Dec. 27, 1935.
9. "Biography," file of Olga Vlasova (Papadopoulou), f. 495, op. 207, d. 159, 16, RGASPI.
10. File of Stella Kerasidou (Olga Ivanova), f. 495, op. 207, d. 169, 2, RGASPI. For an officer's eyewitness account of the Pontian exodus to Russia during the Russo-Turkish Wars see Felix Fonton, *Russia in Asia Minor: The Campaign of Marshal Paskevitch in 1828–29* [in French] (Leneveu, 1840). See also Ioannis F. Kaztaridis, *I "exodos" ton Ellinon tou Kars tis Armenias* [The exodus of the Greek from Kars Armenia] (Kyriakidis 1996); Michel Bruneau, "The Pontic Greeks, from Pontus to the Caucasus, Greece, and the Diaspora: 'Iconography' and Mobile Frontiers," *Journal of Alpine Research* 101, no. 2 (2013), https://doi.org/10.4000/rga.2092; Pratsinakis, "Contesting National Belonging."
11. See, respectively, Speros Vryonis Jr., "The Labour Battalions in the Ottoman Empire," in *Cultural and Ethical Legacies: The Armenian Genocide*, ed. Richard Hovannisian (Routledge, 2006): 275–91; Tanja Penter, "From a Local *Erfahrungsgeschichte* of Ho-

Iodomor to a Global History of Famines," in "Round Table on Soviet Famines," special issue, *Contemporary European History* 27, no. 3 (2018): 447.

12. This quote is based on the observations of a British liaison officer stationed in Greece during the Resistance, who recalled that village women, especially in the mountains, were treated as "not very valuable animals." As recounted in US government report by D. M. Condit, *Assessing Revolutionary and Insurgent Strategies: Case Study in Guerrilla War—Greece during World War Two*, rev. ed. (Army Special Operations Command, 1962), 173. Similar habits and attitudes are recalled by members of my own family about their ancestors in rural Greece.

13. "Letter to Esteemed Comrade Khrushchev" May 31, 1962, File of Olga Vlasova (Papadopoulou), f. 495, op. 207, d. 159, 16, RGASPI.

14. See Francisco J. Beltrán Tapia, and Michail Raftakis, "Sex Ratios and Gender Discrimination in Modern Greece," *Population Studies: A Journal of Demography* 76, no. 2 (2022): 331; see also Violetta Hionidou, "Nuptiality Patterns and Household Structure on the Greek Island of Mykonos, 1859–1959," *Journal of Family History* 20, no. 2 (1995): 67–102; Aglaia E. Kasdagli, "Dowry and Inheritance, Gender and Empowerment in the 'Notarial Societies' of the Early Modern Greek World," *Fund og Forskning i Det Kongelige Biblioteks Samlinger* 44, no. 3 (2005), https://doi.org/10.7146/fof.v44i3.132994.

15. "Registration card," file of Olga Vlasova (Papadopoulou), f. 495, op. 207, d. 159, 32, RGASPI.

16. The fight against tuberculosis was a major driver of the momentum for the complete modernization of Greek social welfare. See Vasiliki Theodorou and Despina Karakatsani, "Health Policy in Interwar Greece: The Intervention by the League of Nations Health Organisation," *Dynamis* (Granada), vol. 28 (2008): 53–66; Katerina Hatzikonstandinou and Lydia Sapounaki-Drakaki, "Two Sanatorium Cases in the Greater Athens Area: Ideal Curative Urban Environments or Perfect Social Exiles?," *Histoire Urbaine* 1, no. 39 (2014): 137–59.

17. *Rizospastis*, Sept. 29, 1928.

18. "Autobiography," file of Olga Ivanova (Kerasidou), f. 495, op. 207, d. 169, 15-16, RGASPI.

19. Gilmartin, "Gender in the Formation," 310.

20. Sara Ann Sewell, "Bolshevising Communist Women: The Red Women and Girls' League in Weimar Germany," *Central European History*, vol. 45 (2012): 272; see also Elizabeth E. Wood, "The Trial of the New Woman: Citizens-in-Training in the New Soviet Republic," *Gender and History* 13, no.3 (2001): 524–46.

21. On the credibility of communist women in relation to the Polish Communist Party between the Wars, see Natalia Jarska, "Women Communists and the Polish Communist Party: From 'Fanatic' Revolutionaries to Invisible Bureaucrats (1918-1945)," *History of Communism in Europe*, vol. 8 (2017): 194.

22. See "Letter to the Politburo of the Central Committee of the Greek Communist Party," June 18, 1932, file of Koula Theou, f. 495, op. 207, d. 303, 1, RGASPI. Theou was married to a member of the Politburo of the time, Kostas Theos.

23. See Sewell, "Bolshevising Communist Women," 287.

24. Eric Weitz coined the term defeminization in reference to German Communism; see Eric D. Weitz, *Creating German Communism 1890-1990: From Popular Front to Socialist State* (Princeton University Press, 1997), 216.
25. Haitas was arrested and probably executed by the NKVD in 1937 as an "enemy of the people," in the context of Stalin's counter-espionage operations, and was never seen again.
26. "Letter to Human Resources of the Comintern," file of Olga Ivanova (Kerasidou), f. 495, op. 207, d. 169, 48, RGASPI.
27. See Vasilis S. Gavalas, "Demographic Reconstruction of a Greek Island Community: Naoussa and Kostos, on Paros 1894–1998" (PhD diss., University of London, London School of Economics and Political Science, 2001). In the Soviet Union, no-fault divorce was introduced by the Bolsheviks one year after they took power; the "Code on Marriage, the Family and Guardianship" was ratified in 1918.
28. As stated in the autobiographical essay of CC member Allegra Felous, whose first attempt to divorce her first husband Solonas Kapetas, in 1944, was "rejected by the Party." "Supplementary Biographical Note," file of Allegra Felous, f. 495, op. 207, d. 1060, 17, RGASPI.
29. Wendy Z. Goldman. *Women, the State and Revolution: Soviet Family Policy and Social Life 1917–1936* (Cambridge University Press, 1993), 49.
30. Richard Stites, *The Women's Liberation Movement in Russia: Feminism. Nihilism, and Bolshevism, 1860–1930* (Princeton University Press, 1978).
31. Wendy Goldman. "Freedom and Its Consequences: The Debate on the Soviet Family Code of 1926," *Russian History* 11, no. 4 (1984): 373.
32. David Hoffman, "Mothers in the Motherland: Stalinist Pronatalism in its Pan-European Context," *Journal of Social History* 34, no. 1 (2000), 47.
33. File of Olga Papadopoulou (Vlasova/ Spiridovna), f. 495, op. 207, d. 159, 16-25, RGASPI.
34. "Letter to Director of KUNMZ from Kaloidis, Ivan Dmitrievich," Sept. 22, 1936, file of Olga Kaloidou, f. 495, op. 207, d. 600, 15-17, RGASPI.
35. Fitzpatrick, *Tear Off the Masks*, 63.
36. Brigitte Studer, "Communism and Feminism," *Clio: Women, Gender, History* 1, no. 41 (2015): 144.
37. File of Olga Papadopoulou (Vlasova /Spiridovna), f. 595, op. 207, d. 159, 16-25, RGASPI.
38. File of Olga Papadopoulou (Vlasova /Spiridovna), f. 595, op. 207, d. 159, 18, RGASPI.
39. File of Olga Papadopoulou (Vlasova /Spiridovna), f. 595, op. 207, d. 159, 19, RGASPI.
40. General Statistical Service of Greece, "Ekpaidefsis, grammata, kalai technai, ekklisia" [Education, letters, arts, religion], in *Statistical Yearbook of Greece (1936)* [in Greek] (General Statistical Service of Greece, 1937), 352–73.
41. Christian Gonsa, "Autobiografika keimena Ellinon kommouniston" [Autobiographical texts of Greek communists] *Mnimon*, vol. 17 (1995): 124.
42. Gonsa, "Autobiografika keimena," 125. 'Katharevousa' is a conservative, now obsolete, form of the modern Greek language conceived in the late eighteenth century as both a literary language and a compromise between Ancient Greek and the contemporary vernacular, demotic Greek.

43. Gonsa, "Autobiografika keimena," 5.
44. Markos Vapheiades, *Apomnimonevmata* [Memoirs], vol. 1 (Difros, 1984), 60.
45. See Donald S. Zagoria, "The Ecology of Peasant Communism in India," *American Political Science Review*, vol. 65 (1971): 144–60; Donald S. Zagoria, "A Note on Landlessness, Literacy and Agrarian Communism in India," *European Journal of Sociology*, vol. 13 (1972): 326–34; Paul R. Brass, "Political Parties of the Radical Left in South Asian Politics," in *Radical Politics in South Asia*, ed. Paul R. Brass and Marcus F. Franda (MIT Press, 1973); Parkes Riley, "Poverty, Literacy and the Communist Vote in India," *Asian Survey* 15 no. 6 (1975) 543–58.
46. File of Chrysanthi Kantzidou (Kaiti Vasiliou), f. 495, op. 207, d. 98, 12-32, RGASPI.
47. It is clear that Vamniatzidou's autobiography is not written in her own handwriting, which was very poor, as evidenced in her *anketa* (written in Greek). "Autobiography of Stella Vamniatzidou," f. 495, op. 207, d. 109, 41, RGASPI.
48. File of Stella Vamniatzidou, f. 495, op. 207, d. 109, 2, 12, 34-35, RGASPI.
49. See Janet G. Chapman, "Real Wages in the Soviet Union 1928–1952," *Review of Economics and Statistics* 36, no. 2 (1954): 144.
50. "Party Characteristics of Graduate Student of the Greek Sector–Dimitrieva," f. 495, op. 207, d. 199, 8, RGASPI.
51. "Autobiography of Clio Dimitrievna Stai," f. 495, op. 207, d. 636, 32, RGASPI.
52. "Autobiography of Clio Dimitrievna Stai," f. 495, op. 207, d. 636, 18, 33, RGASPI.
53. "Autobiography of Clio Dimitrievna Stai," f. 495, op. 207, d. 636, 27, 32, RGASPI.
54. "Character Reference from Comrade Frumkina, Rector of University," file of Clio Christodoulidou (pseud. Nora Irman / Margarita Robopoulou) f. 495, op. 207, d. 583, 20, RGASPI.
55. "Letter to Panov," 20/10/1932, File of Clio Christodoulidou (pseud. Nora Irman / Margarita Robopoulou) f. 495, op. 207, d. 583, 17, RGASPI.
56. "Letter to Comrade Abramov, OMC [International Relations Department]" June 13, 1935, Nov. 13, 1935, file of Clio Christodoulidou (pseud. Nora Irman), f. 495, op. 207, d. 583, 1, 11, RGASPI.
57. KKE, *Dokimio istorias tou KKE* [Essays on the history of the Greek Communist Party], vol. 1, 1919–1949 (Syghroni Epochi, 2012); KKE, *To KKE sto Italo-Elliniko Polemo 1940–1941* [The Greek Communist Party in the Italian-Greek War] (Syghroni Epochi, 2015); Nefeloudis, *Aktina Θ*; Rodakis, *Nikos Zachariadis*; Farakos, *B Pagosmios Polemos*; Haralambidis, *Dekemvriana 1944*, 4; Vasilis Barziotas, *I ethniki adistasi stin adouloti Athina: Merikoi vasikoi stathmoi tis istorias tis KOA tou KKE* [The national resistance in indomitable Athens: Essential points in the history of the Athens organization of the Greek Communist Party] (Syghroni Epochi, 1984), 137.
58. "Reference for Alika Kanda, signed by Vladimirov," Aug. 29, 1940, f. 495, op. 207, d. 99, 18, RGASPI.
59. "Extract of Minutes of the Credentials Committee of the MLS, signed by Klavdiya Kirsanova (Rector)," Oct. 13, 1935, f. 495, op. 207, d. 99, 28, RGASPI.
60. Bakola is mentioned by name in the following volumes: KKE, *Dokimio Istorias tou KKE*; KKE, *To KKE sto Italo-Elliniko Polemo*; Nefeloudis, *Aktina Θ*; Rodakis, *Nikos Zachariadis*; Farakos, *B Pangosmios Polemos*; Haralambidis, *Dekemvriana*.

61. Stavridis, *Ta Paraskinia tou KKE*, 233. See also Nefeloudis, *Martiries*, 194–97. Cited in Markovitis, *Ochi, den eimai echthros*, 141–43.
62. D. Gaxie., "Economie des partis et rétributions du militantisme," *Revue Française de Science Politique* 27, no. 1 (1977): 123–54.
63. Kivisaari, "Communists Are Not Born," 76.
64. Ravandi-Fadai, "Red Mecca," 721.
65. Ravandi-Fadai, "Red Mecca," 718. The anniversary coincided with the 3rd International Conference of Communist women in March 1924.
66. "Autobiography of Olga Kaloidis" (Kaloidou), file of Olga Kaloidou, f. 495, op. 207, d. 600, 21-22, RGASPI.
67. OSOAVIAKHIM (Society for the Assistance of Defense, Aviation, and Chemical Construction of the USSR) was a millions-strong paramilitary organization (1926–1948) established in the context of Soviet mass mobilization campaigns. It was a voluntary mass civil defense society that eventually developed its own airfields, radio clubs, parachuting towers, and firing ranges whose main purpose was to inculcate militarist values into the population, provide strong civil defense, and help modernize the Soviet Union.
68. "Character reference of Olga Kaloidou," signed by Konop (Director), file of Olga Kaloidou, f. 495, op. 207, d. 600, 24, RGASPI.
69. "Letter to Comrade Kornilyev," Academic and Party Member Character Reference of Olga Kaloidou, graduate of Greek Sector, file of Olga Kaloidou, f. 495, op. 207, d. 600, 69-70, RGASPI.
70. File of Olga Ivanova (Kerasidou) f. 495, op. 207, d. 169, 46-47, RGASPI.
71. ECCI personal file of Stella Kerasidou (Ivanova), f. 495, op. 207, d. 169, 15, RGASPI. See Laamanen, "From Communist to Cadre Outsider."
72. See Stavridis, *Ta Paraskinia tou KKE*, 293, 355.
73. "Letter to Human Resources of the Comintern," file of Olga Ivanova (Kerasidou), f. 495, op. 207, d. 169, 46, RGASPI.
74. "Letter from Communist Party of Greece to IKKI (ECCI)," dated May 22, 1930, Athens, f. 495, op. 207, d. 169, 115, RGASPI.
75. All data cited is taken from the *anketa* of Olga Ivanova, f. 495, op. 207, d. 169, RGASPI.
76. "Autobiography," file of Olga Vlasova (Papadopoulou), f. 495, op. 207, d. 159, 41, RGASPI.
77. See John N. Hazard, "The Child under Soviet law," *University of Chicago Law Review* 5, no. 3 (1938): 424–46.
78. "Confirmation of Dependents," file of Olga Vlasova (Papadopoulou), f. 495, op. 207, d. 159, 41, RGASPI.
79. "Letter to Comrade Kupriyanov," dated Oct. 8, 1925, file of Olga Papadopoulou (Vlasova), f. 495, op. 207, d. 159, 40, RGASPI.
80. "Letter to Comrade Gusakova," dated Sept. 28, 1925, file of Olga Papadopoulou (Vlasova), f. 495, op. 207, d.159, 34-38, RGASPI; "Request of Secretary of the Greek Section, Topuzis, to Balkan Sector of IKKI about the Transfer of Comrade Papadopoulou to the International Group," dated Oct. 23, 1925, file of Olga Papadopoulou (Vlasova), f. 495, op. 207, d. 159, 39, RGASPI.

81. "Letter to Comrade Nodev," May 14, 1937, file of Olga Papadopoulou (Vlasova), f. 495, op. 207, d. 159, 43, RGASPI.
82. In the Athens Library there is a collection titled "Publications of the Greeks of the Soviet Union," which contains sixty-eight bound volumes of *Kommunistis* published between 1931 and 1932, in both Pontian and demotic Greek. See Markovitis, *Ochi, den eimai echthros*, 165; Karpozilos, "Pontic Culture." Regarding the effort to replace demotic Greek with Pontic as the official language of the Pontic Greek minority, see also Dawkins, "The Pontic Dialect."
83. File of Olga Papadopoulou (Vlasova), f. 495, op. 207, d. 159, RGASPI.
84. "Letter to Esteemed Comrade Khrushchev," dated May 31, 1962, file of Olga Papadopoulou (Vlasova f. 495, op. 207, d. 159, 16-25, RGASPI.
85. Valesky was one of many members of the apparatus of the ECCI secretariat who were purged in 1937. For more see Tim Rees and Andrew Thorpe, eds., *International Communism and the Communist International 1919–1943* (Manchester University Press, 1998).
86. Haitas was arrested, and probably executed by the KGB in 1937 as an "enemy of the people," in the context of Stalin's counterespionage operations, and was never seen again.
87. "Information on Olga Ivanova, also known as Stella Kerasidou," (Greece), dated May 29, 1938, file of Olga Ivanova (Kerasidou), f. 495, op. 207, d. 169, 52-53, RGASPI.
88. "Letter from Kerasidou to Human Resources of the Comintern," dated Jan. 14, 1938, file of Olga Ivanova (Kerasidou), f. 495, op. 207, d. 169, 49, RGASPI.
89. "Letter from Kerasidou to Human Resources," 48.
90. "Letter from Kerasidou to Human Resources," 75.
91. The EEE refers to the National Union of Greece (Ethniki Enosis Elladas), an antisemitic nationalist party established in Thessaloniki, Greece, in 1927. It was founded by refugee merchants of Asia Minor and was registered as a mutual aid society. According to the organization's constitution, only Christians could join, excluding Thessaloniki's substantial Jewish population. "Letter to Personnel Department IKKI," June 29, 1937, file of Stella Kantzidou (pseud. Kaiti Vasiliou), f. 495, op. 207, d. 98, 35, RGASPI.
92. For more on "ritualistic performances" in which individuals were invited to accept their own failings and to expose the errors of others—as much educative as disciplinary—requiring the participants to learn the latest political formulas, see Rees, "Deviation and Discipline," 147. The process of self-criticism is described vividly and in excruciating detail by Wolfgang Leonhard, *Child of the Revolution* (1957; repr., London: W.M Collins, 1979), 197–208.
93. John Murphy and Bill Gollan, "Loyalty and the Communists: An Interview with Bill Gollan," *Labor History*, no. 66 (1994): 115.
94. Russians were very prolific letter-writers to Soviet authorities, sending missives ranging in nature from complaints, denunciations, statements of opinion, appeals and requests, to threats and confessional outpourings. See Sheila Fitzpatrick, "Supplicants and Citizens: Public Letter-Writing in Soviet Russia in the 1930s," *Slavic Review* 55, no. 1 (1996): 78–105.

95. Golfo Alexopoulos, "The Ritual Lament: A Narrative of Appeal in the 1920s and 1930," *Russian History* 24, no. 1/2 (1997): 117.
96. See, for example, Fitzpatrick, "Supplicants and citizens"; Juliane Furst, "In Search of Soviet Salvation: Young People Write to the Stalinist Authorities," *Contemporary European History* 15, no. 3 (2006): 327–45; Hellbeck, "Working, Struggling."
97. See, for example, Hellbeck, "Working, Struggling"; Fitzpatrick, "Supplicants and Citizens"; Hannah Parker, "Education, Labour and Self-Worth in Women's Letters to Soviet Authorities, 1924–1941," in *Feelings and Work in Modern History: Emotional Labour and Emotions about Labour*, in Agnes Arnold-Forster and Alison Moulds, 99–117 (Bloomsbury, 2022).
98. Vladimir A. Kozlov, "Denunciation and Its Functions in Soviet Governance: A Study of Denunciations and Their Bureaucratic Handling from Soviet Police Archives, 1944-1953," *Journal of Modern History* 68, no. 4 (1996): 867–98.
99. "Letter to Khrushchev," file of Olga Papadopoulou (Vlasova), f. 495, op. 207, d. 159, 23, RGASPI.
100. "Letter from A. Toporikov, Desk Officer of the International Department of the Central Committee of the CPSU," dated Oct. 12, 1963, file of Olga Papadopoulou (Vlasova), f. 495, op. 207, d. 159, 5, RGASPI.
101. "Letter to Khrushchev," file of Olga Papadopoulou (Vlasova), f. 495, op. 207, d. 159, 16, RGASPI.
102. "Letter to Khrushchev," 24. Her expulsion was disputed by the KKE in subsequent correspondence, but the outcome of her appeals is not documented.
103. Nanci Adler, *Keeping the Faith: Communist Believers Return from the Gulag* (Bloomington: Indiana University Press, 2012).
104. Elli Pappa, *Martiries mias diadromis* [Testimonies from a journey] (Benaki Museum, 2010).
105. "Letter to Khrushchev," file of Olga Papadopoulou, f. 495, op. 207, d. 159, 20, RGASPI.

CHAPTER 5

1. "Dido Sotiriou and the Women's Movement—'I cared about living the life'" (interview), *Eleftherotipia*, March 10, 2004; Margarita Lazaridou, *Polemos kai aima: Taxidi sto parelthon, taxidi ston pono* [War and blood: Journey into the past, journey of pain] (Diogenes, 2005).
2. Branko M. Lazitch and Milorad M. Drachkovitch, *Biographical Dictionary of the Comintern* (Hoover Press: Stanford, 1973). Hatzivasiliou's file has been viewed twice, first by Lazitch, and then by me in 2015.
3. Ivo Banac, introduction to *The Diary of Georgi Dimitrov 1933-1949* (Yale University Press, 2003).
4. Hatzivasiliou would not have described herself as a feminist, but, echoing Kristen Ghodsee, "if the goal of feminism is to improve women's lives, along with eliminating discrimination and promoting equality with men," then Hatzivasiliou was committed to that goal. See Chrysa Hatzivasiliou, *To KKE kai to Gynaikeio Zitima* [KKE

and the woman question] (Central Committee of the Greek Communist Party, 1946). See also Kristen R. Ghodsee, "Untangling the Knot: A Response to Nanette Funk," *European Journal of Women's Studies* 22, no. 2 (2015): 248–52.
5. "Aidin, a Vast Sepulchre," *New York Times*, Aug. 29, 1921.
6. See Stavridis, *Ta Paraskinia tou KKE*, 476.
7. Onur Inal, "Levantine Heritage in Izmir" (MA thesis, Koc University, December 2006), 25; Vangelis Kechriotis, "Educating the Nation: Migration and Acculturation on the Two Shores of the Aegean at the Turn of the Twentieth Century," in *Cities of the Mediterranean: From the Ottomans to the Present Day*, ed. Meltem Toksöz and Biray Kolluoglu (I.B. Tauris, 2010).
8. Natalia Novikova and Kristen Ghodsee, "Alexandra Kollontai (1872–1952): Communism as the Only Way towards Women's Liberation," in *The Palgrave Handbook of Communist Women Activists around the World*, ed. Francisca De Haan (Palgrave Macmillan, 2023).
9. "Character Assessments of the 4th Year Students of the Greek Sector of KUNMZ," file of Chrysa Hatzivasiliou (pseud. Alexandra Nikolai Armand), f. 495, op. 207, d. 13, 9, RGASPI.
10. "Character Assessments of the 4th Year Students," 9.
11. Hatzivasiliou and Zachariadis were students at the Comintern at the same time but at different institutions. Constantly hounded by the state, the KKE leadership sent Zachariadis to Moscow in 1928/1929. He spent the period studying at the International Lenin School.
12. Decades later, the KKE elected Alexandra "Aleka" Papariga to the helm, who served as general secretary from 1991 to 2013.
13. See for example, John Lowenhardt, Erik Van Ree, and James Ozinga, *The Rise and Fall of the Soviet Politburo* (St. Martin's Press, 1992); and E. A. Rees, ed., *The Nature of Stalin's Dictatorship: The Politburo, 1924-1953* (Routledge, 2004).
14. "The 7th Congress of KKE," *Dokimio Istorias tou KKE*, vol. 1, 1919-1949 (Syghroni Epochi, 2012). See also the communist daily *Rizospastis*, Jan. 9, 2005.
15. In an article titled "Captain of the Crags," *Time Magazine* refers patronizingly to "Roussos's petite, intense wife Chrysa Hadzivassiliou [sic], who now likes to think of herself as Greece's Ana Pauker." *Time Magazine*, April 4, 1948.
16. Barbara Evans Clements, *Bolshevik Women* (Cambridge University Press, 1997), 198.
17. Clements, *Bolshevik Women*, 190.
18. Kristine Byron, "Writing the Female Revolutionary Self: Dolores Ibárruri and the Spanish Civil War, "Autobiography and Memoir," special issue, *Journal of Modern Literature* 28, no. 1, (2004): 138–65.
19. Petros Roussos (1908–1992; pseud. "Ydraios" and "Polychronidis") was born in Eastern Thrace (Anatolia/ Turkey) and raised in Odessa. He resettled in Greece in 1923 and in 1930 became secretary of the Central Committee of the Communist Union of Youth (OKNE), editor of the communist newspaper *Rizospastis*, and a member of the Central Committee from 1935 till 1973.
20. I refer, for example, to Iro Barziota, Avra Partsalidou, Sofia Nefeloudi, Lilika Papakyrikou Georgiou, Kaiti Zevgou, Domna Papazoglou Ioannidi, Roula Koukoulou,

and Rita Lazaridou whose lives were at once illuminated and eclipsed by their partnerships with high-ranking communist men.

21. Hatzivasiliou's KUNMZ file records breaks in study due to illness, while ex-general secretary of the KKE Eleftherios Stavridis recalls her travels to the Soviet Union to receive treatment for tuberculosis. She died of leukemia in 1950 at forty-six years of age.

22. From an article in *Protagon:* "Prepublication: 'The English Consul' by Petros St. Makris-Staikos," [in Greek] *Protagon,* November 24, 2017, http://www.protagon.gr/epikairotita/politismos/prodimosiefsi-o-agglos-proksenos-petros-st-makris-staikos-wkeanida-10460000000.

23. "Minutes from the 7th Plenum of the Central Committee," August 1950, published in *Neos Kosmos,* File 2, Box. 1, Contemporary Social History Archive, KKE Central Committee materials.

24. "Minutes from the 7th Plenum," cited by Zachariadis at the 7th Plenum.

25. Hatzivasiliou was visited in her last days only by communist leader Kostas Karagiorgis (*Gyftodimos*), another casualty of KKE's post-Civil War purges, who would also be dismissed from his duties and imprisoned in Romania for holding Zachariadis responsible for the defeat. Hatzivasiliou's remains were returned to Greece in 1975 after the collapse of the dictatorship and the end of the Civil War state. She was laid to rest at the First Cemetery in Athens.

26. Roussos' presence at the funeral is disputed across the sources. See for example, Lazaridou, *Polemos kai Aima,* 134.

27. *Foni tis Gynaikas,* December 1950 (monthly publication of the Panellinia Omospondia Dimokratikon Gynaikon [Panhellenic Federation of Democratic Women]), Contemporary Social History Archive (ASKI).

28. *Foni tis Gynaikas,* December 1950.

29. Pappa, *Martiries mias diadromis.*

30. "Chrysa Hatzivasiliou," file of Chrysa Hatzivasiliou (pseud. Alexandra Nikolai Armand), f. 495, op. 207, d. 13, 6, RGASPI.

31. "Memorial for Fighters/Comrades," Nov. 14, 1960, radio station Foni tis Alitheias (Voice of Truth), GR-ASKI-0002, Contemporary Social History Archive (ASKI), Athens, Greece.

32. Angelika Psarra, "I istoria os martirologio: Scholio se mia ekthesi gia tin istoria tou gynaikeiou kinimatos" [History as martyrdom: Comment on an exhibition on the history of the women's movement], *ArcheioTaxio: Publications from the archives of the Contemporary Social History Archive* (ASKI), vol. 9 (2007): 161–74.

33. Hatzivasiliou, "KKE and the Woman Question," Appendix 2 of this book. The Metaxas-Glucksburg axis is not just a reference to state anticommunism but also to the dictator Metaxas's steadfast royalism (antirepublicanism). The monarchy installed in Greece by the Great Powers after the Greek Revolution—as a remedy for internecine strife—was foreign, initially Bavarian, and from 1864, descended from the Danish Glucksburg dynasty, thus the Metaxas-Glucksburg axis.

34. "Memorial for Fighters/Comrades," Nov. 14, 960, radio station Voice of Truth, GR-ASKI- 0002, Contemporary Social History Archive (ASKI), Athens, Greece.

35. See the full English translation of Chrysa's Hatzivasiliou's essay in Appendix 2 of this book.
36. The scholarship on the Greek Civil War and its causes is vast. Some notable English-language works on the British role include John Iatrides, *Revolt in Athens: The Greek Communist "Second Round," 1944–1945* (Princeton University Press, 1972); Nicholas X. Rizopoulos, "The International Dimension of the Greek Civil War," *World Policy Journal* 17, no. 1 (2000): 87–103; G. M. Alexander, *The Prelude to the Truman Doctrine: British Policy in Greece 1944–1947* (Oxford University Press, 1982); Robert Frazier, *Anglo-American Relations with Greece: The Coming of the Cold War 1942–47* (Macmillan, 1991); Christina Goulter-Zervoudakis, "The Politicization of Intelligence: The British Experience in Greece, 1941–1944," *Intelligence and National Security* 13, no. 1 (1998): 165–94; Heinz Richter, *British Intervention in Greece: From Varkiza to Civil War* (Merlin Press, 1985); Athanasios D. Sfikas, *British Labour Government and The Greek Civil War: 1945–1949* (Edinburgh University Press, 2019).
37. The Women's International Democratic Federation (WIDF), was one of the most prominent and active left-identified international women's organizations of the postwar period. It was founded in December 1945, at the World Congress of Women held in Paris, an initiative of the French Union of Antifascist Women led by prominent wartime resistance activists French physicist Eugenie Cotton and photo-journalist Marie-Claude Vaillant-Couturier. Antifascist in origin, it sought to unite feminism and left politics and included many women who had been active in resistance movements during World War II.
38. *Congrès International des Femmes; Compte Rendu des Travaux du Congrès Qui S'est Tenu à Paris du 26 Novembre au 1er Décembre 1945* (Fédération démocratique internationale des femmes, 1946), available through Women and Social Movements, International, 1840–Present, https://alexanderstreet.com/products/women-and-social-movements-international-1840-present.
39. See, for example, Hatzivasiliou's reflections on KKE policy at the 11th Plenum of the KKE (April 5–10, 1945), in *Neos Kosmos*, August 1950, 643. The turning point for the KKE and the civil war was the Truman Doctrine in 1947. Following the withdrawal of British military and economic assistance to the Greek government in its war against the Greek Communist Party, Truman asked Congress to effectively reorient American foreign policy—to support the Greek government against the communists by providing $400,000,000 worth of aid to both the Greek and Turkish governments, and to dispatch American civilian and military personnel and equipment to the region. In the words of the Truman Doctrine, it became "the policy of the United States to support free peoples who are resisting attempted subjugation by armed minorities or by outside pressures."
40. See Appendix 2.
41. Official visual propaganda deployed subtle and effective images to portray communists as savage Ottoman warriors, barbarians, and beasts. See Alexander Kazamias, "The Visual Politics of Fear: Anti-Communist Imagery in Post-War Greece," *Journal of Contemporary History* 1, no. 0 (2022); Margaret Poulos, "From Heroines to Hyenas:

Women Partisans during the Greek Civil War," in "Gender and War in Europe 1918–1949," special issue, *Contemporary European History* 10, no. 3 (2001): 481–501.

42. I take up this theme in Poulos, "'So That Life May Triumph': Communist Feminism and Realpolitik in Civil-War Greece," *Journal of Women's History* 29, no. 1 (2017): 63–86.

CONCLUSION

1. Filatova, "Indoctrination or Scholarship," 65.
2. "Biographical information," signed by Novoselsky and Pozharsky, September 1937, file of Stella Vamniatzidou (pseud., Elena Agneva) f. 495, op. 207, d. 98, 12, RGASPI.
3. "Letter from Papadopoulou (Vlasova) to Khrushchev," May 31, 1962, file of Olga Papadopoulou, f. 495, op. 207, d. 159, 20, RGASPI.
4. John Murphy, *Socialism and Communism* (Rosen Education Service, 2014).
5. "Prisons of the mind" was first used by Lebanese American historian William Haddad, to which Mansel added that the cosmopolitanism and hybridity of "the Levant was a jailbreak." See Philip Mansel, *Levant: Splendour and Catastrophe on the Mediterranean* (John Murray, 2010), 2, 4.
6. Poulos, "Beyond the Ballot Box."
7. The German occupying forces and local security battalions targeted the refugee neighborhoods of Kokkinia, Dourgouti, Nea Ionia (Kalogreza), Vyronas, and Kallithea.
8. Thessaloniki occupies a special place in the history of left-wing militancy in the Ottoman Empire, especially after the 1908 Revolution, prompting scholars to regard it as the "birthplace of Ottoman socialism." See Paul Dumont, "Naissance d'une Socialisme Ottoman," in *Salonique 1850–1918: La "ville des juifs" et le reveil Balkan*, ed. Gilles Veinstein, 195–207 (Editions Autrement, 1992).
9. Converzation with Theodoros Skaloubakas, in Alexandros Dagas, *Gia Mia Koinoniki Istoria tis Ypaithrou: I Perifereia tis Thessalonikis ston Eikosto Aiona—I Periodo eos to 1945* [Toward a social history of the countryside: Regional Thessaloniki in the twentieth century until 1945] (Epikendro, 2010), 464.
10. Chrysa Hatzivasiliou, "KKE and the Woman Question," 19.

APPENDIX 1

1. "Required Knowledge and Skills for Admittance of 1st-Year Students to Year II." f. 532, op. 8, d. 104, 3, RGASPI.

APPENDIX 2

Chrysa Hatzivasiliou, "To KKE kai to Gynaikeio Zitima stin Ellada" (KKE, 1946). Author's translation from the Greek.

1. I have left in Hatzivasiliou's original citations.
2. Kyrou was editor of the conservative Athenian newspaper *Estia*.

3. Organization X, commonly referred to simply as X (Chi in Greek, and its members Chites), was a right-wing, militant resistance organization set up in 1941 during the Axis occupation of Greece. Initially an anti-Axis resistance organization, it gradually shifted its focus toward anticommunism, collaborating with the Axis authorities against the communist-led EAM Resistance movement and its affiliates. Following the end of the Axis occupation, X played an active role in the persecution of communist sympathizers during the White Terror and various military operations of the Greek Civil War. EPON refers to the Enomeni Panellinia Organosi Neon (United Panhellenic Organization of Youth) which was the youth wing of the communist-led National Liberation Front (EAM).

Bibliography

Archives

Archives of Communist Party of Greece (Kommounistiko Komma Elladas/ KKE)
Center for Asia Minor Studies (Kendro Mikrasiatikon Spoudon), Athens
Charilaos Florakis Archive, Athens
Contemporary Social History Archive (Archeio Syghronis Koinonikis Istorias / ASKI), Athens
Eleftherios Venizelos Archive, Benaki Museum, Athens
Fonds Francais de l'Internationale Communiste, Maison des Sciences de l'Homme de Dijon, University of Burgundy, France
Greek Literary and Historical Archive (Elliniko Logotechniko kai Istoriko Archeio / ELIA), Athens
League for the Rights of Women (Syndesmos gia ta Dikaiomata ton Gynaikon), Athens
Library of the Greek Parliament, Athens (including digitized materials)
National Library of Greece, Athens
Rizospastis newspaper archive, Athens (including digitized materials)
Russian State Archive of Socio-Political History (Rossiiskii Gosudarstvennyi Arkhiv Sotsialno-Politicheskoi Istorii / RGASPI), Moscow
Society of Greek Writers (Etaireia Ellinon Logotechnon), Athens
Ungarisches Institut Munchen, Germany
US Foreign Office and CIA documents (including digitized material)

Newspapers

GREECE

Acropolis
Bulletin of the Greek Democratic Army

Ergatiki Boitheia Elladas (EBE) Deltio [Bulletin]
Eleftheros Logos
Eleftherotipia
Foni tis Gynaikas
Neos Kosmos
O Agonas tis Gynaikas
Prosfygikos Kosmos
Protagon
Rizospastis

OTHER

New York Times
Communist International
International Press Correspondence (Produced in multiple languages; published, variously, in Berlin, 1921–1923; Vienna, 1924–1929; Berlin, 1930–32. English edition published in London by H. R. G. Jefferson, 1934–1938)

Autobiography and Memoir

Alexiou, Elli. *Apo poli konda* [Up Close]. Kastaniotis, 1990.
Apostolou, Lefteris. *O Aris Velouchiotis opos ton gnorisa* [Aris Velouchiotis as I knew him]. Filistor, 2003.
Barziotas, Vasilis. *I ethniki adistasi stin adouloti Athina: Merikoi vasikoi stathmoi tis istorias tis KOA tou KKE* [The national resistance in indomitable Athens: Essential points in the history of the Athens organization of the Greek Communist Party] Syghroni Epochi, 1984.
Ciliga, Ante. *The Russian Enigma*. Ink Links, 1979.
Djilas, Milovan. *Rise and Fall*. Harcourt Brace Jovanovich, 1983.
Farakos, Grigoris. *B Pangosmios Polemos: Scheseis tou KKE kai Diethnous Kommounistikou Kendrou* [Second World War: Relations between the Greek Communist Party and the International Communist Center]. Ellinika Grammata, 2004.
Grizonas, Kostas. *Kokkinoi drapetes 1920–1944* [Red fugitives]. Glaros, 1985.
Haywood, Harry. *Black Bolshevik: Autobiography of an Afro-American Communist*. University of Minnesota Press, 1978.
Karliaftis, Loukas [Kostas Kastritis]. "The Birth of Bolshevism in Greece." Encyclopedia of Trotskyism On Line, Marxists International Archive, updated Oct. 25, 2003. https://www.marxists.org/history/etol/revhist/supplem/karliaft.htm.
Kazantzakis, Nikos. *Russia: A Chronicle of Three Journeys in the Aftermath of the Revolution*. Translated by Thanasis Maskeleris and Michael Andonakis. Creative Arts Book Company, 1989.
Lazaridou, Margarita. *Polemos kai Aima: Taxidi sto parelthon, taxidi ston pono* [War and blood: Journey into the past, journey of pain]. Diogenes, 2005.

Leonhard, Wolfgang. *Child of the Revolution.* Translated by C. M. Woodhouse. Collins, 1957.
Markovitis, Marios. *Ochi, den eimai echthros tou laou* [No, I am not an enemy of the people]. Epikendro, 2017.
Metaxas, Ioannis. *Logoi kai Skepseis: 1936–1938*, vol. 1. Govostis, 1969.
Nefeloudis, Vasilis. *Aktina Θ.* Estia, 2007.
———. *Martyiries 1906–1908* [Testimonies 1906–1938]. Okeanida, 1984.
Pappa, Elli. *Martiries mias Diadromis* [Testimonies from a journey]. Benaki Museum, 2010.
Partsalidou, Avra (née Vlassi). *Anamniseis apo tin zoi stin OKNE* [Memories of life in OKNE], 4th ed. Syghroni Epochi, 1983.
Someritis, Stratis. *H megale kampi: Martyries—anamniseis 1924–1974* [The great turning point: Testimonies—recollections], vol. 1. Olkos, 1975.
Stavridis, Eleftherios. *Ta Paraskinia tou KKE* [Behind the scenes of KKE]. Self-published, 1953.
Stogiannis, I. T. *What I Saw in Soviet Russia: Phenomena and Other Things* [in Greek]. Vradini, 1934.
Vapheiades, Markos. *Apomnimonevmata* [Memoirs], vol. 1. Difros, 1984.
Winter, Ella. *Red Virtue: Human Relationships in the New Russia.* Victor Gollancz, 1933.
Zachariadis, Nikos. *Istorika dilimmata, istorikes apandiseis: Apanda ta dimosievmena 1940–1945* [Historical dilemmas, historical responses: Complete published works 1940–1945]. Kastaniotis, 2011.
Zevgou, Kaiti. *Me ton Yianni Zevgo sto epanastatiko kinima* [With Yiannis Zevgos in the revolutionary movement]. Self-published, 1980.

Party Publications

KKE. *Dokimio istorias tou KKE: 1919–1949* [Essays on the history of the KKE], vol. 1. Syghroni Epochi, 2008.
KKE. *Dokimio istorias tou KKE: 1949–1968* [Essays on the history of the KKE], vol. 2. Syghroni Epochi, 2012.
KKE. *Episima Keimena 1925–1928* [KKE: Official Documents], vol. 2. Syghroni Epochi, 1974.
KKE. *Episima Keimena 1918–1924* [KKE: Official Documents], vol. 1. Syghroni Epochi, 1974.
KKE. "To KKE kai to Gynaikeio Zitima stin Ellada" [The Greek Communist Party and the woman question in Greece]. KKE, 1946.
KKE. *To KKE sto Italo-Elliniko Polemo 1940–1941* [KKE during the Italian-Greek war] Syghroni Epochi, 2015.
Kommounistiki Epitheorisi [Communist review] 2, no. 1 (January 1929).
Kommounistiki Epitheorisi [Communist review], no. 7 (April 1933).
PEEA. *Ethniko Symvoulio: Periliptika praktika ergasion tis Protis Synodou tou—Koryschades 14–27 May 1944* [National Council: Summary of the minutes of the First Synod—Koryschades 14–27 May 1944]. Municipality of Koryschades, Euritania, 1988.

"Report of the Central Committee to the Eighth Convention of the Communist Party of the USA." Cleveland, Ohio, April 2–8, 1934. Workers Library Publishers, 1934.

Secondary Sources

Adler, Nancy. *Keeping Faith with the Party: Communist Believers Return from the Gulag* Indiana University Press, 2012.

Agtsidis, Vlassis. "Pontian Refugees in the 'Motherland.'" *Istoria tou Ethnous*, vol. 17 (August 2010): 23.

———. *Parefxinios Diaspora* [Black Sea diaspora]. Adelfoi Kyriakidi, 1997.

———. *Pontiakos Ellinismos: Apo tin genoktonia kai to stalinismo stin perestroika* [Pontic Hellenism: From the genocide and Stalinism to perestroika]. Adelfoi Kyriakidi, 1997.

———. "The Persecution of the Pontic Greeks in the Soviet Union," *Journal of Refugee Studies* 4, no. 4 (1991): 372–82.

Alexander, G. M. *The Prelude to the Truman Doctrine: British Policy in Greece 1944–1947*. Oxford University Press, 1982.

Alexopoulos, Golfo. "Stalin and the Politics of Kinship: Practices of Collective Punishment, 1920s–1940s." *Comparative Studies in Society and History* 50, no. 1 (2008): 91–117.

———. *Stalin's Outcasts: Aliens, Citizens, and the Soviet State 1926–1936*. Cornell University Press, 2003.

———. "The Ritual Lament: A Narrative of Appeal in the 1920s and 1930s," *Russian History* 24, no. 1/2 (1997): 117–29.

Altamirano, Deborah R. "Up in Arms: The Lives and Times of Women Activists in the World War II Greek Resistance." PhD diss., UCLA-Santa Barbara, 1993.

Apostolakou, Lito. "Greek Workers or Communist 'Others': The Contending Identities of Organized Labor, c. 1914–1936." *Journal of Contemporary History* 32, no. 3 (1997): 409–24.

Arendt, Hannah. *The Origins of Totalitarianism*. Penguin Books, 2017.

Ascherson, Neal. *Black Sea: The Birthplace of Civilization and Barbarism*. Vintage, 1996.

Avdela, Efi. "Class, Ethnicity, and Gender in Post-Ottoman Thessaloniki: The Great Tobacco Strike of 1914." In *Borderlines: Gender and Identities in War and Peace 1870–1930*, edited by Billie Melman, 421–38. Psychology Press, 1997.

———. "To the Most Weak and Needy: Women's Protective Labor Legislation in Greece." In *Protecting Women: Labor Legislation in Europe, the United States and Australia (1880–1920)*, edited by Ulla Wikander and Alice Kessler-Harris. University of Illinois Press, 1995.

———. *Public Servants of the Female Sex: The Division of Labor by Gender in the Public Service 1905–1953*. Research and Education Foundation of the Commercial Bank of Greece, 1990.

———. "The Contradictory Content of Social Protection: Legislation on Women's Industrial Work, 19–20th Century." *Istorika*, vol. 11 (1989): 339–60.

Balsoy, Gülhan. "Gendering Ottoman Labor History: The Cibali Régie Factory in the Early Twentieth Century." *International Review of Social History*, vol. 54 (2009): 45–68.

Banac, Ivo. *The Diary of Georgi Dimitrov 1933–1949*. Yale University Press, 2003.

Baranova, Vlada. "Local Language Planners in the Context of Early Soviet Language Policy: The Case of Mariupol Greeks." In "1917 en Russie: La Philologie a l'epreuve de la Revolution," special issue, *Revue des Etudes Slaves* 88, no.1–2 (2017): 97–112.

Bedlek, Emine Yesim. *Imagined Communities in Greece and Turkey: Trauma and the Population Exchanges under Ataturk*. I. B. Tauris, 2015.

Beinin, Joel, and Zachary Lockman. *Workers on the Nile: Nationalism, Communism, Islam, and the Egyptian Working Class, 1882–1954*. Princeton University Press, 1987.

Betas, Thanasis. "From the Tobacco Shop to the Cigarette Factory: Technological Changes, Gender and Surveillance in a Greek Cigarette Form in the Early 20th Century." *Advances in Historical Studies*, vol. 5 (2016): 49–62.

Bogdanović, Irena, and Walter Puchner. *Elliniko Theatro stin Odysso 1814–1914: Agnosta Stoicheia gia Ellinikes Parastaseis stin Poli tis Filikis Etaireias kai stis Parefxeinies Hores apo Rossikes kai Ellinikes Efimerides tis Odysso* [Greek Theater in Odessa 1814–1914: Unknown aspects of Greek performance in the city of the Friendly Society and in the Black Sea areas, as presented in Russian and Greek newspapers of Odessa]. Paravasis, 2013.

Bourrinet, Philippe. "An Ambiguous Journey: Ante Ciliga (1898–1992)." Translated by George Gordon, 1993. Left-Disorder, Dec. 12, 1992. http://www.left-dis.nl/uk/ciliga.htm.

Brass, Paul R. "Political Parties of the Radical Left in South Asian Politics." In *Radical Politics in South Asia*, edited by Paul R. Brass and Marcus F. Franda. MIT Press, 1973.

Bruneau, Michel. "The Pontic Greeks, from Pontus to the Caucasus, Greece, and the Diaspora: 'Iconography' and Mobile Frontiers." *Journal of Alpine Research* 101, no. 2 (2013). https://doi.org/10.4000/rga.2092.

Bryer, Anthony. "Greeks and Turkmens: The Pontic Exception," *Dumbarton Oaks Papers*, vol. 29 (1975): 113–48.

Bugay, Nikolay. *The Deportation of Peoples in the Soviet Union*. Nova Publishers, 1996.

Burmeister, Alfred [Wanda Brońska-Pampuch]. *Dissolution and Aftermath of the Comintern: Experiences and Observations 1937–1947*. Research Program on the USSR East European Fund, 1955.

Byron, Kristine. "Writing the Female Revolutionary Self: Dolores Ibárruri and the Spanish Civil War." In "Autobiography and Memoir," special issue, *Journal of Modern Literature* 28, no. 1 (2004): 138–65.

Campbell, Alan, John McIlroy, Barry McLoughlin, and John Halstead. "The International Lenin School: A Response to Cohen and Morgan." *Twentieth-Century British History* 15, no. 1 (2004): 51–76.

Chapman, Janet G. "Real Wages in the Soviet Union, 1928–1952." *Review of Economics and Statistics* 36, no. 2 (1954) 134–56.

Clements, Barbara Evans. *Bolshevik Women*. Cambridge University Press, 1997.

Cohen, Gidon, and Kevin Morgan, "Stalin's Sausage Machine: British Students at the International Lenin School 1926–1937," *Twentieth Century British History* 13, no. 4 (2002): 327–55.

Condit, D. M. *Assessing Revolutionary and Insurgent Strategies: Case Study in Guerrilla War— Greece during World War Two*, rev. ed. Army Special Operations Command, 1962.

Conquest, Robert. *The Harvest of Sorrow: Soviet Collectivization and the Terror–Famine*. Oxford University Press, 1986.

Dagas, Alexandros. *Gia mia koinoniki istoria tis ypaithrou: I perifereia tis Thessalonikis ston eikosto aiona—i periodo eos to 1945* [Toward a social history of the countryside: Regional Thessaloniki in the twentieth century until 1945]. Epikendro, 2010.

David-Fox, Michael. *Revolution of the Mind: Higher Learning among the Bolsheviks, 1918–1929*. Cornell University Press, 2016.

———. *Showcasing the Great Experiment: Cultural Diplomacy and Western Visitors to the Soviet Union, 1921–1941*. Oxford University Press, 2012.

Dawkins, R. M. "The Pontic Dialect of Modern Greek in Asia Minor and Russia." *Transactions of the Philological Society* 36, no. 1 (1937): 15–52.

de Haan, Francisca. "The Women's International Democratic Federation (WIDF): History, Main Agenda, and Contributions, 1945–1991." Women and Social Movements (WASI) Online Archive, October 2012. http://alexanderstreet.com/products/women-and-social-movements-international.

Dumont, Paul. "Naissance d'une Socialisme Ottoman." In *Salonique 1850–1918: La "ville des juifs" et le reveil Balkan*, ed. Gilles Veinstein, 195–207. Editions Autrement, 1992.

Dzhukha, I. *Grecheskaya operatsiya*. Aleteiya, 2006.

Eichner, Carolyn. *Feminism's Empire*. Cornell University Press, 2022.

Efthimiou, Kostas. *Ergatiki bohtheia kai koinoniki allileggi: Dyo paradigmata taxikis allillegias drasis stin Ellada tou mesopolemou* [Labor Assistance and Social Solidarity: Two examples of Class Solidarity in Interwar Greece]. Ekdoseis ton Synadelfon, 2014.

Elefandis, Angelos. *I epaggelia tis adynatis epanastasis: Ke kai Astismos ston Mesopolemo* [The promise of the impossible revolution: The Greek Communist Party and the bourgeoisie between the wars]. Themelio, 1976.

Farakos, Grigoris. *B Pangosmios Polemos: Scheseis tou KKE kai Diethnous Kommounistikou Kendrou* [Second World War: Relations between the Greek Communist Party and the International Communist Center]. Ellinika Grammata, 2004.

Filatova, Irina. "Indoctrination or Scholarship?: Education of Africans at the Communist University of the Toilers of the East in the Soviet Union 1923–1937." *Pedagogica Historica* 35, no. 1 (1999): 41–66.

Fitzpatrick, Sheila. *Education and Social Mobility in the Soviet Union 1921–1934*. Cambridge University Press, 2010.

———. "Supplicants and Citizens: Public Letter-Writing in Soviet Russia in the 1930s." *Slavic Review* 55, no. 1 (1996): 78–105.

———. *Tear Off the Masks: Identity and Imposture in Twentieth-Century Russia*. Princeton University Press, 2005.

———. *The Commissariat of Enlightenment: Soviet Organization of Education and the Arts under Lunacharsky, October 1917–1921*. Cambridge University Press, 2002.
Foley, Barbara. *Radical Representations: Politics and Form in U.S. Proletarian Fiction, 1929–1941*. Duke University Press, 1993.
Fonton, Felix. *Russia in Asia Minor: The Campaign of Marshal Paskevitch in 1828-29* [in French]. Leneveu, 1840.
Fortouni, Eleni. *Greek Women in Resistance: Journals, Oral Histories*. Delphini Press, 1986.
Fouskas, Vasilis, and C. Dimoulas. *Greece, Financialization and the EU: The Political Economy of Debt and Destruction*. Springer, 2013.
Frazier, Robert. *Anglo-American Relations with Greece: The Coming of the Cold War 1942–47*. Macmillan, 1991.
Funk, Nanette. "A Very Tangled Knot: Official State Socialist Women's Organizations, Women's Agency and Feminism in Eastern European State Socialism." *European Journal of Women's Studies* 21, no. 4 (2014): 344–60.
———. "Knot So: A response to Kristen Ghodsee." *European Journal of Women's Studies* 22, no. 3 (2015): 350–55.
Furst, Juliane. "In Search of Soviet Salvation: Young People Write to the Stalinist Authorities." *Contemporary European History* 15 no. 3 (2006): 327–45.
Gasias, Giorgos. "The Case of the Football Associations in Greek Society between the Wars, 1922–1936." PhD diss., University of Crete, 2005.
Gavalas, Vasilis S. "Demographic Reconstruction of a Greek Island Community: Naoussa and Kostos, on Paros 1894–1998." PhD diss., University of London, 2001.
Gaxie, D. "Economie des partis et rétributions du militantisme," *Revue Française de Science Politique* 27, no. 1 (1977): 123–54.
General Statistical Service of Greece. "Ekpaidefsis, grammata, kalai technai, ekklisia" [Education, letters, arts, religion]. In *Statistical Yearbook of Greece (1936)*. General Statistical Service of Greece, 1937.
Gerolymatos, Andre. *An International Civil War in Greece 1943–1949*. Yale University Press, 2016.
Ghikas, Anastasis. *Rixi kai ensomatosi: Symvoli stin istoria tou ergatikou-kommounistikou kinimatos tou mesopolemou, 1918–1936* [Rupture and integration: A contribution to the history of the labor-communist movement of the interwar period, 1918–1936]. Syghroni Epochi, 2010.
———. "The Politics of Working-Class Communism in Greece 1918–1936." PhD diss., University of York, 2004.
Ghodsee, Kristin R. "Untangling the Knot: A Response to Nanette Funk." *European Journal of Women's Studies* 22, no. 2 (2015): 248–52.
Ghodsee, Kristin R., and Natalia Novikova. "Alexandra Kollontai (1872–1952): Communism as the Only Way towards Women's Liberation." In *The Palgrave Handbook of Communist Women Activists around the World*, edited by Francisca De Haan. Palgrave Macmillan, 2023.
Gilmartin, Christina. "Gender in the Formation of a Communist Body Politic." *Modern China* 19, no. 3 (1993): 299–329.

Goldman, Wendy. *Women, the State and Revolution: Soviet Family Policy and Social Life 1917–1936*. Cambridge University Press, 1993.

Goldman, Wendy. "Freedom and Its Consequences: The Debate on the Soviet Family Code of 1926." *Russian History* 11, no. 4 (1984): 362–88.

Gonsa, Christian. "Autobiografika keimena Ellinon kommouniston kai i istoria tou Ellinikou Kommounistikou Kommatos" [Autobiographical writings of Greek communists and the history of the Greek Communist Party]. *Mnimon*, no. 17 (1995): 107–29.

Goulter-Zervoudakis, Christina. "The Politicization of Intelligence: The British Experience in Greece, 1941–1944." *Intelligence and National Security* 13, no. 1 (1998): 165–94.

Gounod, Andre. "Sport reformiste ou sport revolutionnaire?" In *Les Origines du sport ouvrier en Europe*, edited by Pierre Arnaud. L'Harmattan, 1994.

Grigoriadis, Theocharis N., and Dimitrios Moschos, "Farewell Anatolia: Refugees and the Rise of the Greek Left." *European Journal of Political Economy*, no. 77 (2023): article 102281. https://doi.org/10.1016/j.ejpoleco.2022.102281.

Haralambidis, Menelaos. *Dekembriana 1944, H Machi tis Athinas* [The December Events 1944: The Battle of Athens] Alexandria Press, 2014.

———. "Aspects of the Political Behaviour of the Refugees in Interwar Greece." *O dromos tis Aristeras*, July 27, 2011.

Harsch, Donna. "Communism and Women." In *The Oxford Handbook of the History of Communism*, edited by Stephen A. Smith. Oxford University Press, 2014.

Hart, Janet. *New Voices in the Nation: Women and the Greek Resistance 1941–1964*. Cornell University Press, 1996.

Hasiotis, Ioannis K. *Oi Ellines tis Rossias kai tis Sovietikis Enosis: Metoikesies kai ektopismoi* [The Greeks of Russia and the Soviet Union: Relocations and displacements]. University Studio Press, 1997.

Hastaoglou-Martinidis, Vilma. "A Mediterranean City in Transition: Thessaloniki between the Two World Wars." *Facta Universitatis: Architecture and Civil Engineering* 1, no. 4 (1997): 493–507.

Hatzikonstandinou, Katerina, and Lydia Sapounaki-Drakaki. "Two Sanatorium Cases in the Greater Athens Area: Ideal Curative Urban Environments or Perfect Social Exiles?" *Histoire Urbaine* 1, no. 39 (2014): 137–59.

Hazard, John N. "The Child under Soviet Law." *University of Chicago Law Review* 5, no. 3 (1938): 424–46.

Hellbeck, Jochen. *Revolution on my Mind: Writing a Diary under Stalinism*. Harvard University Press, 2006.

———. "Working, Struggling, Becoming: Stalin-Era Autobiographical Texts." *Russian Review* 60, no. 3 (2001): 340–59.

Halstead, John, and Barry McLoughlin, "British Students at the International Lenin School." Ireland and the Spanish Civil War, accessed July 23, 2024, http://irelandscw.com/ibvol-MLSchool.htm.

Hionidou, Violetta, and David Saunders. "Exiles and Pioneers: Oral Histories of Greeks Deported from the Caucasus to Kazakhstan in 1949." *Europe-Asia Studies* 62, no. 9 (2010): 1479–501.

Hionidou, Violetta. "Nuptiality Patterns and Household Structure on the Greek Island of Mykonos, 1859–1959." *Journal of Family History* 20, no. 2 (1995): 67–102.

Hoffman, David L. *Stalinist Values: The Cultural Norms of Soviet Modernity 1917–1941.* Cornell University Press, 2018.

———. "Mothers in the Motherland: Stalinist Pro-Natalism and Its Pan-European Context." *Journal of Social History* 34, no. 1 (2000): 35–54.

Iatrides, John. *Revolt in Athens: The Greek Communist "Second Round," 1944–1945.* Princeton University Press, 1972.

Illiadou-Tachou, Sofia, and Alexia Orfanou. "From Tsarist Russia to the Soviet Union: The Effects of Civil War on Grecophone Education." In *Democratization of Education: Historical Perspectives,* edited by Zanda Rubene, 131–40. University of Latvia Press, 2015.

Inal, Onur. "Levantine Heritage in Izmir." MA thesis, Koc University, 2006.

Jarska, Natalia. "Women Communists and the Polish Communist Party: From 'Fanatic' Revolutionaries to Invisible Bureaucrats (1918–1945)." *History of Communism in Europe,* no. 8 (2017): 189–210.

Jecchinis, Chris. *Trade Unionism in Greece: A Study in Political Paternalism.* Labor Education Division, Roosevelt University, 1967.

Kabadayi, Mustafa Erdem. "Working in a Fez Factory in Istanbul in the Late Nineteenth Century: Division of Labor and Networks of Migration Formed along Ethno-Religious Lines." *International Review of Social History,* vol. 54 (2009): 69–90.

Karamanou, Anna. "The Changing Role of Women in Greece." In *Greece in the Twentieth Century,* edited by Theodore A. Couloumbis, Theodore C. Kariotis, and Fotini Bellou, 274–93. Frank Cass, 2003.

Karamesinis, Fotis M. "Poinikopoiisi ton ideologikon andilipseon kai staseon stin Elliniki ekpaidefsi: Poines kai metra mesa sta ekpaideftika archeia tis periodou 1925–1929" [The criminalization of ideological perceptions and positions in Greek education: Crimes and punishments from the education archives of the period 1925–1929]. Postgraduate thesis, Ionian University, Corfu, 2015.

Karliaftis, Loukas. "The Birth of Bolshevism in Greece." *Revolutionary History* 3, no. 3 (spring 1991), https://www.marxists.org/history/etol/revhist/supplem/karliaft.htm.

Karliaftis, Loukas. "Stalinism and Trotskyism in Greece." *Revolutionary History* 3, no. 3 (spring 1991). https://www.marxists.org/history/etol/revhist/backiss/vol3/no3/staltrot.html.

Karpozilos, Apostolos. "The Greeks in Russia." In *The Greek Diaspora in the Twentieth Century,* edited by Richard Clogg. Macmillan, 1999.

———. "Pontic Culture in the USSR between the Wars." *Journal of Refugee Studies* 4, no. 4 (1991): 364–71.

Katsiamboura, Yianna. "Proto-Socialist Feminism: Women Communists and Socialists of the Interwar Period." Paper presented at workshop "Democratic or Socialist Revolution in Greece?: 80 Years after Pouliopoulos and His Era." Institute of Political and Social Research Pandelis Pouliopoulos, December 12–13, 2014, Athens. http://ipsr-pouliopoulos.org/sites/ipsr-pouliopoulos.org/files/1412-katsiampoura-pouliopoulos.pdf.

Katz, Zev. "Party Political Education in Soviet Russia 1918–1935." *Soviet Studies* 7, no. 3 (1956): 237–47.
Kasdagli, Aglaia E. "Dowry and Inheritance, Gender and Empowerment in the 'Notarial Societies' of the Early Modern Greek World." *Fund og Forskning i Det Kongelige Biblioteks Samlinger* 44, no. 3 (2005). https://doi.org/10.7146/fof.v44i3.132994.
Kazamias, Alexander. "The Visual Politics of Fear: Anti-Communist Imagery in Postwar Greece." *Journal of Contemporary History* 57, no. 4 (2022): 997–1028.
Kazamias, Andreas M. *Education and modernization in Greece*. ERIC Clearinghouse, 1975. https://files.eric.ed.gov/fulltext/ED097251.pdf.
Kaztaridis, Ioannis F. *I Exodos ton Ellinon tou Kars tis Armenias* [The exodus of the Greek from Kars Armenia]. Kyriakidis, 1996.
Kechriotis, Vangelis. "Educating the Nation: Migration and Acculturation on the Two Shores of the Aegean at the Turn of the Twentieth Century." In *Cities of the Mediterranean: From the Ottomans to the Present Day*, edited by Meltem Toksöz and Biray Kolluoglu. I. B. Tauris: London, 2010).
Kessler, Mario. "Resisting Moscow? Ruth Fischer and the KPD." In *Weimar Communism as Mass Movement 1918–1933*, edited by Ralf Hoffrogge and Norman LaPorte. Lawrence and Wishart, 2017.
Khuri-Makdisi, Illham. *The Eastern Mediterranean and the Making of Global Radicalism, 1860–1914*. University of California Press, 2010.
Kirasirova, Masha "The 'East' as a Category of Bolshevik Ideology and Comintern Administration: The Arab Section of the Communist University of the Toilers of the East." *Kritika: Explorations in Russian and Eurasian History* 18, no. 1 (2017): 7–34.
Kirschenbaum, Lisa A. *International Communism and the Spanish Civil War: Solidarity and Suspicion*. Cambridge University Press, 2015.
Kitroeff, Alexander. "The Greek State and the Diaspora: Venizelism Abroad, 1910–1932." *Classics Journal* 10, no. 1 (2020). https://classics-at.chs.harvard.edu/classics10-alexander-kitroeff-the-greek-state-and-the-diaspora-venizelism-abroad-1910-1932.
Kitromilides, Paschalis. "Greek Irredentism in Asia Minor and Cyprus." *Middle East Studies* 26, no. 1 (1990): 3–17.
Kivisaari, Marja. "Communists Are Not Born, They Are Made: The Political Education System of the French Communist Party." In "Red Lives," special issue, *Socialist History*, no. 21 (2002). http://www.socialist-history-journal.org.uk/SH_21_contents.html.
Kofas, John V. *Authoritarianism in Greece: The Metaxas Regime*. East European Monographs, 1983.
Kofos, Evangelos. "The Impact of the Macedonian Question on Civil Conflict in Greece (1943–1949)." In *Greece at the Crossroads: The Civil War and Its Legacy*, edited by John O. Iatrides. Pennsylvania State University Press, 2010.
Kokkinos, Yiorgos, Vlassis Agtsidis, and Elli Lemonidou. *Memory, Identity, and Ideology amongst Pontian Greeks*. Taxideftis, 2011.
Koliou, Nitsa. *Typo-photographic Panorama of Volos*, vol. 1. Self published, 1991.
Kondaxi, Anastasia. "A Bourgeois Refugee Settlement: Nea Ionia Volou." Master's thesis, Aristotle University, Thessaloniki, 1993.

Kontogiorgi, Elizabeth. *Population Exchange in Macedonia*. Oxford University Press, 2006.
Köstenberger, Julia. "Die Geschichte der Kommunistischen Universität der nationalen Minderheiten des Westens (KUNMZ) in Moskau 1921–1936" [The history of the Communist University for the National Minorities of the West]. *Jahrbuch für historische Kommunismusforschung*, edited by Hermann Weber and Foundation for the Study of the SED Dictatorship, 248–303. Metropol Verl, 1993.
Kostis, Kostas. *History's Spoiled Children: The Story of Modern Greece*. Hurst, 2018.
Kotkin, Stephen. *Magnetic Mountain: Stalinism as a Civilization*. University of California Press, 1997.
Koumandaraki, Anna. "The Greek Trade Union Movement in Controversy: Against a State-Centered Approach to Labor Movement Theory." *Workers of the World: International Journal on Strikes and Social Conflicts* 1, no.1 (2012): 117–32.
Kozlov, Vladimir A. "Denunciation and Its Functions in Soviet Governance: A Study of Denunciations and Their Bureaucratic Handling from Soviet Police Archives, 1944–1953." *Journal of Modern History* 68, no. 4 (1996): 867–98.
Kozlov, Nicholas N., and Eric D. Weitz. "Reflections on the Origins of the 'Third Period': Bukharin, the Comintern, and the Political Economy of Weimar Germany." *Journal of Contemporary History*, vol. 24 (1989): 387–410.
Krekola, Joni, and Ole Martin Running. "International Cadre Education of Nordic Communists." In *Red Star in the North: Communism in the Northern Countries*, edited by Sven Egge and Svend Rybner. Orkana Forlag, 2015.
Kriegel, Annie. *The French Communists: Profile of a People*, translated by Elaine Halperin. University of Chicago Press, 1972.
Kritikos, Giorgos. "From Labor to National Ideals: Ending the War in Asia Minor—Controlling Communism in Greece." *Societies*, vol. 3 (2013): 348–82.
Krylova, Anna. "Bolshevik Feminism and Gender Agendas of Communism." In *World Revolution and Socialism in One Country, 1917–1941*, vol. 1 of The Cambridge History of Communism, edited by Sylvio Pons and Stephen A. Smith, 424–448. Cambridge University Press, 2017.
———. "Beyond the Spontaneity-Consciousness Paradigm: 'Class Instinct' as a Promising Category of Historical Analysis," *Slavic Review* 62, no.1 (2003): 1–23.
Kuromiya, Hiroaki. "Ukraine and Russia in the 1930s," *Harvard Ukrainian Studies* 18, no. 3 (1994): 327–41.
Laamanen, Ville. "From Communist to Cadre Outsider: Ideals, Opportunism, and Coping with Change in Moscow and Stockholm, 1929–1948." *Scandinavian Journal of History* 45, no. 3 (2020): 334–59.
Lazitch, Branko M., and Milorad M. Drachkovitch. *Biographical Dictionary of the Comintern*. Hoover Press, 1973.
Lazitch, Branko, *Les Partis Communistes d'Europe*. Les Illes d'or, 1956.
League of Nations, "The Settlement of Greek Refugees, Scheme for an International Loan, Protocol." Geneva, September 29, 1923. Ungarisches Institut Munchen. http://www.forost.ungarisches-institut.de/pdf/19230929-1.pdf.
Levy, Robert. *Ana Pauker: The Rise and Fall of a Jewish Communist*. University of California Press, 2001.

Lewin, Moshe. "Who Was the Soviet Kulak?" *Europe-Asia Studies* 18, no. 2 (1966): 189–212.

Liakos, Andonis, *Ergasia kai politiki stin Ellada tou mesopolemou* [Labor and politics in interwar Greece]. Nefeli, 1993.

Lowenhardt, John, Erik Van Ree, and James Ozinge. *The Rise and Fall of the Soviet Politburo*. St. Martin's Press, 1992.

Macartney, A. C. *The Work of the League*. League of Nations Union, 1930.

MacFarlane, L. J. *The British Communist Party: Its Origin and Development until 1929*. McGibbon and Kee, 1966.

Macrakis, Lily. *Eleftherios Venizelos 1864–1910: The Making of a National Leader* [in Greek]. MIET, 1992.

Mansel, Philip. *Levant: Splendour and Catastrophe on the Mediterranean*. John Murray, 2010.

Maos, V. "Plythismiakes exelixeis ton Ellinon Pontion stin proin Sovietiki Enosi kai stin Ellada" [Demographic developments of the Greek Pontics in the former Soviet Union and in Greece]. In *Pontic Immigrants from the Former Soviet Union: Social and Economic Integration*, edited by K. Kasimati. Secretary General for Greek Returnees and European Social Fund, 1992.

Marantzidis, Nikos. *Under Stalin's Shadow: A Global History of Greek Communism*. Cornell University Press, 2023.

Markwick, Roger. "Ukraine and Great Russian Power: Christian Rakovsky versus Josef Stalin 1922–1923." *Historical Materialism* (blog), January 27, 2023. https://www.historicalmaterialism.org/blog/ukraine-and-great-russian-power-christian-rakovsky-versus-joseph-stalin-1922-23.

Martin, Terry. "An Affirmative Action Empire: The Soviet Union as the Highest Form of Imperialism." In *A State of Nations: Empire and Nation Making in the Age of Lenin and Stalin*, edited by Ronald G. Suny and T. Martin. Oxford University Press, 2001.

———. "The Origins of Soviet Ethnic Cleansing." *Journal of Modern History* 70, no. 4 (1998): 813–61.

Mavrogordatos, G. T. *Stillborn Republic: Social Coalitions and Party Strategies in Greece, 1922–1936*. University of California Press, 1992.

Mazower, Mark. "The Messiah and the Bourgeoisie: Venizelos and Politics in Greece." *Historical Journal* 35, no. 4 (1992): 885–904.

McDermott, Kevin, and Jeremy Agnew. *The Comintern: A History of International Communism from Lenin to Stalin*. Palgrave, 1996.

McIlroy, John, and Alan Campbell. "Bolshevism, Stalinism and the Comintern: A Historical Controversy Revisited." *Labor History* 60, no. 3 (2019): 165–92.

———. "Forging the Faithful: The British at the International Lenin School." *Labor History Review* 68, no. 1 (2003): 99–128.

McLoughlin, Barry. "Proletarian Academics or Party Functionaries?: Irish Communists at the International Lenin School, 1927–1937," *Saothar: Journal of the Irish Labor History Society*, no. 22 (1997): 63–79.

Mitsopoulou, Anastasia. *Greek Anti-Communism in the Short Twentieth Century*. Epikendro, 2014.

Moschou-Sakorrafou, Sasa. *I istoria tou Ellinikou feministikou kinimatos* [History of the Greek feminist movement]. Private publication, 1990.
Murphy, John. *Socialism and Communism*. Rosen Education Service, 2014.
Murphy, John, and Bill Gollan. "Loyalty and the Communists: An Interview with Bill Gollan." *Labour History*, no. 66 (1994): 114–21.
Murphy, J. T. "The First Year of the Lenin School." *Communist International*, September 30, 1927.
Nacar, Can. "Labor Activism and the State in the Ottoman Tobacco Industry." *International Journal of Middle East Studies* 46, no. 3 (2014): 533–51.
Offerle, M. *Les partis politiques*. Presses universitaires de France, 1987.
O'Sullivan, Michael B. "The Greek Interwar Refugee Crisis as a Cause of the Greek Civil War, 1922–1949," *Historical Perspectives*, series II: vol. 15, article 8 (2010): 49.
Pagratis, N., C. Tsiamis, M. Mandyla, C. Bampounis, and D. Anoyatis-Pele. "Medical, Demographical and Social Aspects of Syphilis: The Case of Infected Sex Workers in Greece during the Interwar." *Giornale italiano di dermatologia e venerealogia* 149, no. 4 (2014): 461–69.
Pantsov, Alexander V., and Daria A. Spichak. "New Light from the Russian Archives: Chinese Stalinists and Trotskyists at the International Lenin School in Moscow 1926–1938." *Twentieth-Century China* 33, no. 2 (2008): 29–50.
Papastefanaki, Leda. *Ergasia, technologia kai fylo stin elliniki viomichania: I klostoyfantourgia tou Pirea 1870–1940* [Labor, technology and gender in Greek industry: The textile industry of Piraeus (1870–1940)]. Crete University Press, 2009.
Parker, Hannah. "Education, Labour and Self-Worth in Women's Letters to Soviet Authorities, 1924–1941." In *Feelings and Work in Modern History: Emotional Labour and Emotions about Labour*, edited by Agnes Arnold-Forster and Alison Moulds, 99–117. Bloomsbury, 2022.
Penter, Tanja. "From a Local *Erfahrungsgeschichte* of *Holodomor* to a Global History of Famines." Round Table on Soviet Famines. *Contemporary European History* 27, no. 3 (2018): 445–49.
Pentzopoulos, Dimitris. *The Balkan Exchange of Minorities and Its Impact on Greece* 1962; repr., De Gruyter Mouton, 2021.
Pobol, N. L., and P. M. Polian, eds. *Stalinskie deportatsii 1928–1953*. Materik, 2005.
Popov, Anton. "From Pindos to Pontos: The Ethnicity and Diversity of Greek Communities in Southern Russia." *Bulletin: Anthropology, Minorities, Multiculturalism*, no. 5 (2004): 84–90.
Popov, Anton. "Making Sense of Home and Homeland: Former Soviet-Greeks' Motivations and Strategies for a Transnational Migrant Circuit." *Journal of Ethnic and Migration Studies* 36, no. 1 (2010): 67–85.
Potamianos, Nikos. "Internationalism and the Emergence of Communist Politics in Greece, 1912–1924." *Journal of Balkan and Near Eastern Studies* 21, no. 5 (2018): 515–31. https://doi.org/10.1080/19448953.2018.1506288.
Poulos, Margarite. "Beyond the Ballot Box: Rethinking Greek Communism between the Wars." *European History Quarterly* 52, no. 1 (2022): 43–64.

———. "'So That Life May Triumph': Communist Feminism and Realpolitik in Civil-War Greece." *Journal of Women's History* 29, no. 1 (2017): 63–86.
———. "Transnational Militancy in Cold-War Europe: Gender, Human Rights, and the WIDF during the Greek Civil War." *European Review of History* 24, no. 1 (2018): 17–35.
———. *Arms and the Woman: Just Warriors and Greek Feminist Identity*. Columbia University Press, 2010.
———. "From Heroines to Hyenas: Women Partisans during the Greek Civil War." In "Gender and War in Europe 1918–1949," special issue of *Contemporary European History* 10, no. 3 (2001): 481–501.
Pratsinakis, E. "Contesting National Belonging: An Established-Outsider Figuration on the Margins of Thessaloniki, Greece." PhD diss., Universiteit van Amsterdam, 2013.
Psarra, Angelika. "I istoria os martirologio: Scholio se mia ekthesi gia tin istoria tou gynaikeiou kinimatos" [History as martyrdom: Comment on an exhibition on the history of the women's movement]. *ArcheioTaxio: Publications from the archives of the Contemporary Social History Archive* (ASKI), vol. 9 (2007): 161–74.
———. "Women in Pursuit of Pleasure and the Vote." In *When Women Have Differences: Contradictions and Conflicts between Women in Contemporary Greece*, edited by Christina Vlachoutsikou and Laurie Kain Hart. Medusa, 2003.
———. "The Different Faces of a Celebration: The Greek Course of International Women's Day, 1924–2010." *Aspasia*, vol. 6 (2012): 43–59.
———. "Feminism and Communism: Notes on the Greek Case." *Aspasia*, vol. 1 (2007): 207–13.
Puchner, Walter. "Greek Cultural Activities in the Black Sea around 1900." In *Ethno-Cultural Diversity in the Balkans and the Caucasus*, edited by Thede Kahl and Ioana Nechiti, 242–56. Austrian Academy of Science, 2019.
Quataert, Donald. "Labor History and the Ottoman Empire, c. 1700–1922." *International Labor and Working-Class History*, no. 60 (2001): 93–109.
Ravandi-Fadai, Lana. "'Red Mecca': The Communist University for Laborers of the East (KUTV): Iranian Scholars and Students in Moscow in the 1920s and 1930s." *Iranian Studies* 48, no. 5 (2015).
Rees, Tim. "Deviation and Discipline: Anti-Trotskyism, Bolshevization, and the Spanish Communist Party 1924–1934." *Historical Research* 82, no. 215 (2009): 131–56.
Rees, Tim, and Andrew Thorpe, eds. *International Communism and the Communist International 1919–1943*. Manchester University Press, 1998.
Rees, E. A., ed. *The Nature of Stalin's Dictatorship: The Politburo, 1924–1953*. Routledge, 2004.
Richards, Edward B. "Soviet Control of the Third International." *Social Science* 36, no. 1 (1961): 26–31.
Richter, Heinz. "The Greek Communist Party and the Communist International." *Jahrbuch für Historische Kommunismusforschung*, 111–40. Aufbau Verlag, 2002.
———. *British Intervention in Greece: From Varkiza to Civil War*. Merlin Press, 1985.
Riginos, M. *Structures of Production and Wages in Greece 1900–1936*. Historical Archives of the Commercial Bank of Greece, 1987.

Riley, Parkes. "Poverty, Literacy and the Communist Vote in India." *Asian Survey* 15, no. 6 (1975): 543–58.
Rizopoulos, Nicholas X. "The International Dimension of the Greek Civil War." *World Policy Journal* 17, no. 1 (2000): 87–103.
Rodakis, Periklis. *Nikos Zachariadis*. Epikairotita, 2007.
Roman, Meredith L. "Race, Politics and US Students in 1930s Soviet Russia." *Race and Class* 53, no. 2 (2011).
Rossi, Jacques, and Michele Sarde. *Jacques the Frenchman: Memories of the Gulag*. University of Toronto Press, 2020.
Saliba, Zizi. *Gynaikes ergatries dtin elliniki biomichania kai biotechnia 1870–1922* [Women workers in the manufacturing and craft industry]. Ethniko Idrima Erevnon (EIE), 2002.
Samiou, Dimitra. "Maria Svolou (born Desypri 1892–1976)." In *Biographical Dictionary of Women's Movements and Feminisms: Central, Eastern, and South Eastern Europe, 19th and 20th Centuries*, 1st ed., edited by Francisca de Haan, Krassimira Daskalova, and Anna Loutfi, 552–57. Central European University Press, 2005.
Sewell, Sara Ann. "Bolshevising Communist Women: The Red Women and Girls' League in Weimar Germany." *Central European History*, vol. 45 (2012): 268–305.
Sewell, William H. *Work and Revolution in France: The Language of Labor from the Old Regime to 1848*. Cambridge University Press, 1980.
Sfikas, Athanasios D. *British Labour Government and the Greek Civil War: 1945–1949*. Edinburgh University Press, 2019.
Sideri, E. *The Greeks of the Former Soviet Republic of Georgia: Memories and Practices of Diaspora*. London: University of London, 2006.
Simpson, J. H. "The Work of the Greek Refugee Settlement Commission." *Journal of the Royal Institute of International Affairs* 8, no. 6 (Nov. 1929): 583–604.
Stratis Someritis, *H megale kampi tou sosialismou* [The great turning point of socialism]. Papazisis, 1978.
Stites, Richard. *The Women's Liberation Movement in Russia: Feminism, Nihilism, and Bolshevism, 1860–1930*. Princeton University Press, 1978.
Strazzeri, Victor, "Beyond the Double-Blind Spot: Relocating Communist Women as Transgressive Subjects in Contemporary Historiography." *Gender and History* 36, no. 2 (2024): 755–74. https://doi.org/10.1111/1468-0424.12675.
Studer, Brigitte. *The Transnational World of the Cominternians*. Palgrave Macmillan, 2015.
———. "Communism and Feminism." *Clio*, no. 41 (2015): 139–52.
Tapia, Francisco J. Beltrán., and Michail Raftakis, "Sex Ratios and Gender Discrimination in Modern Greece." *Population Studies* 76, no. 2 (2021): 329–46.
Theodorou, Vasiliki, and Despina Karakatsani. "Health Policy in Interwar Greece: The Intervention by the League of Nations Health Organization." *Dynamis* (Granada), vol. 28 (2008): 53–75. https://raco.cat/index.php/Dynamis/article/view/118807.
Timofeyeva, Natalya. "Kommunistichyeskii Univyersityet Trudyaschikhsya—tsetr idyeinoi podgotovki ryevolyutsionnykh kadrov" [The Communist University for Toilers of the East: Center for Ideological Preparation for Communist Revolutionary Cadres]. PhD dissertation, Institute of Oriental Studies of the Academy of Sciences, Moscow, 1989.

Tounda-Fergadi, Areti, *Themata Ellinkis Diplomatikis Istorias (1912–1934)*. Paratiritis, 1986.
Tsoucalas, Constantine. *The Greek Tragedy*. Penguin, 1969.
Tsouparopoulos, T. *The Democratic Institutions of the Greek Resistance*. Politeia, 1989.
Tzanaki, Demetra. "Sex Work Is Work: Greek Capitalism and the Syndrome of Electra, 1922–2018." In *Back to the 1930s?: Recurring Crises of Capitalism, Liberalism, and Democracy*, edited by Jeremy Rayner, Susan Falls, George Souvlis, and Taylor C. Nelms. Springer Nature, 2020.
Ulunian, Artiom. "The Communist Party of Greece." In *International Communism and the Communist International*, edited by Tim Rees and Andrew Thorpe. Manchester University Press, 1998.
Unfried, Berthold. "Foreign Communists and the Mechanisms of Soviet Cadre Formation in the USSR," In *Stalin's Terror: High Politics and Mass Repression in the Soviet Union*, edited by Barry McLoughlin and Kevin McDermott. Palgrave Macmillan, 2003.
Vardagli, E. Tutku. "Tobacco Labor Politics in the Province of Thessaloniki: Cross-Communal and Cross-Gender Relations." PhD diss., Bogaziçi University, Turkey, 2011.
Vervenioti, Tasoula. *H Gynaika tis Adistasis: H Eisodos ton Gynaikon sti Politiki* [The reluctant woman: The entry of women into politics]. Odysseus, 1994.
Viola, Lynne. "The Campaign to Eliminate the Kulak as a Class, Winter 1929–1930: A Re-evaluation of the Legislation," *Slavic Review* 45, no. 3 (1986): 503–24.
Voglis, Polymeris. *Becoming a Subject: Political Prisoners during the Greek Civil War*. Berghahn, 2002.
Voutira, Eftichia. *The "Right to Return" and the Meaning of "Home": A Post-Soviet Greek Diaspora Becoming European?* Lit Verlag, 2012.
———. "Post-Soviet Diaspora Politics: The Case of the Soviet Greeks." *Journal of Modern Greek Studies* 24, no. 2 (2006): 379–414.
Vryonis Jr., Speros. "The Labor Battalions in the Ottoman Empire." In *Cultural and Ethical Legacies: The Armenian Genocide*, edited by Richard Hovannisian, 275–91. Routledge, 2006.
Waters, Elizabeth. "In the Shadow of the Comintern." In *Creating German Communism 1890–1990: From Popular Front to Socialist State*, edited by Sonia Kruks, Rayna Rapp, and Eric D. Weitz. Princeton University Press, 1997.
Wood, Elizabeth. *The Baba and the Comrade: Gender and Politics in Revolutionary Russia*. Indiana University Press, 2001.
———. "The Trial of the New Woman: Citizens-in-Training in the New Soviet Republic." *Gender and History* 13, no. 3 (2001): 524–46.
Xanthopoulou-Kyriakou, A. "The Diaspora of the Greeks of the Pontos: Historical Background." *Journal of Refugee Studies* 4, no. 4 (1991) 357–63.
Young, Marilyn B., Sonia Kruks, Rayna Rapp, eds. *Promissory Notes: Women in the Transition to Socialism*. Monthly Review Press, 1989.
Zagoria, Donald S. "A Note on Landlessness, Literacy and Agrarian Communism in India." *European Journal of Sociology*, vol. 13 (1972): 326–34.

———. "The Ecology of Peasant Communism in India." *American Political Science Review*, vol. 65 (1971): 144–60.

Zapantis, Andrew L. *Greek-Soviet Relations, 1917–1941*. East European Monographs, 1982.

Zheng, Wang. *Finding Women in the State: A Socialist Feminist Revolution in the People's Republic of China, 1949–1964*. University California Press, 2016.

Zumoff, Jacob. "The Double-Edged Sword of Bolshevization" in *The Communist International and US Communism 1919–29*. Brill, 2014.

Index

Page numbers in **bold** refers to tables. Page numbers in *italics* refers to figures.

Akropolis (Athens newspaper), 52
Alexiou, Elli, 16–17
Anatolian Greeks
   refugees, 6, 18–20, 23, 116, 127, 161, 164
   students in Comintern universities, 3, 83, 87, 97, 100
Anemelou, Lena (pseud., Nikolaevna Dimitrieva/Dimitrova), 38–39, 70, 87, 97, 128, 130
Ankara Agreement of 1930, 28, 30
antifascist resistance, 16–17, 158
Apostolou, Electra, 8, 10, 34, 42, 62
Athens
   refugees and, 18, 20, 22–23, 117–18
   University of Athens, 51, 181
   World War 2 and, 3, 156–57
autobiographies, 13, 16, 38, 60
Avdela, Efi, 25–27, 39–40
Axis occupation, 7, 17, 153, 165

Bakola, Olga, 47–48, 61, 98, 133–36
Balkan Communist Federation, 70
Balkan Wars, 20, 29, 127
Battle of Athens (Dekemvriana), 156–57
Battle of Aydin, 147
biography
   Anemelou, Lena (pseud., Nikolaevna Dimitrieva/Dimitrova), 130
   Bakola, Olga (pseud., Aliki Kanda), 133–34
   Christodoulidou, Clio Stylianou (pseud., Nora Irman), 131–33
   Hatzivasiliou, Chrysa (pseud., Alexandra Nikolai Armand, Mary), 147–58
   Kaloidou, Olga, 136–37
   Kantzidou, Chrysanthi (pseud., Kaiti Vasiliou), 127–28, 142–44
   Kerasidou, Stella (pseud., Olga Nikolaevna Ivanova), 114, 137–39
   Kritikou, Smaro, 114–15
   Papadopoulou, Olga (pseud., Olga Vlasova), 2, 115–17, 139–40, 143
   Paterouli, Olga, 114
   Stai, Clio Dimitrievna, 130–31
   Theou, Koula, 120
   Vamniatzidou, Stella (pseud., Elena Arnova), 38–39, 98, 128–29
   See also professional revolutionaries
Bolshevization
   aims and, 49, 57–58, 64, 71
   definition and, 5, 12

Bolshevization (cont'd.)
  education and, 53, 63–64, 67
  history and, 7, 14
  refugee crisis and, 4, 17, 71, 100, 148, 161
  social impacts and, 15
  women and, 31, 55–56
  See also KKE (Kommounistiko Komma Elladas; Greek Communist Party)
Britain. See Great Britain
Byzantine Civil Code (Roman law), 180–81

cadre universities. See Comintern university system
capitalism, 40, 157, 176–77, 182
Catherine the Great, 101
Caucasus, 110, 115, 132, 136–37
Central Athens organization (Kendriki Organosi Athinas, KOA), 8
child labor, 25, 27, 29, 139
Chinese Communist Party (CCP), 55, 118
Christodoulidou, Clio Stylianou, 131–33
Churchill, Winston, 157
Cibali Régie Factory, 38
Ciliga, Ante, 79
Comintern Archives, 13–15
Comintern university system
  cadre education approach to and, 73, 78
  challenge, shortcomings and, 64, 67–68, 77–78, 111, 134
  closure and, 3, 72, 87, 112, 134
  curricula. See specific universities
  disband for Western European countries and, 111–12
  educational standards and, 76–78
  ethnic composition and, 100–102, 106–8, 163
  fourth period, 1934: repressive policy of Stalin and, 111–13
  graduates and, 6–7, 60–62, 77, 118
  Greek sectors: KUTV and the KUNMZ and, 71–72, 75, 105–6, 111
  Greek students and, 59–61, 111–13
  history and, 54–58
  International communist movement and, 64, 77, 97
  international students and, 63–64, 67, 71–72, 105
  objectives and, 12, 14, 57, 63–66, 73, 75, 134
  outcomes and, 61–62, 78–80, 106–11, 161–62, 164
  social welfare relief and, 98
  Soviet Greeks, Greeks and, 100–102, 105–8, 113, 136–45
  student categories and, 57–58
  student characteristics and, 114
  student living conditions and, 78–79
  student requirements. See specific universities
  student selection and, 58, 82
  third period, 1928–1933: expansion and, 87, 97
  See also specific universities
communist movement, Greece, repression and, 33, 49, 52
communist party, Bulgaria (BKP), 151
communist party, China, 55, 118
communist party, France (PCF), 58
communist Party, Germany (KPD), 82, 120, 151–52
communist party, Great Britain (CPGB), 58, 65
communist party, Greece. See KKE (Kommounistiko Komma Elladas; Greek Communist Party)
communist party, Romania, 151
communist party, Soviet Union (CPSU), 5, 30, 56–57, 60, 86–87, 118, 137
communist women. See women and communism
Communist Women's International, 32, 138
communist youth, 30, 33, 61–62, 155

Congress of the World Committee of
   Women Against War and Fascism, 17
Converzations with Lenin (Zetkin), 32
Crimea, 101–2
Cyprus, 83, 97, 131–32
Czechoslovakia, 12

demotic Greek, 104–5
de-Stalinization, 144, 155
Dimokratikos Stratos Elladas (Greek
   Democratic Army), 8, 10–11, 126
displacement, 115, 117, 124, 127, 139, 148,
   164–65
divorce, 122–23, 177
Domontovich, Alexandra Mikhailovna
   (Kollontai), 148–49
Donbas, 99, 112, 116

EAM Resistance Movement, 7–8, 10, 159,
   166
Eastern bloc, 8, 30
Eastern Orthodox, 18, 38, 161
EBE budget, 1934, **47** (table 2)
EBE (Ergatiki Boitheia Elladas; Labor
   Assistance Greece), 45–49
economic crisis, 30–31, 42–43
EGSEE/Enotiki (Unitary Greek General
   Workers' Confederation), 41
Enosis Hiron kai Orfanon Dikaiouchon
   Andallaximon (Union of Entitled
   Widows and Orphans), 36
Ergatiko Kendro Pirea (EKP; Labor
   Center Piraeus), 49
Ergatria (Woman Worker; newspaper), 41,
   132
ethnic cleansing, 3, 161
ethnic identity, 22, 56, 103, 105, 113
Ethniko peleftherotiko Metopo (EAM;
   National Liberation Front), 7
Ethniko Symvoulio (National Council), 8
Ethnikos Dichasmos (National Schism),
   29
Executive Committee of the Communist
   International (ECCI), 63–64, 71

fascism, 4, 7, 17, 47, 177, 187, 197
Federation of Greek Communist Youth
   (Omospondia Kommounistikon
   Neolaion Elladas, OKNE), 32–35
Felous, Allegra, 10–11, 110
female refugee labor force
   communist party and, 31–32, 38–40, 49,
      161
   expansion and, 18–22
   exploitation and, 14, 25–28, 35–36, 161,
      174, 176
   plight of and, 23–26, 28, 35, 41, 49, 110
   politics and, 14, 19, 28–29
   prostitution and, 25
   tobacco industry and, 37–40
   trade unions and, 36–40
   unprotected labor and, 28, 35, 49, 161
   unregulated conditions and, 19, 23
   working conditions and, 23–25, 27, 40
feminism
   activists and, 17, 24, 26, 159
   movements and, 16, 26, 35, 37, 118, 147
   society and, 26–27, 50, 56, 120, 157–59
Fillipidi, Foteini, 8
Fischer, Ruth, 32, 138, 151–52
Fitzpatrick, Sheila, 13, 53, 56, 66, 143–44
Foni tis Gynaikas (Woman's Voice;
   newspaper), 154

gender
   competition and, 25–26
   conflict and, 39–40, 56
   discrimination and, 100, 117–18, 125, 153
   equality and, 10, 31–32, 120
   ideals in Soviet society and, 56–57
   ratios in Soviet cadre universities and,
      69, 72
   relations and, 123
   social injustice and, 118
   students and, 113
   understanding of women and, 160–61
   vulnerability of female labor force and,
      19
   woman's place in historiography and, 17

General Metaxa, 53
Gonsa, Christian, 16, 62, 125
Great Britain, 29, 58, 109, 157
Great Terror, 66, 71, 108, 111, 122, 139, 141, 163
Grecophone schools, 102, 104
Greco-Turkish Friendship Treaty, 29
Greco-Turkish war, 3–4, 18, 30, 102, 116, 163
Greece
  Balkan wars and, 29
  carpet industry and, 21–24, 37, 40–41, 52
  elections 1932 and 1936 and, 52
  employment data for 1907, 21 (table 1)
  government and, 28–29, 50, 52
  health and social welfare situation and, 117–18
  population, growth, composition and, 18–19
  society and, 18, 20, 53, 56
  tobacco industry and, 37–40
  trade and industry and, 20–24, 161
  woman question and, 35, 156–58
Greek archival material, 16
Greek Civil War, 7–9, 30, 61, 153, 157
Greek communism, 2–3, 7, 12, 16, 19, 164
Greek Communist autobiographies, 13–16
Greek Communist Party of the Interior (KKE Esoterikou, later Synaspismos), 11
Greek Communist Party. *See* KKE (Kommounistiko Komma Elladas; Greek Communist Party)
Greek dialects, 105
Greek education system, restructuring, 50–52, 102–3, 125
Greek language, 104
Greek Ministry of the National Economy, 24
Greek Parliament, 19, 30, 35
Greek population in Russia, 101–5

Greek Refugee Resettlement Commission (RSC; Epitropi Apokatastasis Prosfygon), 20–21, 28
Greek settlements in Russia. *See* Russia, Greek settlements
Greek student sector expansion: KUNMZ and MLS, 87
Greek students in Russia, 83, 86
Greek students, individual personal files, 12–13
Greek Tobacco Workers' Federation (Red Trade Union of Tobacco Workers), 37–40
Gritsi-Milliex, Tatiana, 158

Haravgi (newspaper), 140
Hatzivasiliou, Chrysa (pseud., Alexandra Nikolai Armand, Mary)
  background, historical sources and, 146–48
  Central Committee and Politburo of communist party and, 55, 150
  communist-feminist, role and, 110, 118, 153, 157–58
  death of, 154, 156
  education and, 36, 147–48
  health issues and, 149, 153
  KUNMZ and, 148–49
  leadership and, 109–11, 148
  marriage and, 152–53
  Women's movement, role and, 156
Hitler, 157, 193

Idionymon Special Crimes Act, 50, 52
illiteracy, 27, 50, 105, 127, 129, 137, 139
individual personnel files (*lichnye dela*), 12–13
Inside Hitler's Greece (Mazower), 153
International communist movement, 64, 77, 97
International Congress of Women, 158
International Women's Day (IWD)
  introduction in Greece, 31

Istanbul (Constantinople), 30, 32, 38, 76, 87, 99, 109, 114

Kalevras, Achilleas, 34–35
Kaloidou, Olga, 136–37
Kantzidou, Chrysanthi (pseud., Kaiti Vasiliou), 127–28, 142–44
katharevousa (form of language), 102, 105, 126
Katou, Rodi, 10–11
Kavala, 19, 38–39, 43, 46, 52, 76, 98–99
Kazantzaki, Galateia, 17
Kerasidou, Stella (pseud., Olga Nikolaevna Ivanova), 114, 118–22, 141–43
Khrushchev
    de-Stalinzation and, 144, 155
    letters by Olga Papaddopoulu and, 2, 143, 162
    secret speech of 1956 and, 30
KKE (Kommounistiko Komma Elladas; Greek Communist Party)
    Bolshevization and, 49, 54, 57, 68, 71, 82, 100
    Comintern principles and, 15, 17, 54–56, 67, 68, 104, 160
    educational aims and, 57–58, 68
    factionalism and, 5, 30, 122, 132, 141–42
    family values and, 122–24
    female refugee labor force and, 31–40
    history and, 18, 184
    illegality and, 18, 33, 53, 68, 82, 97, 119
    KUTVists and, 62–63, 81–82
    leadership and, 5, 8, 29, 82, 109, 153, 155, 164
    OKNE: relationship with, 32–33
    recruitment and membership and, 16, 19, 31–33, 99–100
    refugees and, 19–22, 27–31
    revolutionary party of the proletariat and, 17, 27, 160
    Stalin and Trotsky split and, 82
    women and, 31–49, 51–53, 119–25, 158, 160
    See also women and communism
"KKE and the Woman Question in Greece, The" (Hatzivasiliou), 156–59
Komioti, Ioanna, 32
Kommounistiki Epitheorisi (KOMEP: Communist review; journal), 10, 32, 44
Kommunistis (newspaper), 140–41
Kremlin, 12, 54, 63–64
Kresinski, Magda, 138
Kritikou, Smaro, 114–15
KUNMZ (Kommunistichesky Universitet Natsionalnykh Menshinstv Zapada; Communist University for National Minorities of the West): Greek Sector
    curriculum content and, 73–74
    establishment and aims and, 69–71, 87, 97
    student requirements and, 71
    students 1928–1936, **88–93** (table 4)
    students and employees and, 87–102
KUTV (Kommunistichesky Universitet Trudiashchikhsia Vostoka; Communist University for the Toilers of the East)
    alumni, 77
    curriculum content, 73–74
    establishment, aims and students and, 68–69
    first cohort of students and, 87
    first female militants from Greece and, 32
    Greek sector: students and employees and, 87–102
    renamed as J. V. Stalin Communist University for Toilers of the East, 69
    student information: Greek students international group, KUTV and, 1924–1925, **84–85** (table 3)
    student requirements and, 71
    value of the education and, 161–62

KUTVists
   ethnicity of students and, 83–87, **84–85** (table 3), 113
   female students contribution to the party and, 98–100
   KKE and, 62–63, 81–83

labor movement, 30, 53, 130
Lausanne, Treaty of, 3, 18, 28, 50, 163
League for Women's Rights (Syndesmos Gia ta Dikaiomata ton Gynaikon), 8, 26–27
League of Nations, 3, 23
Lenin, 75, 87, 123, 148, 152, 177, 185
Leonhard, Wolfgang, 1, 79, 147
liberals, 29, 49, 53, 159. *See also* Venizelism
literacy, 68, 78, 112–13, 125, 127, 140, 144

Macartney, C. A., 21
Macedonia, 22, 37, 82
Makropoulou, Anna, 25
Makroyiannis, Dimitris, 61, 76, 112
marriage, 117, 123
Marxism and the National Question and *The National Question and Leninism* (trans., Hatzivasiliou), 154
Marxism-Leninism, 57, 107, 145, 156
Mavroeidi-Hiourea, Machi, 8
memoirs as a historical source, 16, 62
Metaxas dictatorship, 2, 4, 10, 19, 50, 86
migration, 20, 56, 103, 115
MLS (Mezhdunarodnaia leninskaia shkola; International Lenin School)
   alumni and, 109
   curriculum and, 74
   establishment and courses and, 71–72
   MLS female students, Greek sector, **94–96** (table 5)
   prestigious status and, 71, 77
   student classification and, 58
   student requirements and, 74–75
monarchy, 4, 157, 180
Moscow, 2, 3, 12, 57, 65, 86

Nazi, 61, 157, 163, 166
Neolaia (Youth) communist youth newspaper, 8, 40

O Agonas tis Gynaikas (Woman's struggle; journal), 27
Omospondia Ergatikou Athlitismou (Greek Workers' Sports Federation), 44
Omospondia Kommounistikon Neolaion Elladas (OKNE), 5, 30, 32–34, 42
Orthodox Christian, 18, 38, 161
Ottoman Empire, 15, 30, 38, 76, 97, 101, 103, 162

Panelladiki Dimokratiki Enosi Gynaikon (PDEG; Panhellenic Democratic Union of Women), 10, 158–59
Pangalos dictatorship, 33, 52, 62
Panhellenic Anti-fascist Congress, 17
Panhellenic Committee of Women Against War and Fascism, 17
Panhellenic Federation of Women (POG; Panellinia Omospondia Gynaikon), 158
Panhellenic Women's Conference, 10
Papadopoulou, Olga (pseud., Olga Vlasova)
   background, 115–17, 125, 143
   education, employment and, 81, 139–40
   letters to Khrushchev and, 2, 143, 162
Partsalidou, Avra (née Vlassi), 10, 16, 34, 61
Pateroul, Olga, 114–15
Pauker, Ana, 151
Petrova, Lidia Ivanovna, 61, 72, 97, 99, 112
Piraeus, 8, 20–22, 40, 49
Politiki Epitropi Ethnikis Apeleftherosis (PEEA; Political Committee of National Liberation), 8, 10
Pontic Greeks, 83, 100–102, 105–6, 115, 131, 164
Pouliopoulos, Pandelis, 35, 67, 82, 108, 122, 141
poverty, 14, 30, 79, 113, 126–27, 164

professional revolutionaries
  autobiographies as a source and, 113–15
  family issues and, 118–20, 136
  gender discrimination and, 117–18, 125
  Greek communist party and, 119–20, 134
  Greek interwar communism and, 161–62
  male dominance and, 117, 123, 125
  personal narratives and, 13, 56, 113
  personnel files (*lichnye dela*) of individual Greek students and, 12–13
  poverty social and health status and, 116–17, 126, 136
  students Group A and, 136–45
  students group B and, 127–36. See also biography
Profintern (Red International of Labor Unions), 43
Profintern 8th Central Conference, Lusovsky proposal of election of women workers to factory committees, 43–44
Prosfygikos Kosmos (Refugee world; journal), 26, 36

Radek, Karl, 69
radicalization, 4–5, 19, 27, 37, 43, 50, 164
Raika (pseud.), 34–35
Red Aid, 114, 119
Red Trade Union of Tobacco Workers, 37, 39–40, 129
refugees
  communist party and, 27–31, 37–40, 165–66
  constraints and, 23–25, 27–28
  contribution to economy and, 20–21, 37–38, 161
  employment and, 18–19, 21–22, 165
  influx after Greco-Turkish War and, 4–5, 17–18, 161
  radicalization and, 4, 19, 27, 37, 164
  resettlement and, 18–23, 165
  rural refugees and, 19
  unprotected labor and, 23, 28–29, 161
  working conditions and, 23–25
  See also female refugee labor force
Rizospastis (newspaper), 28, 32, 40, 48, 134
Roussaki, Eleni, 34
Roussos, Petros, 152–53
Russia, Greek settlements
  Demotic as the official language and, 105
  Greek ethnic minority and education system and, 101–4, 163
  settlements on the shores of Black Sea, 103
Russian Communist Party. *See* Communist Party, Soviet Union (CPSU)
Russian empire, 101
Russian Revolution, 102, 103, 105, 115, 125–26, 148, 164
Russo-Turkish War, 101, 115

Second Hellenic Republic, 29
Simpson, Sir John Hope, 20
Smyrna, 4, 21, 68, 147, 165
social inequality, 51
social injustice, 100, 118, 126
Socialist Labor Party (Sosialistiko Ergatiko Komma Elladas, SEKE/KEKE), 18, 27, 31, 57
sources for the study, 12–16
Soviet foreign policy, 3, 83
Soviet Greek students group B: Greek nationals in Russia, 86–87, 97, 100–101, 105–6, 127–36
Soviet Greek students: Soviet nationals group A, 105–6, 136–45
Soviet Greeks, 100, 106–7, 115, 132, 136, 163
Soviet Greeks and Greek citizenship, 85–86
Soviet Union, 12, 14, 30, 50, 57, 60, 102, 162
Soviet-Greek school network, 103
Soviet-Greek communist women, 2–3
Spartakos (newspaper), 141

Stai, Clio, 130–31
Stalin
  deportation policies and, 112
  ethnic minorities and, 104
  industries and five-year plan and, 53, 116
  KUTV and, 69
  repressive policy (Greek operation) and, 112–13
  Stalin and Trotsky split and, 82
  Stalinization and, 5, 55–56, 82
  See also de-Stalinization; Great Terror
Stalin and German Communism (Fischer), 152
Stavridis, Eleftherios, 29, 59, 80, 83, 134, 138, 147
strike actions, 39, 41–43, 53, 134, 162
Sverdlov University, 79
Svolos, Alexandros, 8
Svolou, Maria Desypri, 8, 24–25, 27, 159
Syndicalistis (trade union paper), 40–41

Thessaloniki, 19, 22, 36–38, 43, 44, 53
tobacco industry, 38–40
trade unions, 23, 25–26, 36, 40
tuberculosis, 24, 40, 59, 109, 117–18, 131, 141
Turkey, 3–4
Turkish War of Independence. *See* Greco-Turkish war

Ukrainian Greeks, 105, 116, 163
unemployment, 28, 40, 98, 115–16, 193
University of Athens, 51

Vamniatzidou, Stella (pseud., Elena Agneva, Stella Vudanya, Yiannoula Nikolaidou, and Elena Arnova), 38–39, 98, 128–29
Venizelism, 28–29
Venizelon government
  "Bourgeois revolution": rise of class-based professions and enterprises, 29
  Greco-Turkish Friendship Treaty and, 29
  Greek education system, restructure and, 50–52, 105, 125
  Idionymon (Special Crimes Act) and, 50
  Metax taking over the government and, 53
  political vision and, 29
  protective laws (1912) for women and children, 25–26
  refugee support and, 28–29
  voting rights to Greek women and, 52
Venizelos, Eleftherios, 28–29
Volos, 19, 37–38, 43, 48

woman question
  KKE and the woman question in Greece and, 156–58
  woman question, 32
  woman question and (Raika pseud.), 35
  woman question in 1946 and, 156–59
women
  femininity and image and, 120
  gender and women's place and, 17
  gender equality and, 10, 31–32
  political and civil rights and, 10
  voting rights and, 52
  See also feminism
women and children, 17, 23–28, 36, 124, 126, 166. *See also* child labor; Venizelon government: protective laws (1912) for women and children
women and communism
  Bolshevization and, 56–57, 63
  Comintern education and, 2–3, 14, 55, 97, 114–44
  See also KKE: women and
women and employment, 18–21, 24–35, 36, 40. *See also* female refugee workforce; Greece: carpet industry and; Greece: tobacco industry and; refugees
women and youth, 14, 17, 23, 25, 52, 132, 161, 165
women workers, 27, 31–32, 35–37, 41–43, 44–49

women's movements, 36, 40–41, 48, 138, 151, 157–59
women's participation, 17–18, 41, 45, 152–56, 160–61
Women's International Democratic Federation (WIDF), 10, 154, 157
Work amongst Women (conference), 32
World Committee of Women Against War and Fascism, Congress of, 17

World War I, 115
World War II, 3, 29, 61, 156–57

Yugoslavia, 79

Zachariadis, Nikos, 5–6, 30, 82, 109, 150, 155
Zetkin, Clara, 151–52
Zevgou, Kaiti (née Nisiriou), 8, 10, 16, 61

www.ingramcontent.com/pod-product-compliance
Lightning Source LLC
Chambersburg PA
CBHW030532230426
43665CB00010B/861